The World of Fish

The World of Fish

GENERAL EDITOR: JOHN HONDERS

PEEBLES PRESS

New York: London

First published 1975
by
Peebles Press International
U.S.: 10 Columbus Circle, New York, N.Y. 10019
U.K.: 12 Thayer Street, London, WIM 5LD

ISBN 0-85690-037-0

Distributed by
Walden Books, Resale Division, in the
U.S. and Canada
WHS Distributors in the U.K., Ireland,
Australia, New Zealand and South Africa

Printed and bound in the U.S.A.

A

ACANTHODIANS, fossil shark-like fishes that first made an appearance in the Silurian. One of the best known genera is *Climatius* of the Lower Devonian. Some authorities consider the acanthodians to have been ancestral to the shark-like fishes (Chondrichthyes) but others believe them to be early members of the bony fishes (Pisces or Osteichthyes). The acanthodians survived until the Lower Permian.
SUBCLASS: Acanthodii, CLASS: Pisces.

ACARA, the common name given to certain freshwater fishes of the genus *Aequidens* (family Cichlidae). They are found in Brazil and Venezuela and certain species are now imported into Europe and North America as aquarium fishes. The best known are the Blue acara *Aequidens pulcher* and the Black acara *A. portalegrensis*. In the wild they grow to 8 in (22 cm) in length, but are very much smaller when kept in aquaria. The young tend to be rather pugnacious but older fishes will settle down well in a community tank. FAMILY: Cichlidae, ORDER: Perciformes, CLASS: Pisces.

ACTINOPTERYGIANS or ray-finned fishes, a broad grouping (subclass) within the class Pisces or bony fishes.
See fishes.   SUBCLASS: Actinopterygii, CLASS: Pisces.

ADIPOSE FIN, a small fleshy fin on the back of some of the more primitive fishes, such as salmon and trout, near the tail, that is to say behind the normal dorsal fin. It is often little more than a small lobe whose function appears to be the control of the small eddies that are formed by any solid body when it moves through water. In some of the catfishes the adipose fin is large and may be preceded by a sharp spine, as in the African genus *Clarotes*. Many of the more advanced fishes have a second dorsal fin in place of an adipose fin but this is a very different structure since it is a membrane supported by finrays which

Blue acara, a popular aquarium fish with blue-green spangled scales.

The adipose fin, typical of salmon-like fishes, lies between the dorsal fin and the tail.

are in turn supported internally by a series of small bones, the pterygiophores.

AIR-BREATHING FISHES, species able to breathe atmospheric air directly. In the vast majority of fishes breathing, that is to say the absorption of oxygen and the elimination of carbon dioxide, is accomplished by the gills. The air-breathing habit is known only in the bony fishes (the teleosts) but fossil remains from up to 250 million years ago show that many of the earliest fishes had lungs and breathed air. During the long evolution of the fishes, most groups passed from using the lungs as breathing organs to using them as a hydrostatic organ, that is to say, a swimbladder (see separate entry). The living lungfishes, however, did not lose this primitive air-breathing habit, but in other fishes it was lost and then later regained, this time with structures other than a 'lung' to absorb the oxygen from the air.

Mudskippers, which spend a considerable

part of their time out of water, have evolved a fairly simple alternative to strict air-breathing. Before emerging into the air, the fish fills its gill chamber with water so that it can still absorb oxygen with its gills. To increase absorption, there are numerous small blood vessels close to the surface of the skin lining the roof of the mouth and a certain amount of gas exchange takes place there. These vascularizations, or concentrations of fine blood vessels just beneath the surface of the skin, are often found lining the gill covers of certain catfishes.

In one group of catfishes, the Loricariidae or Mailed catfishes, and also in some of the loaches, air is taken in and passed down into the intestine. The walls of a part of the intestine are vascularized and gas exchange can take place here, the used-up air later being voided via the vent.

The anabantid or labyrinthfishes of the tropical Old World have a labyrinthine breathing organ at the top of the gill cham-

ber, hence their common name. Some members of this group are so strictly adapted to air-breathing that they will actually drown if prevented from reaching the surface, a most unexpected failing in a fish! A major problem in using the gills as air-breathing organs is that in air the fine lamellae or plates of the gills tend to collapse. This is overcome in certain catfishes (e.g. some species of *Clarias*) by a stiffening of the gill filaments. In addition, the gills may bear spongy arborescent organs supported by cartilage and these are able to absorb oxygen that has been taken into the gill cavity. Some of the symbranchid eels and the snakeheads have similar air-breathing organs.

Lungs are typically paired structures lying below the alimentary canal, while the swimbladder lies above the alimentary canal and just below the backbone. There are some primitive fishes in which the swimbladder, by its shape and position, is clearly a swimbladder but is used like a lung. Some of the osteoglossids or Bony tongues, the tarpon and certain characins such as *Erythrinus,* use the swimbladder in this manner. The inner lining of the swimbladder is spongy in appearance and this gives a large surface area for the absorption of oxygen and removal of carbon dioxide. Under 'Fishes' it is explained how the modern bony fishes, the teleosts, evolved from a more primitive radiation of the fishes known as holosteans. The few surviving holosteans all have a swimbladder and use it as a lung.

The question arises, why should fishes, which appear to be well adapted to life in water, have gone to such lengths to re-develop organs to enable them to breathe air directly? The answer is that other specializations enabled fishes to explore and colonize a very wide variety of habitats. With growing competition for food and living space there were still some niches that were not yet filled, namely those in which air-breathing was an advantage or even a necessity. Most of the air-breathing fishes live in water where the concentration of oxygen is low, either temporarily or permanently. The snakeheads and symbranchid eels live in small streams running through marshes where oxygen levels become very low and the streams themselves may dry up. The mudskippers are able to skip from one small pool to another within the mangrove swamps when the tide is out. The habits of the lungfishes are worth more detailed discussion and this can be found in the 'lungfish' entry.

ALBACORE, a name given to certain large Tuna-like fishes with long dorsal and anal fins in adults.

ALEWIFE *Alosa pseudoharengus,* a herring-like fish of the western north Atlantic and related to the shads of Europe. Two explana-

Air breathing catfish *Clarias batrachus.*

Air breathing Dwarf gourami *Colisa lalia.*

tions have been given for its common name: it may be a 17th century corruption of the American Indian name for the fish *Aloofe,* or it may be derived in some way from the French word *Alose* meaning a shad. The alewife is a silvery fish resembling a herring but with marked striations radiating across the gill cover. It rarely reaches 12 in (30 cm) in length. It is found both in the sea and in freshwaters, the populations often migrating back and forth. Normally they live in deep water but in June or July they come into the shallows or feeder streams to breed. Alewife are also found in Lake Ontario, from whence they migrated via the Welland Canal into Lake Erie in 1931. Since then the Lake Erie population has grown considerably. The alewife plays a fairly important part in fisheries along the Atlantic coast of the United States and in the lakes. FAMILY: Clupeidae, ORDER: Clupeiformes, CLASS: Pisces.

ALFONSINOS, a common name for members of the Berycidae, a family of primitive fishes in many ways intermediate between the soft-finned fishes and the more advanced spiny-finned groups of the superorder Acanthopterygii. The earliest berycids, from rocks of the Cretaceous period 70–135 million years old, are little different from the modern alfonsinos, so that the latter are of great interest to students of fish evolution.

The alfonsinos are ocean-living fishes of moderately deep waters down to 2,500 ft (750 m) and are found in the Atlantic and Indo-Pacific regions. *Beryx splendens* is world-wide and *B. decadactylus* is not uncommon off the continental shelf of the North Atlantic. Both have silvery bodies

with reddish fins and forked tails. As in the acanthopterygians, the first ray of the pelvic fins is spiny but there are many more soft rays (up to 13). The body is deep and compressed and the eyes are large. These fishes are rarely used for food except in Japan where *Beryx splendens,* which reaches 2 ft (60 cm) in length, is a popular table fish. FAMILY: Berycidae, ORDER: Beryciformes, CLASS: Pisces.

ALLIGATOR GARS, see 'garpikes' for which it is an alternative name.

ALPINE CHAR *Salvelinus alpinus,* a member of the large salmon family, often referred to merely as char. In Great Britain the populations of Alpine char are entirely land-locked in the deep and cool lakes of Scotland, Northern England, Wales and Ireland. Off Greenland, however, the fishes feed in the open sea but return to freshwater to breed, a habit commonly found amongst the Salmonidae.

During the final cold period of the Ice Age, the Alpine char became isolated in lakes as the ice sheet receded. As often happens, this isolation has led to slight differences in body form between the populations in the various lakes, which encouraged zoologists of the last century to refer to each lake population as a different species. It is now recognized, however, that all the British char belong to the same species.

Alpine char are fairly large fishes, a good specimen from British waters weighing up to 3 lb (1·4 kg), but they are caught by British

Annual fish of the genus *Aphyosemion.*

anglers more by accident than design. The flesh is most delicate, however, and they are actively fished for in northern Norway when they leave the deep waters of the lakes and make their way into the feeder streams to breed (a relict of their former migratory habit). One of the most attractive features of the Alpine char is its beautiful colouring. During the spawning season the males assume a bright breeding dress of intense scarlet on the belly and flanks while the back becomes jet black. FAMILY: Salmonidae, ORDER: Salmoniformes, CLASS: Pisces.

AMBERJACKS, marine fishes related to the Horse mackerels, scads and pompanos. They have fairly deep, compressed bodies, slender and crescentic tail fins. Unlike many other carangid fishes, they lack bony scutes along the lateral line. A typical species, *Seriola dumerilii* is found on both sides of the tropical Atlantic including the Mediterranean and the West Indies. Its back is a violet-blue, the flanks reddish-gold and the fins yellow but the juvenile has brilliant vertical bands of gold down the body. Amberjacks live in shoals and are voracious fish, especially when after mackerel. They can be caught by trolling with a spoon or whole mackerel and can provide considerable sport since they grow to over 100 lb (45 kg). FAMILY: Carangidae, ORDER: Perciformes, CLASS: Pisces.

AMERICAN BROOK TROUT *Salvelinus fontinalis,* strictly speaking not a trout but a char. Its native home is America and Canada,

where it inhabits the eastward-flowing rivers and grows to 14 lb (6·4 kg) in weight. It is an attractive fish, with the fins and body mottled and barred. Because of its appearance and edibility, it was introduced into Europe in 1889 as a sporting fish. The introductions have generally been successful except in Great Britain, where the fishes usually escape to the sea and are lost to sight or, if in lakes, fail to thrive. They are strongly cannibalistic and great care must be exercised if a fishery is to be maintained. FAMILY: Salmonidae, ORDER: Salmoniformes, CLASS: Pisces.

The anchovy, a small, herring-like fish that exists in enormous numbers, especially in tropical seas.

ANCHOVIES, a family of usually small and silvery fishes allied to the herrings and found in temperate and tropical seas with a few species passing into freshwater or with permanent populations in rivers. Anchovies can be immediately distinguished from any small herring-like fishes by the pointed snout that overhangs the mouth and the long and slender lower jaw. The body is slender, more or less compressed depending on the species, there is a single soft-rayed dorsal and anal fin and the tail is forked. The silvery scales are often easily shed. The majority of species are small, usually growing to 4–6 in (10–15 cm), but a few species may reach 12 in (30 cm). The anchovies, of which about a hundred species are known, are essentially tropical fishes with a few species in temperate waters. The best known of the latter is the European anchovy *Engraulis encrasicolus,* an elongated, round-bodied species that forms large shoals and is found from Norway southwards to the Mediterranean and the west coast of Africa and forms the basis for large fisheries. A very similar fish is found off the American Atlantic coast and in the Caribbean, as well as off the coasts of South Africa, Japan and southern Australia. It forms one of the three principal species in the great 'Iwashi' fisheries of Japan. Along the Pacific coasts of the Americas *Engraulis mordax* in the north and *E. ringens* in the south are also of considerable economic im-

portance, the catches off the Peruvian coasts at one time being the highest for any single species of fish in the world (not excepting the famous menhaden of the American Atlantic). The anchovies of the tropical New World all have smooth bellies without the series of saw-edged scutes found in herrings and in the anchovies of the Indo-Pacific region. The anchovies in the latter area show a number of curious specializations. In some species of *Thryssa* the body is greatly compressed, the anal fin is very long and the principal bone of the upper jaw, the maxilla, is extended back to reach beyond the head to the base of the pectoral fins or even to halfway along the anal fin (*T. setirostris*). The function of this long maxilla is not known. The most highly specialized of the Indo-Pacific forms are the species of *Coilia,* the Rat-tailed anchovies, in which the body tapers to a long filament with a very small tail fin on the end, the anal fin running the entire length and containing over a hundred finrays. In addition, the upper rays of the pectoral fins are filamentous. Although members of *Coilia* are found in shallow coastal waters or muddy estuaries, one species has very prominent rows of silvery light organs (photophores) along the lower flanks.

In addition to the anchovy fisheries of temperate waters, fairly large local fisheries are found in the Indo-Pacific region concentrating on the small, 4–5 in (10–13 cm) species of *Stolephorus.* The anchovies are also an important source of live bait for the tuna fisheries, especially off the Pacific coasts of Central America where the anchoveta *Cetengraulis mysticetus* is commonly used. FAMILY: Engraulidae, ORDER: Clupeiformes, CLASS: Pisces.

ANEMONEFISH, alternative name for the clownfish.

ANGEL FISHES, name used for three different groups of fish:
a) common name in the United States for members of the Chaetodontidae, a family of coral fishes here termed the butterflyfishes;
b) alternative name for the monkfish;
c) to the aquarist, Angel fishes are members of the freshwater genus *Pterophyllum* of the

Freshwater Angel fishes, popular with aquarists.

family Cichlidae. These are highly compressed, deep-bodied fishes with slender, filamentous pelvic rays. When seen head-on through a growth of water plants, the extreme narrowness of the body makes the fish look like just another plant stem. The light brown flanks are marked with four darker vertical bars, so that even from the side the fish blends with its surroundings.

There are still problems concerning the numbers of species in the genus *Pterophyllum,* but three are usually recognized, *P. eimeki, P. altum* and *P. scalare.* Identification is difficult for the amateur and will become more so because the hybrids between *P. eimeki* and *P. scalare* are commonly sold. *P. altum* is imported less often than the other two species.

P. scalare is the largest of the three species in the Amazon, grows to a total length of 6 in (15 cm) and has a body height (including fins) of 10¼ in (26 cm). However when kept in an aquarium it does not grow so large. Breeding in captivity is not difficult, the main problem being to recognize the sexes and this is best overcome by allowing the fishes to pair off themselves. They spawn on broad-leaved plants which have previously been cleaned by the fishes themselves. After the eggs have been deposited, the parents continually fan them and at 86°F (30°C) the young hatch in about 30 hours. The parents assist the young to hatch by chewing at the eggs and spitting the young onto leaves. There they hang suspended from short threads until the parents remove them to a shallow depression or nest in the sand. After four to five days the young, who may number as many as a thousand, are able to swim and the parents lead their brood out of the nest. FAMILY: Cichlidae, ORDER: Perciformes, CLASS: Pisces.

ANGEL SHARKS or monkfishes, sharks, the large pectoral fins of which give them a 'hybrid' appearance between a shark and a ray. Unlike the rays, the pectoral fins of Angel sharks are not joined to the head. There are two dorsal fins, no anal fin and the nostrils have two barbels that extend into the mouth. The latter is almost terminal and not underslung as in most sharks. Angel sharks are found principally in temperate waters and they feed mainly on fishes. The monkfish *Squatina squatina* of European waters is the largest, reaching 8 ft (2·4 m) in length and weighing 160 lb (73 kg). It is found in British waters, chiefly off the south coast, and enters shallow waters in summer. Of the several species known, *S. dumeril* occurs off American Atlantic coasts and *S. californica* off American Pacific coasts. FAMILY: Squatinidae, ORDER: Pleurotremata, CLASS: Chondrichthyes.

ANGLERFISHES, a highly specialized

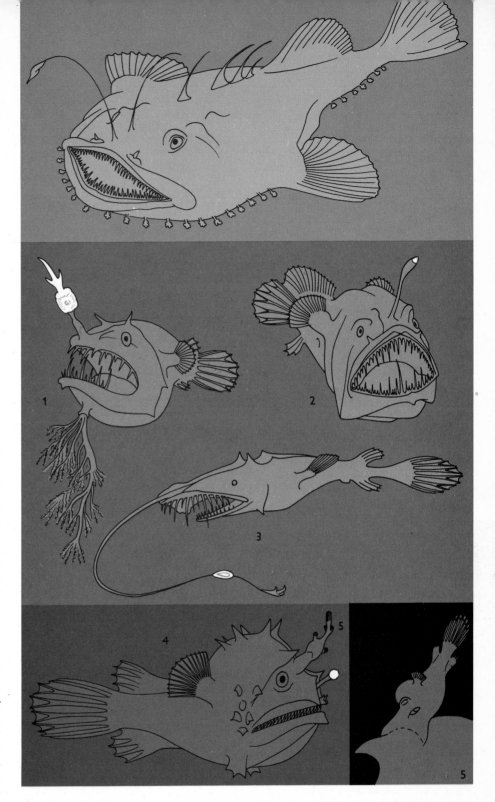

Types of anglerfishes: Common anglerfish (top), deep-sea anglerfishes (centre) including 1) *Linophryne arboriper,* 2) *Melanocetus johnsoni,* 3) *Lasiognathus saccostoma,* with various forms of lure, and (bottom) female ceratioid anglerfish *Photocorynus spiniceps,* bearing a dwarf male (5), shown enlarged to right.

group of marine fishes found in all oceans and at all depths, from shallow waters down to the abyssal trenches. The anglerfishes can be divided into three main suborders: the Lophioidea, the Antennarioidea and the Ceratioidea. The three groups share certain anatomical features, the most outstanding and the one that has given them their common name being the tendency for the first ray of the dorsal fin to be long and to develop a lure at its tip with which the anglerfish 'angles' for its prey. In addition, the pectoral fins in many species are borne on a fleshy limb, which adds to the bizarre appearance of the fish and gave rise to a former scientific name for the whole group, the Pediculati.

The first group of anglerfishes, the Lophioidea, are shallow water fishes. The Common anglerfish *Lophius piscatorius,* sometimes known as the Fishing frog, is found around European and American coasts. It is a greatly flattened fish, lying like a huge disc on the sea bottom. The mouth is enormous and the jaws are lined with sharp, needle-like teeth. The eyes are on the top of the head and the brown body is fringed with small flaps of skin so that the outline of the fish is broken and the fish itself rendered inconspicuous. The anterior rays of the dorsal fin are very long and are separated from the rest of the fin. They function as the fishing rod or illicium, the first ray having a small flap of tissue at its tip to act as a lure. This lure is dangled in front of the mouth and when small fishes come to investigate the huge mouth is suddenly opened and then closed over them. The mouth is capacious and food can be stored there until it is swallowed. It is interesting to note that Aristotle, who well merits the title of Father of Zoology, recorded this curious feeding habit over 2,000 years ago. Anglers seem to eat anything that is available. In spite of their rather sluggish appearance, they have been seen at the surface and it is not uncommon to find seagulls in their stomachs. They are large fishes, reaching 4 ft (120 cm) in length. The spawn of the anglerfish is also peculiar. The eggs are contained in a long ribbon of mucus 1–3 ft (30–90 cm) wide and up to 50 ft (16 m) long. These long ribbons are often reported floating at the surface of the sea.

The second group of anglers, the Antennarioidea, includes two important families. The family Antennariidae comprises species that are flattened from side to side (not from top to bottom as in the lophioids). One of the best known members is the Sargassum weed fish *Histrio* spp. The second family is the Ogcocephalidae, often called the batfishes (a name also used for the genus *Platax*). The batfishes are flattened like the lophioids and have large heads and fairly small bodies. The most striking feature is the limb-like pectoral fins which are muscular and are used to crawl about the bottom with a slow, deliberate waddle. The lure is hidden in a tube above the mouth and it can be projected out when the fish is hungry; the tube gives the fish a rather sharp-nosed appearance. Batfishes grow to about 15 in (38 cm) and are found in both the Atlantic and Pacific Oceans.

There is no doubt that the third suborder of anglers, the Ceratioidea or Deep-sea anglers, are amongst the most fascinating of all fishes. They are clearly separated from the other anglers by the absence of pelvic fins. Unlike the other two groups, the cerati-

An anglerfish *Antennarius* lies in wait on the sea-bed to catch passing prey.

oids do not stay on the bottom but are essentially midwater fishes of the deep seas. In this group, the body is rounded and not flattened, but the characteristic fishing lure is present. The existence of these fishes was not suspected until the 1830s when a Danish sea captain discovered one washed up on the shores of Greenland. Captain Holboell's discovery has been commemorated in the naming of one of the giants of this group, *Ceratias holboelli,* a species that grows to 36 in (90 cm). Most of the ceratioids, however, are only a few inches long. They are usually dark brown or black, without scales and with a fragile, velvety skin, although some have warty projections on the body.

It is one thing to fish with a lure in clear, shallow water but obviously this would be ineffective in depths where little or no light penetrates. The Deep-sea anglerfishes have overcome this in a remarkable way, the lure being luminescent. In members of the genus *Linophryne* there is also a luminescent, tree-like barbel hanging from the chin, as well as the luminescent lure. In *Ceratias* and *Lasiognathus* there is a further specialization. The illicium can be slowly retracted so that the prey is drawn closer to the jaws

before it is finally seized. Considering that the illicium is merely a modified finray, it is remarkable that it can be manoeuvred in this manner. In *Lasiognathus saccostoma* there is a slender line beyond the luminous bait, at the end of which is a series of horny

Veil-tailed goldfish.

hooks; these are not, however, used like fishing hooks. The ultimate sophistication in lures is found in the bottom-living *Galatheathauma*, a fish that lives at depths of 12,000 ft (about 4,000 m). In this fish the luminescent organ is on the roof of the mouth, thus tempting the prey right inside.

The extraordinary breeding habits of the Deep-sea anglerfishes, in which the male becomes parasitic on the female, have been described in the article on deep-sea fishes. The young, which look fairly 'normal' by comparison with the adults, spend their larval life in tropical and subtropical surface waters. The eyes are normal in size, but as the juveniles metamorphose into the adult they sink slowly into the deeper waters and the eyes cease to grow larger. Thereafter, the eyes become smaller and smaller in comparison with the body, so that they are often hard to find in the adult.

Food is not easy to come by in the ocean depths and the anglerfishes cannot afford to miss any opportunities, even if the prey is larger than the predator. A specimen of *Melanocoetus,* for example, measuring only 3½ in (9 cm) in length, has been found with a 6 in (15 cm) lanternfish coiled up in its elastic stomach. These anglers are for the most part small and are not rapid swimmers, relying on their lures to attract their prey to them. ORDER: Lophiiformes, CLASS: Pisces.

ANNUAL FISHES, species that, for climatic reasons, complete their life cycle in a single year. In hot countries which have one or two well defined rainy seasons with an intervening rainless period, many of the smaller pools dry up between the rains. Nevertheless, such pools are often colonized by fishes, the so-called annual fishes, which deposit their eggs in the mud before the start of the dry season. As the pools dry out, the parents die but their eggs remain in the hardened mud, protected from desiccation by their tough outer membranes. Months later, with the onset of the rains, the pools refill and the eggs complete their development and hatch. Even when they are kept in an aquarium, the parents still die because their entire metabolic cycle is geared to this short period of life. Further, to raise the eggs in an aquarium it is essential to siphon out the water in order to provide the necessary dry period. There are four New World genera of toothcarps (Cyprinodontidae), comprising about 24 species, which are annual fishes (*Austrofundulus, Cynolebias, Pterolebias* and *Rachovia*), including the beautiful Argentine pearlfishes. African annual fishes include members of the genera *Nothobranchius* and *Aphyosemion.*

ANTARCTIC CODS, fishes belonging to the family Nototheniidae, but in no way related to the true cods. They are placed in a

suborder that includes the icefishes. The Antarctic cods are confined to the ocean surrounding Antarctica and live in waters which are permanently only just above freezing. They are generally sluggish bottom-living forms with large heads and jaws and show their relationship to other perch-like fishes in the presence of spines on the first part of the dorsal fin. FAMILY: Nototheniidae, ORDER: Perciformes, CLASS: Pisces.

AQUARIUM FISHES, usually small species, often very colourful, which can be suitably kept in tanks. The aquarium itself is

quite as important as the fish that will live in it, both for aesthetic reasons and for the welfare of its inhabitants. The shape of the aquarium greatly affects the amount of oxygen that can diffuse into the water. When filled to the brim, the old-fashioned round goldfish bowl is most unsuitable because of the very small surface area in relation to the depth of the bowl. The best kind of aquarium is one made of angle-iron with glass bottom and sides; its length should be about twice its width and the width about the same as the depth. This will ensure an adequate surface area for the diffusion of oxygen. In deeper

Cichlid fishes from opposite sides of the Atlantic: *Pelmatochromis* (above) from West Africa, and *Symphysodon discus* (below) from the Amazon.

Rasbora, a well known tropical aquarium fish, during copulation. With many fishes a brief courtship precedes copulation during which the males particularly show their breeding dress to great advantage. In egg-laying fishes copulation is accompanied by the release of the reproductive cells into the water, where the eggs are fertilized.

A well stocked aquarium contains both fish and plants so that natural conditions are reproduced.

tanks and in those which have a high density of fishes, a small air pump should be used. The tank should be covered, both to keep out dust and to prevent certain tropical fishes from jumping out. The cover also provides a screen for whatever lighting is used to illuminate the tank. The type of lighting used is a matter of taste. Some aquarists favour various proprietary brands of strip lighting that simulate daylight, while others insist that ordinary household bulbs, together with daylight, are cheaper and just as good. It is important to remember that light stimulates the growth of algae on the sides of the tank (which can be scraped off with a razor blade or wiped with cotton wool from time to time). Also, a period of darkness is necessary for the well-being of some species of fishes and snails, so that constant lighting is to be avoided. The bottom of the tank should be lined with about 1½ in (4 cm) of coarse sand or gravel which has been sterilized and very thoroughly washed in a bucket under a running tap (the water will cloud if the sand is not clean). The aquarium can be filled either with rain water or with tap water, although the latter should be allowed to stand for a while before the fish are introduced. During the filling of the tank, a sheet of brown paper or plastic spread over the sand will prevent the water clouding. Any decorative stones should be well washed and sterilized before being placed in the tank.

The tank is now ready for plants. Plants from clean but still or sluggish waters can be used but those from fast-flowing streams usually do not survive long in an aquarium. A great range of plants can be bought from dealers, some of them suitable for unheated aquaria but others requiring warm water. The Canadian pond weed *Elodea canadensis* is a cold water species that can adapt well to heated aquaria. The roots should be well anchored in the sand and a small stone can be placed on top of them if there is any tendency for the plant to float upwards. Plants serve three functions in an aquarium. They diffuse oxygen into the water, they provide shelter for the fishes and they add greatly to the appearance of the aquarium. When stocking with fishes overcrowding should be avoided. A useful rule of thumb is to allow 1 gal (4·5 1) of water for 1 in (2·5 cm) of fish. Above this limit it is advisable to use artificial aeration.

There are three kinds of aquaria: coldwater, tropical and marine. The first is in many ways the simplest, the second the most decorative and the third the greatest challenge to the skill of the aquarist.

Suitable fishes for a coldwater aquarium include the common goldfish *Carassius auratus* (but not the more highly bred varieties), and many of the European and American carp-like fishes found wild in slow-flowing waters. These have the great advan-

Catfish *Corydoras elegans*, useful members of the aquarium community as they keep the tank bottom clear of detritus.

tage that they are not carnivorous and will thrive on the easily obtainable commercial fish foods (but not on the standard 'ants eggs'). In Europe, the Golden orfe as well as the tench, rudd and roach are commonly kept in tanks, but once experience is gained many more species can be tried. The North American catfish *Ictalurus* spp. is a most useful addition to the coldwater aquarium because it feeds on the food that has dropped to the bottom and thus keeps the tank clean. Some of the North American sunfishes, such

as the pumpkinseed, are also amenable to aquarium life. Inevitably, however, the aquarist will be drawn to the tropical fishes.

The tropical species are undeniably prettier and more diverse than the coldwater species. For the tropical tank a small heater and thermostat are required to keep the temperature of the water at about 72–78°F (22–25°C). Many more exotic plants can be grown than in the coldwater tank; but unfortunately there will also be a tendency for the glass to become more quickly clouded with

Most characins are carnivores, but *Myleus* sp, shown here, a relative of the fierce piranha, eats only plants and is quite inoffensive.

algae. The range of fishes available for tropical tanks is now very large and most beginners start with a community tank, that is to say one containing several different but compatible species. The suitability of different species for a community tank has been noted in individual articles in the encyclopedia but as a general rule one is safe with the smaller fishes such as the live-bearing toothcarps (guppies, swordtails, mollies and platys). These fishes will most likely breed in the tank provided that there is enough cover and this adds both to the interest and to the appearance of the tank. Many of the smaller characins (Neon tetras, X-ray fishes, Beacon fishes and Black widows) will make beautiful living patches of colour, particularly the Neon, Glowlight and Cardinal tetras. The smaller barbs are peaceful fishes and fit in well, as also do many of the danios. The cichlids, on the other hand, should be treated with caution since many of them will attack small fishes. Essential to the tropical aquarium are the small catfishes, for example,

Firemouth cichlid, of Yucatan, with its fry. This species has a fiery orange colour along the belly and this extends even into the mouth.

members of the genus *Corydoras,* since they grub around the bottom and thus keep the tank clean. Another useful addition to the community tank is either a Sucking loach *Gyrinocheilus* spp. or one of the Sucking catfishes (*Otocinclus* or *Plecostomus*). These fishes browse on the algae that grow on the glass or on stones and they again will help to keep the tank clean. Such fishes have the lips expanded to form a disc and when they adhere to the glass it is possible to see their jaws rasping away at the algae.

The larger, and more costly, tropical fishes are best left until experience has been gained with the less expensive ones. Suitable food can be obtained from dealers who sell excellent preparations of dried foods. It is advisable to supplement this occasionally with live food such as *Daphnia,* tubifex worms or finely chopped garden worms. The tropical aquarium is not difficult to maintain provided that it is kept properly heated, clean and not overstocked. Various filtering devices, which are inexpensive and run off the aerating pump, can be used to prevent an accumulation of excess food and faeces on the bottom. The skill, however, is in producing a balanced unit, with the plants supplying oxygen and the fishes keeping the film of algae down to a minimum.

The marine aquarium is the most difficult of all. The problem of obtaining seawater can be resolved by making up the correct solution using sea salt products from a dealer. Nevertheless, it is better if real seawater can be used. The commercial sea fishes are not usually kept as they grow too large, but there are many pretty coral reef fishes that do well in tanks. Compared with freshwater aquaria, seawater aquaria have become popular in relatively recent times and the range of species is still rather small. They are more expensive to keep and dealers usually invest only in species which are easily kept. Malayan angels and Sea horses are always popular and if small live food is available the latter are fairly easy to keep alive. The marine aquarium is not advised for those with limited means.

Fish are very sensitive to certain substances in the water. Copper and zinc are highly toxic and the use of copper or brass pipes for filling the tank should be avoided. Fish are also prone to various diseases, and

15

Arapaima, largest freshwater fish.

reaching about 9 ft (2·8 m) in length (reports of fishes reaching 15 ft (4·3 m) are probably exaggerated). It has a long, sinuous body, with the dorsal and anal fins set far back, the scales on the body thick and large, and the mouth not protrusible. The family to which the arapaima belongs is of considerable scientific interest because it appears to have been fairly widespread in Eocene times but is now represented by species isolated in South America, Africa, Australia and parts of the Indo-Australian Archipelago.

There are two species of osteoglossids in South America, the arapaima and the related arawana *Osteoglossum bicirrhosum.* Curiously enough, the most suitable bait for the arapaima seems to be the arawana. The arapaima is an avid fish-eater and even the armoured catfishes are readily taken. The front part of the body is a bronze-green, but nearer the tail red patches appear and the tail itself can be mottled orange and green. Arapaima live in murky waters and the swimbladder has been adapted for breathing atmospheric oxygen, the adult fishes coming to the surface about once every 12 minutes to breathe.

Male arapaima guard the eggs, which are laid in holes dug out of the soft bottom of the river bed. An interesting method has been evolved to prevent the newly hatched larvae from straying too far and thus being snapped up by predators. For three months the young fishes stay with the father and during that time they remain close to his head. What keeps them there is a substance secreted by the male from glands opening from the back of the head. This was formerly thought to be a kind of 'milk' on which the young fed but it is now known to be merely a substance that attracts the young. Should the male be killed while looking after the young, the latter will disperse until they encounter another male and will join his brood. The males apparently do not eat the young of their own species.

The arapaima has a rapid growth and a 6 in (15 cm) specimen at the London Zoo grew to nearly 6 ft (1·8 m) in a period of six years. FAMILY: Osteoglossidae, ORDER: Osteoglossiformes, CLASS: Pisces.

it is most important to buy fish that appear to be in good condition. A healthy fish swims smoothly and lithely, whereas one that is sickly is dull, listless or erratic, with the fins not erect and their edges often ragged. Avoid buying a fish from an aquarium that contains a sickly fish. Fishes are prone to white spot *Ichthiophthyrius,* fin rot, dropsy and a host of other diseases, for which bathing in solutions of potassium permanganate or salt may provide a cure. The most important thing is to isolate the affected fishes in a separate tank and to diagnose the disease with the aid of one of the many books now available.

There is some evidence that the Egyptians kept fishes not only for eating but also for the pleasure of watching them. The keeping of aquarium fishes has been practised for many centuries in China and the Far East. In Europe and the United States fish keeping has become increasingly popular since the last war and as a result the number of species available has increased enormously. With just a little care and common sense a well-balanced community of fishes can bring colour, interest and beauty into the home.

ARAPAIMA *Arapaima gigas,* a large and rather primitive fish of the Amazon basin. The arapaima is the largest member of the family Osteoglossidae or bonytongues and is one of the largest of all freshwater fishes,

ARCHERFISH *Toxotes jaculatus* and related species, perciform fishes from southeast Asian freshwaters that shoot down insects with droplets of water. The archerfishes are small, rarely reaching more than 7 in (18 cm) in length in the wild. They have fairly deep bodies and the dorsal and anal fins are set far back near the tail. The body is generally silvery with three or four broad dark bars on the flanks.

The archerfishes live in muddy water and swim just below the surface searching for insects that rest on leaves overhanging the water. When a suitable insect is spotted, the fish pushes its snout out of the water and

Archerfish *Toxotes jaculatus* and, above, showing how insect prey is brought down into the water.

squirts droplets at the insect until it falls into the water and can be eaten. A small archerfish can only shoot a few inches but an adult can hit a fly up to 3 ft (90 cm) away. Their aim is remarkable when it is considered that their line of sight is diffracted as it passes from water to air. It has been found, however, that before 'shooting' an archerfish manoeuvres to place its body in as nearly a vertical line as possible, to minimize refraction. The jet of water is squirted between the tongue and the roof of the mouth. Along the tongue there is a ridge and above it a groove along the palate; water is forced through the narrow channel between the two and emerges as a fine stream.

Archerfishes will eat other foods if no insects are available, but they retain their shooting habits in the aquarium and can be trained to shoot for their food. They usually hit with the first shot but will alter their position in the water and try again if they fail. The act of shooting seems to be induced by hunger since a well-fed fish will not shoot whereas a hungry one will do so, even aiming at blemishes on the glass of the aquarium above the water-line. The force of the jet cannot be controlled with any accuracy. On occasions, if the jet is too powerful, the insect will be knocked out of reach so that it would seem that instinct rather than learned skill plays a major part in their shooting abilities. FAMILY: Toxotidae, ORDER: Perciformes, CLASS: Pisces.

ARCTIC CHAR, an alternative name for the Alpine char *Salvelinus alpinus,* but a name that is also used in the United States for other species or races of char found in the cold arctic lakes of Canada and Alaska. FAMILY: Salmonidae, ORDER: Salmoniformes, CLASS: Pisces.

ARGENTINE PEARLFISH *Cynolebias belotti,* an egg-laying toothcarp from the La Plata basin in South America. All species of *Cynolebias* are annual fishes (see separate entry) and have a life span of only eight months, the adults dying while the eggs survive until the next season buried in the mud. The Argentine pearlfish, which grows to about $2\frac{1}{2}$ in (7 cm) in length, has a moderately deep and stocky body. In the male, the back is a dark slaty blue and during the breeding season the underside is a deep emerald green. A series of vertical rows of white pearl-like spots cover the median fins and the tail. The female is duller in colour, with a yellow-brown body and irregular dark brown spots.

These are splendid fishes to keep in an aquarium (remembering always to get young ones since their life span is so short). Breeding is stimulated by gradually lowering the water-level in the tank. The courtship and deposition of eggs are interesting to watch since the pair burrow down into the substrate (peat is an ideal medium). After the eggs have been laid, the peat should be removed, placed in a small bowl and kept slightly moist. After some weeks the peat (and thus the eggs) should be replaced in the tank in slightly acid water and the young will hatch out fairly soon after. FAMILY: Cyprinodontidae, ORDER: Atheriniformes, CLASS: Pisces.

ARGENTINES, living in the midwaters of the North Atlantic. They resemble salmon and trout in having a small adipose fin behind the dorsal fin. Two species are occasionally trawled off European coasts, *Argentina silus* and *A. sphyraena.* The former is the larger of the two and reaches 2 ft (60 cm) in length. Its flesh is very palatable and it is known to live in shoals off the west coast of Ireland where it may in the future form the basis for an important fishery.

The name 'argentine' comes from the intensely silver colouring of these fishes, particularly in the form of a wide band down the flanks. FAMILY: Argentinidae, ORDER: Salmoniformes, CLASS: Pisces.

ARGUS, a name given to certain species of the marine perch-like fishes known as grouper. The Blue-spotted argus *Cephalopholis argus* is perhaps the best known. It is found in the tropical Pacific and reaches a maximum length of 18 in (46 cm). The body is brown or olive passing into a deep blue on the fins with many small light blue spots edged with darker blue over both body and fins. There are also four to six whitish circular bands around the body, but these fishes are renowned for their quick colour changes and the bands will appear and disappear in rapid succession. The Blue-spotted argus has now been introduced into Hawaiian waters where it was previously unknown. FAMILY: Serranidae, ORDER: Perciformes, CLASS: Pisces.

AYSHEAIA *Aysheaia pedunculata,* a fossil onychophoran known only from the Middle Cambrian Burgess Shales of western Canada. It was a soft-bodied animal related to the living genus *Peripatus,* which it seems to have resembled in most respects, but had branched antennae and only ten body segments compared with the unbranched antennae and 15—43 body segments of the living forms. CLASS: Onychophora, PHYLUM: Arthropoda.

AYU, the common name for *Plecoglossus altivelis,* a peculiar salmon-like fish found in Japan. Most of the salmonid fishes have pointed teeth but the ayu, amongst other anatomical peculiarities, has plate-like teeth. Because of this, it is placed in a family of its own, the Plecoglossidae.

The ayu, which grows to about 12 in (30 cm), migrates into freshwater to spawn. During the upstream migration, Japanese fishermen used to bring their trained cormorants at night to the rivers, attach rings round the throats of the birds and then release them into the water. The ring prevents the cormorant from completely swallowing the ayu and on the return of the bird the fisherman takes the fish from the cormorant and sends it off on another foray. FAMILY: Plecoglossidae, ORDER: Salmoniformes, CLASS: Pisces.

Cynolebias nigripinnis, related to the Argentine pearlfish.

B

BARBEL *Barbus barbus,* one of Europe's largest members of the carp-like family Cyprinidae. It is also the only European member of the genus *Barbus* found outside the Danube basin. Like other cyprinids, the barbel is streamlined and a good swimmer, well adapted to the swift waters near weirs and in rapid stretches of rivers. It reaches about 14 lb (over 6 kg) in weight. Its name derives from the four mouthbarbels.

Pollution has sadly restricted the distribution of the barbel but re-stocking programmes have been fairly successful. In 1955 parts of the English rivers Trent, Welland, Bristol Avon and Severn were stocked with barbel, but only in the latter have they bred freely and expanded their range. FAMILY: Cyprinidae, ORDER: Cypriniformes, CLASS: Pisces.

BARBS, term loosely applied to certain members of the carp-like family Cyprinidae, referring to the small barbels round the mouth. Barbs include not only the genus *Barbus* but also the related genera *Hemibarbus, Spinibarbus, Puntius* and *Capoeta*. In Europe, the only barb is the barbel. Barbs are found throughout the temperate and tropical regions of the Old World and many of the smaller species are imported into Europe and the United States as aquarium fishes.

Barbs show a surprising range in size. The mahseer, the classic game fish of India, grows to about 9 ft (3 m) in length, while many aquarium barbs are fully grown at 3 in (7 cm). Identification of the species is often difficult, even for the specialist, because the shape and appearance of an individual often depend on the conditions in which it lives. In Africa, there are forms with thick, rubbery lips, forms with sharp, chisel-edged lips, and others with normal lips. Recent work has shown that the shape of the lips is in many, if not all, cases dependent on the nature of the lake or river bottom. Fishes living over rocks require a hard edge to the mouth to scrape off algae, while those with rubbery lips probably grub in the mud. There is also some evidence that lake dwellers are deeper-bodied than those that live in rivers.

Members of the Cyprinidae lack teeth in the jaws but are equipped with a set of teeth in the throat, the pharyngeal teeth. The number, size and shape of these reflect the diet of the fish and the degree to which the food must be chewed before swallowing. The pharyngeal teeth are a useful aid in identifying barbs, but this method is obviously of little help to the aquarist.

All the barbs lay eggs and many are quite easy to breed in an aquarium provided the parents are removed after they have scattered and fertilized the usually sticky eggs. Even the prettiest of barbs can become cannibals.

Most of the imported barbs come from India, Ceylon and the Indo-Malayan Archi-pelago. The commonest are the Rosy barb *Barbus concharius* from northern India; the Checkered barb *B. oligolepis* from Sumatra; the Black ruby *B. nigrofasciatus* from Ceylon; the Tiger barb *B. pentazona hexagona* from Sumatra; and the Two-spot barb *B.ficto* from Sumatra. The Golden barb, referred to as *'Barbus schuberti',* is not a distinct species but seems to be a hybrid that suddenly appeared in aquaria in the United States and is closely related to a species from Singapore.

African barbs are less frequently imported but have been keenly studied because of their importance as food fishes in inland areas. An interesting species is the Blind barb *Caecobarbus geertsi* from the Congo. See Blind

The barbel of the clear-running rivers of Europe feeds only at night.

Two Tiger barbs *Barbus pentazona hexagona*, of Sumatra and Borneo, now to be found in aquaria in Europe and North America.

fishes. FAMILY: Cyprinidae, ORDER: Cypriniformes, CLASS: Pisces.

BARBUDAS, of the genus *Polymixia,* these are small-scaled marine fishes found in both the Atlantic and Indo-Pacific regions at depths of about 600 ft (180 m). They grow to about 12 in (30 cm) in length, have two long barbels on the chin and are of little commercial importance. FAMILY: Polymixiidae, ORDER: Beryciformes, CLASS: Pisces.

BARRACUDAS, tropical marine fishes related to the much more peaceable Grey mullets (family Mugilidae). The barracudas are fierce predators which, in some areas such as the West Indies, are more feared than sharks. The body is elongated and powerful, with two dorsal fins. The jaws are lined with sharp dagger-like teeth which make a neat, clean bite. There are many records of barracudas attacking divers and they appear to be attracted to anything that makes erratic movements or is highly coloured. They feed on fishes and have been seen to herd shoals of fish, rather after the manner of sheepdogs, until they are ready to attack.

The smallest of the barracuda *Sphyraena borealis* grows to about 18 in (46 cm) and is found along the North American Atlantic coast. The Great barracuda *Sphyraena barracuda* which grows to 8 ft (2·4 m) in length, is found in the western Pacific and on both sides of the tropical Atlantic. A certain mystery surrounds its habits, for it is known to attack divers in the West Indies but in the Pacific region, and particularly in Hawaii, it has the reputation of being harmless to man. The truth of this, however, has never been properly examined, since it is difficult to obtain accurate information from people who treat the fish with such great, and perhaps well advised, respect. In the Mediterranean there is a single species, *S. sphyraena,* which reaches 5 ft (1·5 m) in length.

Barracudas are good to eat and one Pacific species is regularly fished off the coast of California. In all, there are about a dozen species which are rather similar in appearance and habits but which rarely venture into temperate waters. FAMILY: Sphyraenidae, ORDER: Perciformes, CLASS: Pisces.

BARRACUDINAS, deep-sea fishes found in all oceans, belonging to the family Paralepididae, containing half a dozen genera. They are not related to the barracudas but are superficially similar although much smaller. The majority never exceed 2 ft (61 cm) length. Their slender bodies are in many cases scaleless, except for the lateral line and in some species a luminous duct is present along the underside of the stomach although the genus *Paralepis* contains species with scaly bodies. *Lestidium ringens* is found at depths down to 1500 ft (500 m) off the American Pacific coast. Like most barracudinas, it grows to 8 in (20 cm) long and is a fish eater. Like many deep-sea fishes barracudinas make considerable vertical migrations at night, some species in the south Pacific coming so close to the surface that fishermen attract them to lights to catch them. A large part of our knowledge of these fishes comes

Golden barbs, of still waters of Central India.

The Great barracuda *Sphyraena barracuda*, of both sides of the Atlantic, has a reputation for ferocity.

from specimens spat up by tunas caught in deep water. FAMILY: Paralepididae, ORDER: Salmoniformes, CLASS: Pisces.

BARRELFISH, one of the several common names applied to butterfishes or stromateids. The barrelfish *Hyperoglyphe perciforma* is also called the logfish, rudderfish or Black rudderfish. *Schedophilus medusophagus,* sometimes known as the portrush or Portuguese barrelfish, has now been identified as the young of *Centrolophus britannicus* (see blackfish). The former is an Atlantic fish found along both American and European coasts, with occasional British records. It has a compressed, fairly deep body of a general purplish-black colour and is distinguished from the second species by the presence of a series of unconnected spines in front of the dorsal fin. Like all stromateids, these fishes have a muscular oesophagus armed with ridges or teeth. The name barrelfish derives from this fish's habit of accompanying floating objects and often entering boxes or barrels; logfish refers to individuals found swimming near barnacle covered logs. *Schedophilus perciformis* feeds on barnacles while *S. medusophagus,* as its name implies, feeds largely on jellyfishes. FAMILY: Stromateidae, ORDER: Perciformes, CLASS: Pisces.

BASKING SHARK *Cetorhinus maximus,* second only to the Whale shark in size and immediately recognizable by its very long gill clefts which extend from the upper to the lower surface of the body. There are two dorsal fins and one anal fin, very small teeth in the jaws, and the general body colour is a grey-brown. The maximum size of these sharks is usually given as 45 ft (13·5 m) and certainly fishes of 30 ft (9 m) are not uncommon. Unlike most of its relatives, the Basking shark is not carnivorous but feeds by straining plankton from the water. The gill arches are equipped with rows of fine rakers (up to 4 in/10 cm long and over 1,000 in each row) and these form a fine sieve through which the water is strained before leaving by the gill clefts. This system is clearly an efficient one since it can provide enough food for an animal that may weigh over 4 tons (4,000 kg). Basking sharks lacking gillrakers are sometimes found and it is thought that the rakers may be shed in winter and regrown every spring. They derive their name from their habit of lying at the surface. They are not dangerous to man, except perhaps accidentally when in collision with small boats.

The Basking shark is the only member of its family and appears to be found everywhere, but chiefly in temperate waters. It is fished commercially off the western coasts of Ireland (where they are known as muldoans) and Scotland, as well as off the coasts of New England, California, Peru and Ecuador. The fishes are mainly caught by harpoon as they 'bask' at the surface. The flesh is less important than the oils from the liver, which are used in tanning processes. The liver itself may comprise a tenth of the total weight of the fish and it is the buoyancy this affords that enables the Basking shark to lie motionless at the surface. Little is known about its breeding but a Basking shark off Norway in 1923 immediately gave birth to six live young when hooked. FAMILY: Cetorhinidae, ORDER: Pleurotremata, CLASS: Chondrichthyes.

BASS, a term used in Europe for the Sea perch *Dicentrarchus labrax* and its close relative the Black-spotted bass *D. punctatus* (both erroneously placed in the genus *Morone* in the older literature). The bass is considered by many to be one of the best of European angling fishes. It is a coastal fish that often enters estuaries and even ascends rivers. It is found in the Mediterranean and off the coasts of Spain and Portugal but reaches the southern coasts of the British Isles. It is found off shelving sand or shingle beaches and is often fished for in the breakers, where it feeds on fishes (sandeels, sprat and herring). Specimens of 18 lb (8 kg) have been caught but fishes of 2–7 lb (0·9–3 kg) are more usual. There are two dorsal fins, the first spiny and separated from the second. The back is blue-green, the flanks silver with a black lateral line and a white belly. This fish is considered excellent eating. The Black-spotted bass is a smaller fish, reaching 2 ft (60 cm) in length and the body is speckled with black spots. This species does not reach as far north as the British Isles. See also Black bass. FAMILY: Serranidae, ORDER: Perciformes, CLASS: Pisces.

BATFISHES, a common name given to two rather different groups of fishes. Members of

Bass of the coastal seas of northwest Europe, excellent angling fishes.

A shoal of Sea bass.

the family Ogcocephalidae, a family of the anglerfishes, are sometimes referred to as batfishes although the term is more appropriately used for members of the Platacidae, a family containing marine perch-like fishes with greatly extended wing-like dorsal and anal fins. Species of *Platax* have highly compressed, almost circular bodies and their long fins give them a bat-like appearance when swimming. They grow to about 2 ft (60 cm) and are found in the Indo-Pacific region. They are beautiful fishes with red-yellow colouring, and dark vertical bands in the young which disappear with age. Such colouring would seem to make them more conspicuous but in fact these fishes strongly resemble floating and yellowing leaves of the Red mangrove. When chased by a predator in a mangrove swamp, the fishes stop swimming and drift motionless like leaves. They feed on small crustaceans and the general detritus of coastal and mangrove swamp areas. FAMILY: Platacidae, ORDER: Perciformes, CLASS: Pisces.

BELUGA, derived from the Russian for 'white' is the name for two animals. The beluga *Huso huso* is the largest of the *sturgeons and probably the largest of all freshwater fishes. It is found in the seas and rivers of the Soviet Union and reaches 29 ft (8·8 m). The beluga *Delphinapterus leucas,* or White whale, is a relative of the narwhal. It lives in northern seas, grows to 18 ft (5·5 m).

The batfish *Platax*, one of several kinds of remarkable fishes that have winglike fins.

Bichir *Polypterus ornatipinnis* of the Congo Basin, up to 37 cm long, characteristically supports itself on its fanlike pectoral fins, when resting.

BICHIRS *Polypterus,* a genus of primitive freshwater fishes of Africa comprising about ten species. The reedfish *Erpetoichthys* (formerly known as *Calamoichthys*) is the only near relative of the primitive bichirs. The name *Polypterus* signifies 'many fins', for when these fishes are alarmed or excited a row of 8–15 little finlets are erected along the back. These are not displayed during normal swimming. The body is covered by thick, rhombic scales of a type known as ganoid (with a covering of ganoine as in certain extinct forms). A pair of spiracles (the vestigial first gill slits in most bony fishes) are conspicuous. In the larvae there are leaf-like external gills such as are known in the South American and African (but not Australian) lungfishes and also in amphibians but in no other bony fishes. In some species of *Polypterus* these gills later disappear. The intestine has a spiral valve which serves to increase the absorbent surface of the gut. This, too, is a primitive feature that is now found only in sharks and in such bony fishes as the sturgeons, lungfishes, the coelacanth and such fishes as the bowfin in the order Holostei. Bichirs can live out of water for a while breathing air into their lungs which are large but not quite so efficient as those of the lungfishes. The pectoral fins are constructed in a way similar to those of the coelacanth and its fossil relatives, that is to say with the finrays arising from a fleshy lobe. *Erpetoich-thys* is basically similar to *Polypterus* but has a more eel-like body.

The bichirs are clearly very primitive fishes but their exact relationship to living and fossil forms has been disputed. In the last century it was thought that the bichirs were related to the lungfishes. In 1929 C. Tate Regan placed the bichirs in the subclass Palaeopterygii (ancient fins) of the order Cladista. The great Russian ichthyologist Leon Berg, 20 years later, decided that the bichirs were so remote from other fishes that they deserved to be in a subclass of their own, the Brachiopterygii (short fins), that is equivalent to the subclass of lungfishes (Dipnoi) and the subclass containing all the ray-finned fishes (Actinopterygii). (See also under fishes, classification). Currently, there is a school of thought that considers the aberrant bichirs to be descendants of the Crossopterygii, the order that includes the coelacanth. As sometimes happens with interesting forms, however, there are no fossils and the true relationships of the bichirs must await the discovery of some fossil link. FAMILY: Polypteridae, ORDER: Polypteri-formes, CLASS: Pisces.

BILLFISHES, a term chiefly used in the United States for the swordfish and the sail-fish but sometimes used for some of the marlins (in which the snout may also be extended into a 'bill').

BITTERLING *Rhodeus sericeus,* a 3 in (8 cm) carp-like fish from lowland waters of Europe, the breeding cycle of which involves a freshwater mussel. The bitterling is normally silvery but in the breeding season the male develops violet and blue iridescence along the flanks and red on the belly, the fins becoming bright red edged with black. In colour, the female is less spectacular but develops a long pink ovipositor from the anal fin. It is this ovipositor, a 2 in (5 cm) tube for depositing the eggs, that gives a clue to the extraordinary breeding biology of the bitter-ling. Most fishes of the family Cyprinidae merely scatter their eggs, but the female bitterling carefully deposits its eggs inside a freshwater mussel, hence the need for the long ovipositor. The male then sheds its milt and this is drawn in by the inhalant siphon of the mussel and the eggs are fertilized inside. Normally, one has only to touch these mussels and the two halves of the shell are snapped shut. The female bitterling, how-ever, conditions the mussel by repeatedly nudging it with its mouth. This remarkable nursery for the eggs is clearly of great value to fishes that would otherwise lose a large percentage of the eggs through predators. It is difficult to see how this association be-tween the mussel and fish arose, but in return

Male and female bitterling, renowned for the way they co-operate with a mussel in breeding.

The bitterling *Rhodeus sericeus,* a carp-like freshwater fish from Europe, inspecting a fresh-water mussel.

the mussel releases its larvae while the bitter-ling is laying its eggs. These fasten onto the skin of the bitterling, which carries them around until they change into young mussels and fall to the bottom.

Attempts have been made to introduce the bitterling into England but they have not been successful. FAMILY: Cyprinidae, ORDER: Cypriniformes, CLASS: Pisces.

BLACK BASS, freshwater fishes of North America belonging to the genus *Micropterus.* The Large-mouthed black bass *M. salmoides* and the Small-mouthed black bass *M. dolomieu* both reach about 2 ft (61 cm) in length and are good sporting fishes. The two species were introduced into Europe in 1883 but neither has been particularly successful. They are most commonly found in southern

Europe. In England they have not become naturalized except for a small colony of Large-mouthed black bass which is appar-ently thriving in Dorset. The same species was also introduced into East Africa and has done well in ponds and lakes in colder areas above 4,000 ft (1,200 m). Bass were chiefly introduced into Europe for sport but they have not found favour with European anglers because they seem to be very wary and retire to the deepest parts of lakes when they grow to any size.

Bass have strong teeth in the jaws and are predatory fishes which lurk amongst stones or weeds and pounce on their prey (fishes, frogs, etc.) occasionally playing with their food as a cat does with a mouse. Both species are nest builders, constructing a large shallow nest which in the Small-mouthed bass is lined with leaves. FAMILY: Cen-trarchidae, ORDER: Perciformes, CLASS: Pisces.

BLACK BREAM, or Black sea bream *Spondyliosoma cantharus,* a marine fish of the eastern Atlantic and Mediterranean; family Sparidae; not related to the fresh-water bream, which is a carp-like fish. The Sea breams, which include the gilthead *Sparus auratus* and the gold-line *Sarpa salpa,* are deep, compressed fishes with sharp cutting teeth at the front of the jaws, often with molar-like teeth at the rear. The Black bream has a deep body which is iron-grey above and silver on the flanks with numbers of dark horizontal bands. It reaches 2 ft (61 cm) in length and when abundant is considered good eating. The young fishes approach close to the shore and may enter ports and estuaries. FAMILY: Sparidae, ORDER: Perciformes, CLASS: Pisces.

BLACKFISH, a name used for two very different fishes, one freshwater and the other marine.

1 Alaska blackfish *Dallia pectoralis,* a small freshwater fish related to the pike and found in Siberia, Alaska and northern Canada. It has a large mouth and the dorsal and anal fins are set far back on the body enabling it, like the pike, to accelerate rapidly towards its prey. Although it only reaches 8 in (20 cm) and in appearance is not very distinctive, it has been of immense interest to zoologists and naturalists because of its alleged ability to withstand being frozen. These blackfishes were formerly said to be able to survive after being frozen solid in ice for the entire winter. Laboratory experiments at the Steinhart Aquarium in California, have shown that when individuals were frozen solid for 12 hours and were then slowly thawed, they were capable of movement after some hours and later swam normally. Nevertheless, they died the following day. It is most likely that the speed of freezing and of formation of ice

Alaska blackfish with a reputation for freezing.

crystals in the cells of the body are of critical importance in the ability of these fishes to revive. FAMILY: Umbridae, ORDER: Salmoniformes, CLASS: Pisces.

2 Blackfish *Centrolophus niger,* and its close relative the Cornish blackfish, *C. britannicus* are marine stromateid fishes related to the barrelfish. These species are found in the eastern North Atlantic and Mediterranean. In *C. niger,* which reaches 3 ft (90 cm) in length, the body is elongated and purplish-black but paler on the head and belly. Little is known of the feeding habits of these fishes but young specimens have been found which had fed on pollack.

In certain parts of the British Isles the name blackfish is also used for ripe female salmon. FAMILY: Stromateidae, ORDER: Perciformes, CLASS: Pisces.

BLACK SWALLOWER *Chiasmodus niger,* also known as the Great swallower, is a deep-sea fish related to the weeverfishes. It is a small species reaching 6 in (15 cm) in length with two dorsal fins and a moderately long anal fin. Its most striking peculiarity is its ability to swallow fishes larger than itself. A fish of 6 in (15 cm) is able to swallow a prey of 10 in (25 cm). It manages this by means of two modifications. The first is an enormously distensible stomach. When the stomach is empty, the Black swallower has the shape of a slim mackerel, but when it has eaten, the stomach bulges out and the prey can usually be seen coiled up inside. The other aid to this method of feeding is the jaws, which are also distensible and elastic. Fishes usually swallow by using the muscles in the throat, but the Black swallower eases itself along the prey by using its jaws in much the same manner as a snake. Inching itself forward, it finally manages to cram the

Tompot blenny *Blennius gattorugine,* of European seas.

Common blenny or shanny out of water.

whole fish inside. Living in the deep seas where all animals are relatively scarce and well spaced out, the swallower must be able to take prey when the opportunity is presented, whether the prey be small or large. FAMILY: Chiasmodontidae, ORDER: Perciformes, CLASS: Pisces.

BLEAK *Alburnus alburnus,* a small freshwater carp-like fish found in slow-flowing waters and large lakes in Europe north of the Alps, but which has also been reported from brackish water in the Baltic. Although found over most of England and Wales, it is rare in Scotland and absent from Ireland. The bleak is gregarious and is frequently seen shoaling at the surface and catching insects; it will also browse on the bottom for aquatic larvae. During the breeding season of April to June the males develop a green-blue colouration on the back and the fins become orange. The sticky eggs are laid between stones in shallow running water. Lake-dwelling bleak migrate up feeder streams to breed. In Europe, large numbers of bleak were formerly caught and their silvery scales used in the manufacture of artificial pearls. Since the adults are only about 8 in (20 cm) long and are practically tasteless, bleak are rarely caught for any other purpose. FAMILY: Cyprinidae, ORDER: Cypriniformes, CLASS: Pisces.

BLENNIES, a group of fairly small elongated marine and brackish water fishes comprising 15 families grouped in the suborder Blennioidei. The name blenny comes from the Latin *blennius* (the scientific name used for one of the principal genera) and indicates a worthless sea fish. Blennies have very long dorsal fins and the pelvic fins, when present, are located in front of the pectoral fins under the head. Typically, the head is large, with a steeply rising forehead, and the body tapers evenly to the tail. A fleshy flap, the orbital tentacle, is often present just above the eyes. Blennies are carnivorous, bottom-living fishes, frequently well camouflaged for a life amongst rocks and in shallow waters. They are almost world-wide in their distribution.

The Scaleless blennies (family Blenniidae) are amongst the most common shore fishes of the North Atlantic but are also found in most other seas. The Tompot blenny or gattorugine *Blennius gattorugine* is the largest of the British species of blenny, its range extending southwards to the Mediterranean. It grows to 12 in (30 cm) in length. The Butterfly blenny has a similar range but only reaches 6 in (15 cm) in length. The first part of the dorsal fin is high and bears a black spot with a light border round it. The shanny *Blennius pholis* derives its name from the Cornish branch of the Celtic language. It is probably the most common of the British blennies and is frequently found in rock pools, which may have given rise to the legend that it basks on rocks in the sunshine. The male shanny exhibits parental care, looking after the eggs until they hatch. Many of the Scaleless blennies pass through a juvenile or ophioblennius stage that is so different from that of the adult that they were at first thought to be distinct species.

The Scaled blennies or klipfishes (family Clinidae) occur mostly in the southern hemisphere. These, often highly coloured, fishes are live-bearers, the male having an intromittent organ, formed from the spines of the anal fin, for introducing sperms into the female. *Heterostichus rostratus* from the Pacific coasts of North America grows to 2 ft (60 cm) in length and is able to change its colour to match its surroundings. *Neoclinus blanchardi* from the American Pacific has a

greatly enlarged mouth with the lower jaw elongated resembling what Dr Earl Herald terms a 'vast scoop shovel'. Some of the clinid fishes have fights while defending their territories, the jaws being opened wide and the gill covers extended to display two spots like eyes. After several sessions of display and aggression, one may bite the other or merely give way and swim off.

The gunnels (family Pholidae) include eel-like species found offshore in the northern hemisphere. One of the best known is the butterfish *Pholis gunnelus* which is described elsewhere. A considerable amount of parental care is shown by members of this family, the female, sometimes the male, wrapping its body around the eggs which lie in a mass on the seabed.

The wolf-fishes (family Anarhichadidae) from the North Atlantic are the giants of the blennioid tribe. As a rule, all teeth in a fish's jaws are approximately the same shape, but in the wolf-fishes the teeth at the front of the jaws are long and pointed while those at the back are flattened, crushing teeth. Two species of wolf-fish are found in the northern Atlantic and both are fished commercially. The wolf-fish *Anarhichas lupus* is the more common in the North Sea and reaches 5 ft (1·5 m) in length. The Spotted wolf-fish *A. minor* grows to about 6 ft (1·8 m) long. Both species are sometimes known as catfishes. ORDER: Perciformes, CLASS: Pisces.

BLIND FISHES, species with degenerate eyes usually found either in caves or in the deep sea. Not all deep-sea fishes are blind, but a large proportion of those that spend their time permanently in the lightless zones lack eyes. Eyes are of use, however, in those species whose prey or mate possess light organs (see Deep-sea fishes).

The Blind cave barb *Caecobarbus geertsi* is found in caves near Thysville in the Congo. It resembles its surface-living relatives of the genus *Barbus* in general shape but is flesh-coloured and lacks eyes. A few

Blind cave characins of Mexico.

were imported into Europe in 1956 but the export of these fishes is now rigidly controlled to prevent their extinction. The most common blind fish kept by aquarists is the Blind cave characin *Astynax jordani,* a species found in caves near San Luis Potosi in Mexico. The species from which it most likely evolved is a Mexican subspecies of *Astynax fasciatus* which is found in surface streams in the same area. Apart from the colouring and the absence of eyes, the cave species is remarkably similar to the surface form. Small eyes are present in the young blind fish but these become covered by skin as the fish grows, even if kept in the light.

BLUEFISH *Pomatomus saltatrix,* a marine perch-like species amongst the most savage and bloodthirsty of all fishes. It does not attack humans, however, and never achieved the notoriety of the barracudas. Bluefishes are deep-chested, slender-tailed and derive their name from their colour. They live in fast moving shoals in all tropical and sub-tropical waters except the eastern Pacific. Anglers hunt for bluefishes both for sport and for food and since these fishes reach 30 lb (13 kg) in weight they are a worthy challenge to the sportsman.

The large shoals of bluefishes that move up and down the American Atlantic shores principally feed on the enormous shoals of menhaden *Brevoortia,* species related to the shads. The bluefishes have the reputation for

Bluefish, a large killer fish of the western Atlantic.

being animated chopping machines the sole aim of which appears to be to cut to pieces, or otherwise mutilate, as many fish as possible in a short time. They have been seen to act like a pack of wolves, driving part of a shoal of menhaden into shallow coves from which they cannot escape. The menhaden apparently fling themselves onto the beach in an effort to escape from these savage predators. The sea is bloodstained and littered with pieces of fish after the bluefishes have eaten. Various impressive statistics have been cited to illustrate the destructive powers of the bluefishes. As many as 1,000 million bluefishes may occur each summer season off American coasts and if each eats only ten menhaden a day and the season lasts for 120 days, then the stock of menhaden must be depleted by 1,200,000,000,000 individuals during that time and this does not take into account the juvenile menhaden that fail to live to adulthood from other causes. FAMILY: Pomatomidae, ORDER: Perciformes, CLASS: Pisces.

BOARFISH *Capros aper,* an oceanic fish related to the John dory. It has a deep, compressed body, $6\frac{1}{4}$ in (16 cm) long, and a pointed snout. It is found throughout most of the Atlantic Ocean and also occurs in the Pacific. FAMILY: Zeidae, ORDER: Zeiformes, CLASS: Pisces.

BOMBAY DUCK *Harpodon nehereus,* a marine fish also known as the bummalow which is eaten seasoned and dried in India. The Bombay duck is one of the myctophoid fishes, a group that includes the deep-sea lantern-fishes. It is found in estuaries round the coasts of India, Burma and China. It reaches about 16 in (40 cm) in length, has long pectoral and pelvic fins and a row of enlarged scales along the lateral line. There are several other species of *Harpodon* but only *H. nehereus* is of commercial importance, mainly because of the proximity of large shoals of these fishes to centres of population. It is also eaten fresh as well as dried. FAMILY: Harpodontidae, ORDER: Salmoniformes, CLASS: Pisces.

BONITOS (sometimes spelt bonitas in the United States), a name used for certain of the smaller tuna-like fishes but not with any consistency, the name being arbitrarily applied to some of the striped fishes of the family Scombridae. In Europe, *Katsuwonus pelamis* is known as the Oceanic bonito, but in the United States this species is referred to as the skipjack. The bonitos, in the broad sense of the term, are found in both the Atlantic and the Indo-Pacific region. They are highly streamlined fishes, often with the fins folding into grooves, and the tail is crescentic. Their bodies are superbly adapted for an oceanic life. The pelamid or Belted bonito *Sarda sarda,* known in the United States as the Atlantic bonito, is found on both sides of the Atlantic as well as in the Mediterranean and sometimes reaches British coasts. It attains 3 ft (10 cm) in length and its high quality white meat is canned in the United States. The Oceanic bonito has a similar distribution and reaches about the same size. It differs from the Belted bonito in having bluish bands running horizontally along the lower part of the body (the bands run obliquely on the upper part of the body in the Belted bonito). It has a remarkable turn of speed, about 25 mph (40 kph) which enables it to chase flying fishes, often leaping clear out of the water to do so. It is also said to circle shoals of fishes and will then charge into the middle of the shoal. Occasionally specimens have been washed onto British coasts (Wales) but the species is essentially

Arawana, South American Bony tongue.

one of warm water and 68°F (20°C) seems to be its optimum temperature. FAMILY: Scombridae, ORDER: Perciformes, CLASS: Pisces.

BONY TONGUES, a family of freshwater bony fishes found in South America, Africa and Australasia and characterized by the fact that the fishes use the teeth of the tongue and those on the roof of the mouth when biting rather than utilizing the upper and lower jaws. The distribution of the Bony tongues, which parallels that of the lungfishes is both confirmation of the primitiveness of the group and also evidence for the theory of Continental Drift proposed by Wegener.

The South American Bony tongues are the arapaima *Arapaima gigas* and the arawana *Osteoglossum bicirrhosum,* the former being one of the largest of all freshwater fishes. The arawana swims at the

The distribution of the Bony tongues: I. *Osteoglossum bicirrhosum,* 2. *Arapaima gigas,* 3. *Clupisudis niloticus,* 4. *Scleropages leichhardtii.*

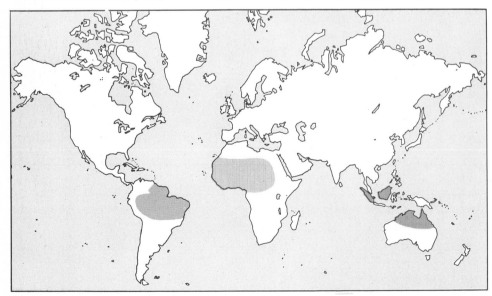

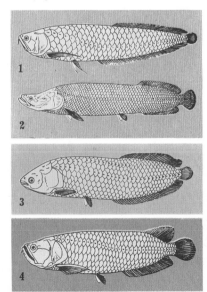

surface and has two leaf-like processes under the chin. These are held in front of it and appear to register any disturbances in the water such as might be caused by a struggling insect, which is then promptly eaten.

The single African Bony tongue *Clupisudis niloticus* lives in central and west Africa, chiefly to the north of the equator. Unlike other members of this family, *Clupisudis* has a small mouth and feeds on tiny organisms. It reaches 3 ft (10 cm) in length and constructs nests up to 4 ft (1·3 m) in diameter with thick walls made from vegetation cleared from the centre of the mass selected, the floor of the nest being the bare bottom of the swamp.

The Australian Bony tongue *Scleropages leichhardtii* is found in Australia and New Guinea, while its close relative *S. formosus* lives in Borneo and Sumatra. Both have shorter dorsal fins than the African and South American species. The mouth is inclined downwards and as in the arawana there are two small barbels. The two species of *Scleropages* are mouth brooders, as may be the arawana, the eggs being incubated in the mouth of the fish and not in a nest. *Scleropages* reach over 3 ft (10 cm) in length.

The Bony tongues show many primitive anatomical features and are of great interest

Bowfin, of North America, sole surviving species of a family that was once widespread.

in tracing the evolution of the more advanced bony fishes. Their closest relatives amongst modern fishes appear to be the Elephant-snout fishes or Mormyriformes. FAMILY: Osteoglossidae, ORDER: Osteoglossiformes, CLASS: Pisces.

BOWFIN *Amia calva*, a member of one of the two surviving groups of Holostei, primi-

tive ray-finned fishes that gave rise to all the modern bony fishes (see fishes and Fossil fishes). Fossil bowfins have been found in Europe but the only surviving species is now confined to the eastern side of North America. It is a cylindrical, solid-looking fish with a long dorsal fin and a heavy armour of scales. The body is dull brownish-green in colour, lighter underneath, with several dark

The boxfish or trunkfish *Ostracion cornutus*, encased in bony armour, indulges in chemical warfare.

Another species of the boxfishes or trunkfishes, *Ostracion lentiginosus.*

vertical stripes. A black spot is found near the base of the tail, margined in males with yellow.

There are certain anatomical features which are of interest in the bowfin. Underneath the lower jaw is a bony plate, the gular plate, a relict from its more primitive ancestors. In the intestine there are remnants of a spiral valve, a device that is found in many primitive fishes increasing considerably the digestive surface of the intestine. A spiral valve is also found in sharks. The swim-

bladder has a cellular structure that enables the bowfin to breathe atmospheric oxygen. Whereas most fishes swim by undulations of the body, the bowfin cruises majestically by a series of waves passing along its long dorsal fin. The normal method is adopted, however, for faster swimming.

Bowfins live in warm sluggish waters, especially in shallow and weedy areas. In the breeding season in early summer the males make a round nest on sandy or gravelly bottoms or in clearings in weed patches.

Bream *Abramis brama,* valued as a sport fish. It favours the lower reaches of large rivers.

They then mate with several females and after the eggs are laid guard them until the fry hatch and can swim well. They are carnivorous and seem to have a particular liking for game fishes. A large bowfin may reach almost 3 ft (10 cm) in length.

Bowfins are of little economic importance. They are eaten in the southern parts of the United States but are elsewhere regarded more as pests. Throughout the United States there is only a single species but it has received a variety of common names such as dogfish, mudfish, lawyer, grindle, choupique, Speckled cat and spot-fin. FAMILY: Amiidae, ORDER: Holostei, CLASS: Pisces.

BOXFISHES or trunkfishes, fishes belonging to the genus *Ostracion,* the head and body of which are enclosed in a solid box of bony plates with only the fins, jaws and the end of the tail projecting and free to move. In cross-section the box-like body is triangular, rectangular or pentagonal, the underside being flat. There are several species, growing to 20 in (50 cm) found around the coral reefs and coasts of the Indo-Pacific area. Since the body is rigid, swimming can only be accomplished by sculling movements of the unpaired fins, with the pectoral fins helping to stabilize what would otherwise be highly erratic movements. Many of the boxfishes are brightly coloured with patterns and spots of red and blue, yellow and blue, blue with a red band, and so on. These bright colours probably serve to warn predatory fishes that the owner is not edible. When boxfishes are attacked they secrete a virulent poison into the water which can kill other fishes. FAMILY: Ostraciontidae, ORDER: Tetraodontiformes, CLASS: Pisces. (Ill. p. 27, 28.)

BRAMBLE SHARK *Echinorhinus brucus,* sometimes known as the Alligator dogfish, a large shark found in tropical and temperate waters in most parts of the world. This fish has two dorsal fins, set rather far back on the body, and there is no anal fin. The body is covered with the usual denticles found in sharks but each one bears one or two sharp spines to give the fish its prickly appearance. Bramble sharks grow to about 10 ft (3 m) in length and although very rare in the western North Atlantic they are fairly common off the Atlantic coasts of Africa and Europe reaching as far north as the British Isles. FAMILY: Echinorhinidae, ORDER: Pleurotremata, CLASS: Chondrichthyes.

BREAMS, deep-bodied carp-like fishes of European freshwaters. They are unrelated to the Sea breams (family Sparidae). In England there are two species, the Common bream *Abramis brama* and the Silver bream *Blicca bjoerkna* which has been described elsewhere. The Common bream has a compressed body with a very high back and short head. The upper parts are grey to black, the sides lighter, the belly silvery and the fins grey or blue-black. It is found chiefly in sluggish weedy waters throughout most of Europe north of the Pyrenees. Bream normally swim in shoals, each shoal made up of individuals of about the same size, usually near the bottom except in hot weather when they tend to lie still near the surface. They grow to over 12 lb (5·4 kg) in weight and are cunning and difficult to catch. They feed on insect larvae, molluscs and worms which they extract from great mouthfuls of mud sucked up from the bottom. The Common bream often shoal with Silver bream and when small the two species are difficult to distinguish. The pharyngeal or throat teeth of the Silver bream are in two rows whereas those of the Common bream are in a single row.

From the angler's point of view, the relative ease with which the bream will hybridize with the roach is a source of considerable annoyance. The hybrids strongly resemble the roach but grow to a much larger size, so that potentially record roach have, on closer examination, proved to be merely hybrids of the two species. From the roach, the hybrids can be distinguished fairly easily, having 15–19 branched rays in the anal fin (9–12 in the roach, but 23–29 in the bream). FAMILY: Cyprinidae, ORDER: Cypriniformes, CLASS: Pisces.

BRILL *Scophthalmus rhombus,* a flatfish from the Mediterranean and eastern North Atlantic. It lies on its right side and is similar to the turbot, but is more oval in shape and has smooth scales with no tubercles. The general colour is grey, brown or greenish with darker patches or mottlings and usually speckled with white spots. The brill, which is common round British coasts, lives on sandy bottoms at depths of 180–240 ft (54–72 m) and is often caught on the same grounds as the turbot. It grows to about 2 ft (60 cm) in length and the flesh is considered most delicately flavoured. In the North Sea spawning takes place in spring and summer, the adult female producing about 800,000 eggs. After hatching, the young come inshore, but move back into deeper water after they have completed their metamorphosis and have attained the flat form of the adult. FAMILY: Pleuronectidae, ORDER: Pleuronectiformes, CLASS: Pisces.

BRISTLEMOUTHS, a name for small deepsea fishes with thin fragile bodies, rarely more than 3 in (7·5 cm) long, of the family Gonostomatidae. Although very abundant they are rarely seen except by fish specialists. Their alternative name, lightfishes, expresses the fact that they have luminous organs which in some genera are grouped together in glands whilst in others they are separate.

The Pearl or Mosaic gourami of southeast Asia, a bubble nest Builder.

The genus *Cyclothone* has species all over the world and many authors have voiced the opinion that they are amongst the most numerous fishes in the seas but because of their unsubstantial bodies and the depths at which they live they are not likely ever to be of any economic importance. Some species take five years to reach 2 in (5 cm) in length. Little is known of their breeding but at least one species of the genus *Vinciguerra* has floating eggs and larvae that are difficult to distinguish from those of sardines. FAMILY: Gonostomatidae, ORDER: Salmoniformes, CLASS: Pisces.

BUBBLE NEST, a very distinctive type of nest made by some of the labyrinth fishes. The nest is formed by blowing bubbles of air and sticky mucus at the surface of the water, resulting in a small heap of foam that is sufficiently firm to keep its shape in still waters until the eggs have hatched. The adult fishes mate below the nest and if the eggs are heavier than water, as in the Siamese fighting fish, the male takes them in its mouth once they have been fertilized and blows them onto the underside of the nest. The eggs become coated with mucus while in the mouth of the male and this helps them to adhere to the nest. The male then guards the nest and the young until they can fend for themselves. In some of the gouramis, strands of algae may be woven into the nest. The eggs of some gouramis and also some Paradise fishes (*Macropodus* species) contain oil droplets so that they are lighter than water

and as they are laid they float up into the nest.

Although these bubble nests are made in still waters, usually amongst floating plants, they are not permanent enough to withstand a long incubation period. In most species, therefore, the young hatch in only 24–36 hours and are able to swim in three days. After this period, the female (if she has not already been driven away by the male) appears to lose her maternal instincts and will eat any young that escape from the guardianship of the male.

BULLHEADS, a name used for two widely separated groups of freshwater fishes having in common broad heads heavy in relation to the rest of the body. They also share the alternative name of *Miller's thumb. In Europe the bullheads are fishes of the family Cottidae (see Miller's thumb). The bullheads of the United States belong to the family Ictaluridae, more or less tadpole-shaped freshwater fishes. They are naked catfishes with four pairs of moderately long barbels. The dorsal fin is short and high, with a strong erectile spine and a long-based anal fin. The tailfin is rounded or square-ended. There are four kinds, the Black bullhead *Ameiurus melas,* Yellow bullhead *A. nebulosus* and the Marbled bullhead *A. n. marmoratus.*

The Black bullhead, up to 12 in (30 cm) or more long, variable in colour, from green to slaty-olive, lives in standing water or slow-moving rivers, from the Great Lakes to Kansas and Texas. The Yellow bullhead, up

Indonesian bumblebee fish, imported into the United States and Europe as an aquarium fish.

Siamese fighting fish *Betta splendens* at bubble nest, shown at the top of the picture.

Burbot, the only freshwater cod.

Butterfish, of the coasts of western Europe, so called for its slippery, slimy skin.

to 14 in (35 cm), coloured yellow to greyish green with dark blotches, inhabits the Great Lakes region and the Mississippi Basin. The Brown bullhead, up to 16 in (40 cm), is also found in the Great Lakes region and the eastern United States, and its related species, the Marbled bullhead, up to 18 in (45 cm), is found farther south, to Carolina and Florida.

The Brown bullhead has been introduced into European waters, where it has flour-ished. It has been described as providing the fisherman with a low-cost supply of protein and like its relatives it feeds mostly on young fishes, worms, insect larvae and also fish spawn. FAMILY: Ictaluridae, ORDER: Siluriformes, CLASS: Pisces.　　　　M.B.

BUMBLEBEE FISH *Brachygobius xanthozona*, $1\frac{3}{4}$ in (4 cm) long, a brightly coloured brackish water goby from Sumatra and Borneo. In the wild, it lives in estuaries clinging to wracks with its sucker-like pelvic fins. This species is well known in Europe and the United States because it is commonly imported as an aquarium fish. It thrives much better if a little sea salt is added to the water. It is prettily marked with vertical bands of yellow and black but is something of a liability in a community tank since it is an inveterate fin-nipper and will sometimes eat young fishes. FAMILY: Gobidae ORDER: Perciformes, CLASS: Pisces.

BURBOT *Lota lota*, the only freshwater member of the cod family. It derives its common name from the Latin for a beard, a reference to the barbel on its chin. The burbot lives in most European rivers except those in the extreme north and south. Its nearest relative is the ling. It has an elongated, subcylindrical body blotched with shades of brown and its general form has given rise to an alternative name, eelpout. It was formerly found in most eastward flowing rivers in England and its grea stronghold was the Norfolk Broads. In recent times a variety of factors such as draining the land and other works have led to the burbot becoming very rare in England and for several years there have been no reliable reports of specimens having been caught. A rather secretive fish, it lurks near the bottom among weeds during the day but comes out at night to feed on frogs and small fishes. The burbot is also found in Asia and there are two subspecies in North America. It usually grows to 24 in (60 cm) but sometimes to as much as 39 in (98 cm). FAMILY: Gadidae, ORDER: Gadifcrmes, CLASS: Pisces.

BUTTERFISH, or gunnel *Pholis gunnellus*, an elongated blenny-like fish commonly found hiding under stones along European and North American coasts when the tide is out. Generally it is buff-coloured with a row of black spots along the base of the long dorsal fin; the pectoral fin may be orange or yellowish. The body is covered with fine scales and is slimy; anybody trying to pick it up will be in no doubt why it is called the butterfish.

The breeding of this fish is quite unusual. The female lays the eggs in a small clump about 1 in (2·5 cm) in diameter, the eggs being compacted into a ball by the female curving her body into a loop and laying the eggs within the circle. The ball of eggs is then thrust into a hole in the rocks or into an empty shell. Both parents (which is a rare procedure in fishes) take turns in guarding the eggs until the young hatch after about four weeks. The young swim out to sea for several months and then return to the shore. Most fishes have paired ovaries, but in the butterfish there is a single long ovary. These fishes grow to about 10–12 in (25–30 cm) in length. FAMILY: Pholididae, ORDER: Perciformes, CLASS: Pisces.

BUTTERFLYFISHES, a common name used for two quite distinct groups of fishes, an African freshwater flying fish and a group of marine, coral reef fishes of the family Chaetodontidae.

1. Freshwater. The butterflyfish *Pantodon buchholzi*, a species from central West Africa related to the Bony tongues. It has the distinction of being one of the few freshwater flying fishes. Growing to 4 in (10 cm) in length, it has the head and body flattened somewhat on top and rounded below. The back and sides are mottled brown and dark green. The pectoral fins, from which the fish derives its name, are large and are coloured brown and white, while the pelvic fins are reduced to four long finrays ringed alternately with brown and white. The latter are spread like a fan when the fish is cruising gently in water. The central rays of the tail are also elongated.

Imperial angelfish, one of the marine butterflyfishes noted for their bright colours.

The flight of the butterflyfish is interesting. The pectoral skeleton is enlarged to allow for the greatly developed muscles that operate the pectoral fins, which are actually flapped in flight (see Flight in fishes). In the wild, this species is found in lakes, ponds and sluggish weedy waters. It feeds on small fishes and also insects which have dropped into the water and is reported to be able to catch insects while it is out of the water. Butterfly-

Butterflyfish, a freshwater flying fish, using actual beats of the fins rather than gliding.

fishes can be kept in large and fairly shallow aquaria, which must of course be covered. They need live food and it is advisable to keep a culture of cockroaches or flies for this purpose.

Breeding is also possible in captivity. The male at first holds the female with his elongated pelvic rays but later wraps himself around her. The middle rays of his anal fin are elongated to form a tube so that it is easy to recognize the sexes. The eggs float on the surface of the water and hatch in three days at 86°F (30°C). Very small insects such as greenfly (aphids) should be provided for the young. FAMILY: Pantodontidae, ORDER: Osteoglossiformes, CLASS: Pisces.

2. Marine. Small and highly coloured marine fishes belonging to the family Chaetodontidae and found chiefly on coral

Marine butterflyfish *Pomacanthus arcuatus*, usually black with yellow bands, but sometimes with black scales edged with white.

reefs. They are also known as angelfishes. These butterflyfishes are deep-bodied and compressed with a long dorsal fin (the anterior rays are spiny) and a long anal fin (with the first three rays spiny). The deep body allows for considerable agility and they seem to flutter around coral heads, diving into cracks at the first sign of danger. Often they have a dark vertical bar across the eyes making them inconspicuous and near the tail there is a large eye-spot. It is thought that predators mistake the tail of the fish for the head, an illusion that is encouraged by some species which on occasion will swim slowly backwards.

The colours of these fishes are often quite splendid and are well shown in the accompanying pictures. In some species, such as the Imperial angelfish *Pomacanthus imperator*, the colouration in the young is quite different from that of the adult. Their ability to disappear into crevices in the coral suggests that their bright colouration is used not for camouflage but to advertise their terri-

tories, which they defend with vigour. In some areas the reef population works in shifts, some species occupying particular areas during the day and other species moving in at night. The Blue angelfish *Pomacanthus semicirculatus* has a series of odd markings on the tail. One particular specimen brought to the fish market in Zanzibar had the markings arranged in what appeared to be Arabic script. On one side of the tail pious Muslims read *Laillaha Illalah* (There is no God but Allah) but on the reverse side was written *Shani-Allah* (A warning sent from Allah). The fish was eventually sold for 5,000 rupees.

The mouths of butterflyfishes are small and have sharp teeth for picking small worms and other invertebrates out of cracks in the coral. In certain species, such as *Chelmon rostratus*, the snout is elongated and tube-like with the small mouth at the end, enabling the fish to poke even deeper into crevices. FAMILY: Chaetodontidae, ORDER: Perciformes, CLASS: Pisces.

CANDIRU or carnero, a small South American catfish which becomes parasitic on larger fish. Habitually it lives in the gill cavities, and with its sharp teeth and the spines on its gill covers it induces a flow of blood on which it feeds. The best known species and one that is greatly feared by the peoples of Brazil is *Vandellia cirrhosa*. This little fish enters the urinogenital apertures of men and women, particularly if they happen to urinate in the water. It seems likely that this is accidental, the fish mistaking the flow of urine for the exhalant stream of water from a fish's gills. Having penetrated, however, it is almost impossible to remove the candiru without surgery because of the erectile spines on the gill cover. The South American Indians often wear special sheaths of palm fibres to protect themselves. The candiru thus has the distinction of being the only vertebrate to parasitize man. FAMILY: Trichomycteridae, ORDER: Cypriniformes, CLASS: Pisces.

CAPELIN *Mallotus villosus,* a small member of the salmon family from the northern Pacific coasts of North America and Asia. It is notable for the great shoals of adults that swim ashore to lay their eggs on the sand, the beach often being covered by masses of fish and eggs. A rather similar phenomenon is seen in the grunion *Leuresthes tenuis,* a small fish the life cycle of which is closely tied to the phases of the moon. The fishes swim as far up the beach as possible during high spring tides and bury their eggs in the sand; the eggs hatch and the larvae make their escape to the sea within a few minutes of the next high spring tide reaching them. FAMILY: Salmonidae, ORDER: Salmoniformes, CLASS: Pisces.

CARDINALFISHES, a family of small marine fishes mainly from the tropical Atlantic and Indo-Pacific, although a few species enter freshwater. They have two dorsal fins, the first spiny, and two spines at the front of the anal fin. Most species are only a few inches long. Some have luminous organs and many species brood the eggs in the mouth. *Apogon endekataenia* lives

amongst the spines of certain long-spined Sea urchins while *A. stellatus* lives in the mantle cavity of giant conch shells. In *A. ellioti* there is a luminous gland near the front of the abdominal cavity. The light is provided by cultures of luminous bacteria and the photophore or light organ has a lens and reflector. Two more photophores are found near the end of the intestine. The muscles surrounding the anterior photophore are translucent and it is they that act as the lens.

Cardinalfishes are often extremely numerous. Professor W. Gosline reported catching over 1,000 specimens of a 3 in (8 cm) species, *A. brachygrammus,* within a very small area of the reef.

The cardinalfishes are predominantly brown and red in colour. In those species that care for the eggs, it is sometimes the male that takes the eggs into the mouth. FAMILY: Apogonidae, ORDER: Perciformes, CLASS: Pisces. (Ill. p. 52.)

CARPET SHARKS, a family of moderately sized but occasionally large sharks characterized by a prominent groove running from each corner of the mouth forward to the nostril where there is a thick and fleshy barbel. Other fleshy appendages are often found around the margin of the head and these, together with the mottled or marbled body colours, help to conceal the fish against the background of the seabed. There are two dorsal fins and, unlike most sharks, the tail is not turned upwards but continues the general line of the body. The Carpet sharks are also unusual in that they show habits transitional between the oviparous or egg-laying sharks and the ovoviviparous or live-bearing sharks. Members of the genera *Stegostoma, Nebrius, Chiloscyllium, Hemiscyllium* and *Parascyllium* lay eggs, while live young are produced by species of *Ginglymostoma, Orectolobus* and *Brachyaeturus*. There are between 20 and 30 species of Carpet sharks, all from the Indo-Pacific area except the Atlantic Nurse shark *Ginglymostoma cirratum*. The latter is one of the largest members of this family, reaching 14 ft (4·2 m) in length, and it occurs in tropical waters on both sides of the Atlantic. The

Zebra shark *Stegostoma fasciatum* of the Pacific is another large species (up to 11 ft or 3·3 m) and is recognizable by the dark stripes on the body. The majority of sharks are rather nondescript in their colouration, but the Carpet sharks are exceptional and especially in the case of the species from Australian waters, where they are known as 'wobbegongs'. In these the body is marked with green, brown and white and the colour pattern is so striking that their skins have been tanned for leather. The Carpet sharks feed on a variety of invertebrates (prawns, lobsters, cuttlefish, Sea urchins) and also on fishes. Two or three rows of teeth are usually functional in each jaw. In spite of their sometimes large size, the Carpet sharks are not aggressive but have been known to use their teeth in defence. FAMILY: Orectolobidae, ORDER: Pleurotremata, CLASS: Chondrichthyes.

CARPS or carp-like fishes, slender streamlined fishes almost entirely found in freshwater, although a few will occasionally go into brackish water, as in the Baltic Sea. Their main centre of distribution is southern Asia from whence they may have originally evolved. Carp-like fishes are entirely absent from South America, Australia and also Madagascar, which was isolated from the mainland before the carps entered Africa. In South America, the ecological niches normally occupied by carps are taken by the related ostariophysin family of Characidae (which may have been ancestral to the Cyprinidae).

Typically, the carps are fairly slender, with silvery scales, a single dorsal fin set at about the midpoint of the body and a forked caudal fin. There are no teeth in the jaws, but these may develop a horny cutting edge for scraping algae or may bear disc-like lips which act as a sucker. One or two pairs of short barbels may be present at the corners of the mouth. Mastication of food, such as insects, plants, detritus, is achieved by a set of teeth in the throat, the pharyngeal teeth (see separate entry). Identification of these fishes is often extremely difficult, especially those in Africa and parts of Asia about which little has been recorded and the collections of which in museums are small. In many cases, the description of their colours in life has had to wait until quite recently when certain species have become better known through the efforts of aquarists.

The larger carp-like fishes have long been an important source of food in inland areas. As a result, some have been artificially introduced into many parts of Europe, North America and certain tropical countries, sometimes to the detriment of the indigenous species. The Common carp *Cyprinus carpio* is a native of Asia but was introduced into England via Europe, presumably by monks who kept these fishes in monastery tanks, in about the 12th century.

In Ethiopia a scaleless domesticated variety of the Common carp has recently been found and this too must have been an introduction and is thought to have been brought in by Italians in 1942. The Crucian carp *Carassius carassius,* a close relative of the goldfish, is a native of Asia and Europe that was introduced into England in about the 17th century. There was an interesting report from Essen in 1806 of a Crucian carp found inside a hailstone, but clearly this is not a normal method of introduction. The Common carp is now widespread in the United States and its introduction dates from fishes imported into California from Germany in the 1870s. Conditions in America seem to suit it and a magnificent specimen of 55 lb (25 kg) has been recorded from American waters. Wild goldfish, which escaped from ponds and aquaria, have now become established in some parts of America. In Japan, the Common carp has for centuries been regarded as a symbol of fertility, but the earliest record of this fish is from China in 500 BC. The first European record seems to be that of Theodoric (475–526 AD), King of the Ostrogoths, whose secretary Cassiderus was compelled to issue a circular to provincial rulers urging them to improve the supply of carp for the king's table.

The carp-like fishes are all egg layers. The so-called Viviparous barb *Barbus viviparus* was at first thought to produce live young (like the toothcarps) but it is now known to reproduce like other cyprinids. Some species lay eggs in shallow water, some in deep, some attach their eggs to aquatic plants, while yet others release their eggs into the water so that they float downstream with the current while the embryos develop. In tropical countries the period of embryonic development may be very short, the larvae hatching in only 36 hours. Other species, such as the bitterling, have formed strange associations with other animals for the care of their eggs.

There are 14 species of carp-like fishes in Great Britain, many of them meriting a separate entry (see barbel, bream, bleak, chub, dace, gudgeon, minnow, roach, rudd, tench and White bream). All of these are also found on the continent of Europe and a few, such as the roach and the minnow, reach right across to Asia. The slow spread of the carp-like fishes from Asia is shown by the fact that there are many more species in Asia than in Europe, more in Europe than in England and more in England than Ireland, to which island very many of the species never reached before it separated from the mainland. The European forms show a number of interesting adaptations. The rapfen is unusual in having an underslung lower jaw and predacious habits. The bream, the White bream and the vimba are highly flattened (laterally compressed) forms, a body shape that gives them great manoeuverability. The zeige *Pelecus cultratus,* an insectivorous and surface-living form, is very similar in appearance and habits to the Asiatic genus *Culter* (the two genera are fairly closely related). Other European forms are adapted to life in swift streams, for example the gudgeon, or to still waters, for example the tench. Finally, there are many more generalized forms, typified by the minnow *Phoxinus phoxinus.*

The Common carp is a moderately deep, laterally compressed fish with a large dorsal fin, short anal fin and two pairs of barbels round the mouth. The scales in wild carp are large, there being about 35–37 along the lateral line, but in the domesticated varieties there are either just a few large scattered scales (Mirror carp) or no scales at all (Leather carp). Carp are very commonly used in fish culture, especially in eastern Europe. By breeding resistant strains, it has been possible to grow them near to the Arctic Circle as well as under tropical conditions. The Common carp grows to a large size and, in addition to the American record already quoted, an English specimen weighed 44 lb (20 kg) and one from South Africa weighed no less than 85 lb (40 kg). Carp are hardy fishes and in winter tend to form shoals of 50 or more which cluster together in the deep waters of lakes or ponds. At this time their metabolic rate drops sharply so that they can be said to 'hibernate', although it is now more usual to speak of this as 'winter torpidity'.

The Near East represents a zone of mixing, with carp-like fishes derived from the European, African and Asiatic faunas. Few of the genera are limited solely to this region, but the genus *Cyprinion,* a form in which scales are lacking, probably has the centre of its distribution in the Near East, as may the minnow-like *Phoxinellus.* The shoaling cyprinid *Acanthobrama* of Lake Galilee could have been the fish that accounted for the 'miraculous draught of fishes' recorded in the Gospels. *Acanthobrama* swims in large shoals near the surface and such shoals can be seen at some distance by anyone standing in a boat or on the shore.

As might be expected, the carp-like fishes of the Asiatic continent are numerous and very diverse. They range in size from the small barbs and danios, which may mature at only a few inches, to the huge mahseer of India which reaches 9 ft (2·7 m). In *Osteochilus* of the East Indies the lower jaw projects as a sharp edge beyond the upper, the mouth being directed upwards and fringed by papillae. In Lake Tung Ting in China there is a predacious cyprinid, *Luciobrama macrocephalus,* that has evolved the pike-like body typical of lurking predators that make a sudden lunge towards their prey. Other carp-like fishes are adapted to the torrential streams of the Himalayas. The majority, however, live in rivers, streams and lakes and provide a most important source of food in inland areas.

The carp-like fishes of Africa are clearly derived from immigrants that made their way to the continent from Asia. Genera such as *Barbus, Labeo* and *Garra* are common to both Africa and the southern parts of Asia, including the Near East. In the rivers of Africa, the carp-like fishes have had to compete with the characins and catfishes, and in the lakes they have had to contend with the very numerous species of cichlids. Perhaps as a result of this, there are fewer genera than in Asia. The genus *Barbus* includes many species, of which a few grow to a length of 18 in (46 cm) or more and form the basis for important fisheries in the rivers and lakes. *Labeo* spp., with soft, underslung jaws, and *Varicorhinus* spp., with scraping jaws, are widespread. In species of the genus *Garra* the mouth is bordered by disc-like lips for attaching to stones in fast streams, while the pectoral and pelvic fins are set low on the body to provide greater friction against rocks (a form of specialization most highly developed in the Hillstream fishes—see separate entry). Rather primitive in appearance, the species of *Barilius* take the place of the minnow in African waters. One of the most surprising adaptations is found in *Caecobarbus* spp., the Blind barbs of the Congo. After the great lake fisheries for cichlids, the carp-like fishes are next in importance as a source of food in many of the African territories.

The carps of North America share few genera with Asia. They appear to have entered the continent from the northwest via the Bering Bridge and from the few forms that did this have evolved the present-day American cyprinids. Strictly speaking, *Catostomus* and the other American suckers should be dealt with separately since they belong to the family Catostomidae, but it is more convenient to mention them here because they are closely related to the cyprinids and share many features. As their name implies, they have protrusile, sucking mouths. There are a few Asiatic species, mainly in eastern USSR, and these are more generalized in form than the American species.

The White sucker *Catostomus commersonii* is extremely widespread in North America, being found throughout Canada and as far south as Mexico. Like most suckers, it is not brightly coloured. It reaches about 6 lb (2·7 kg) in weight, as also does the Long-nose sucker *Catostomus catostomus*. The latter supports a commercial fishery on Lake Superior, where it is found at depths of 600 ft (180 m). The Quillback sucker *Carpoides cyprinus* can be easily identified by its highly flattened (laterally compressed) body and the elongation of the first few dorsal rays, from which it gets its name. The largest of all the suckers is the Bigmouth buffalo sucker *Ictiobus cyprinellus*. Average specimens weigh about 3 lb (1·4 kg), but the record fish (from Spirit Lake, Iowa) weighed over 80 lb (36 kg). The Buffalo sucker differs from other members of the family by having a terminal mouth, that is at the end of the snout and not underneath. As a result, it can make use of a much more varied diet. Seeds of plants are often eaten, and in Iowa these fishes eat the 'cotton' from the cottonwood trees in springtime. Small fishes are also taken. The Humpback sucker *Xyrauchen texanus* from the Colorado river shows an interesting parallel with one of the few Chinese suckers, *Myxocyprinus asiaticus*. Both fishes are very deep-bodied, a shape usually evolved in fishes that live in still waters, and one that presents serious problems in fast rivers. In each case the fishes have, so to speak, solved the problem in the same way. The body is not the same thickness at the top and the bottom but is sharply keeled along the high back. Water streaming past the fish tends to force it closer to the bottom where presumably the fish finds it easier to keep its station against the flow of water. One other species deserves mention, the Northern hogsucker *Hypentelium nigricans* of the United States. This species has the more usual dorso-ventral flattening of the body found in fishes that live in fast water. It frequently enjoys the company of trout which swim after it eating the insect larvae that it dislodges while it roots around stones at the bottom.

The other large group of American carp-like fishes are those referred to as minnows, although they are often large and are not closely related to the European minnows. Often called dace, chub or shiners, they will be dealt with under the heading minnows.

As one of the principal freshwater groups of fishes, it is natural that the cyprinids should provide many of our commonest aquarium fishes. The vast majority of those imported by dealers come from India and the Far East, although some of the African species are becoming popular. Details of some of these are given under barbs and danios and a quick glance at the number of *Barbus* species now available in pet shops shows something of the success of this genus in the tropics. An unusual member of this group is the so-called Flying barb *Esomus danrica* from India, Ceylon, Thailand and Singapore. This is a slim, silvery fish with a red and violet iridescent sheen. One pair of barbels are extremely long and reach back to the mid-point of the body. Its common name alludes to its very large pectoral fins, but although these fishes are prone to leaping, there is no evidence that they actually 'fly'.

The widespread genus *Labeo* provides many aquarium fishes from India and South-east Asia. In *Labeo* the mouth is ventral, lying under the snout, and the lips form a sucking disc lined with sharp, horny ridges. *Labeo bicolor*, known as the Red-tailed black shark, has a velvety black body, dorsal, anal and pelvic fins, while the caudal fin is a vivid red. The species is easy to keep provided that soft, peaty water and plenty of shade are available. It grows to at least 6 in (15 cm) and, although an algal feeder, will happily accept lettuce leaves as a substitute. While kindly disposed to other fishes, it is advisable not to have more than one large specimen in a tank since they tend to attack members of their own species. The Black shark *Morulius chrysophekadion*, a close relative of *Labeo bicolor*, is jet black with a faint red or yellow spot on each scale and a large dorsal fin. It grows to 22 in (56 cm) in the wild. Another species that is often imported is *Labeo frenatus*, a peaceable fish with a brown body and pale red fins.

The genus *Rasbora* is widespread throughout east and south Asia and is common on many of the islands of the Indo-Malayan Archipelago. The rasboras are mostly shoaling fishes with slim bodies, one of the few exceptions being the deep-bodied harlequinfish. The Brilliant rasbora *Rasbora einthoveni*, from Thailand and the Malayan islands, has a yellow-olive back and flanks with a bluish sheen on which runs a shining band of black, dark green or emerald from the snout to the base of the tail. The Pigmy rasbora *R. maculata*, from southern Malaya, is a tiny species which reaches only 1 in (2·5 cm) in length. The body is red to yellow (redder in males than females) with dark blotches at the base of the fins. The Scissor-tail *R. trilineata* receives its name from its habit of closing the forks of the tail as it swims, the movement being made more obvious by the black band on either lobe of the otherwise colourless tail. FAMILY: Cyprinidae, ORDER: Cypriniformes, CLASS: Pisces. (Ill. p. 56, 57, 60.)

CARTILAGINOUS FISHES, members of the class Chondrichthyes which includes the sharks, rays and chimaeras as well as certain fossil fishes.

CASTOR OIL FISH *Ruvettus pretiosus,* an oceanic fish related to the Snake mackerels. It is known to the Spanish as escolar. The Castor oil fish is found in deep waters in most parts of the world, usually occurring at depths of about 2,400 ft (700 m). It reaches 6 ft (1·8 m) in length and the flesh is extremely oily and has purgative properties, hence the common name (true castor oil comes from a plant). FAMILY: Gempylidae, ORDER: Perciformes, CLASS: Pisces.

CATADROMOUS FISHES, species which pass downstream from freshwaters into the sea to breed, a good example being the freshwater eel. The majority of eels inhabit tropical waters but the anguillids (the freshwater eel and its relatives) and also the congrids (Conger eels) are exceptional in living in temperate waters. However, both groups make a fairly long migration between the feeding and the breeding grounds which are in tropical waters. It would seem, therefore, that the delicate eggs and larvae have been tied to the ancestral breeding areas and that any extension in the range of the fishes has involved only the larger juveniles and adults. One can infer, therefore, that fishes that are catadromous have evolved in the sea and have only later colonized freshwaters. The reverse is probably the case with the anadromous fishes.

CATFISHES, widespread chiefly freshwater fishes with barbels round the mouth. There are 31 families from all parts of the world except the colder regions of the northern hemisphere. Some have completely naked, scaleless bodies while others have a heavy armour of bony plates. There is a single dorsal fin followed by an adipose fin (see separate entry) which in some families (e.g. armoured catfishes) is supported by a spine. The common name for these fishes refers to the barbels round the mouth which look like whiskers and serve a sensory function in detecting food. Anatomically, the catfishes are interesting since the bones of the upper jaw (premaxilla and maxilla) have, to varying degrees, been reduced or are even absent. Where present they form a basal support for a pair of barbels. The vast majority of catfishes are found in freshwaters but two families are marine.

Europe has only two catfishes, both of which spread into Europe from Asia after the last Ice Age but which never reached the British Isles. The larger of the two, and one of the largest of the European freshwater fishes, is the wels *Silurus glanis* which is also found in Asiatic USSR. The second is *Parasilurus aristotelis*, an Asiatic species that is found in a few rivers in Greece. It was named after Aristotle whose very accurate account of its biology was doubted for 2,000 years until it was realized that his descriptions referred to *Parasilurus* and not to the wels. Both these catfishes belong to the family Siluridae the members of which are found across Asia south of latitude 40°N and north of the Himalayas to Thailand. The silurids are naked catfishes with the dorsal and adipose fins short, small or even absent. The anal fin may be very long and may be continuous with the tail. The Glass catfish *Kryptopterus bicirrhus* from Burma is familiar to aquarists. The body is completely transparent and slightly yellow and the dorsal fin is reduced to a single ray. There is a single pair of long barbels. In the aquarium, these fishes are peaceful and thrive on live foods but several individuals should be kept since solitary fish appear to become 'unhappy'. This species grows to about 4 in (10 cm) in length. The young of *Ompok bimaculatus* are also transparent and might be mistaken for the Glass catfish except that there are several rays in the dorsal fin. In the wild, it grows to 16 in (40 cm) and loses its transparency, but it stays much smaller than this in an aquarium. This fish is usually imported and sold in mistake for the Glass catfish.

In the southern part of its range the Siluridae overlaps with another family of naked catfishes, the Bagridae. In this family the dorsal fin is preceded by a stout spine, an adipose fin is always present and the anal fin is usually short. The family ranges through Asia Minor to south and east Asia, Africa, Japan and Malaysia. Many of the species of *Bagrus* in Africa grow up to 3 ft (90 cm) and are important in local fisheries. The genus *Leiocassis* from Thailand and Malaya contains several species commonly imported into Europe and the United States for aquarists. *Leiocassis siamensis* has a thick-set dark brown or blue-grey body with four irregular pale yellow vertical bands. *Leiocassis poecilopterus,* sometimes called the Bumblebee fish, has a brown-blue body with irregular yellow blotches. Both these species adopt the most unlikely resting positions, sometimes almost vertical. *Mystus tengara,* from northern India, has a greenish-yellow body with a brown back. The young are amenable to life in a community tank but the adults are liable to become predacious.

The family Ictaluridae contains freshwater catfishes from North America and Southeast Asia. The ictalurids have a naked body and a large head. In the United States they are called Tadpole madtoms or bullheads and are suitable for cold water aquaria (some have been introduced into Europe). These American catfishes are discussed under madtoms.

The family Schilbeidae contains Asiatic and African catfishes which resemble the silurids except that the dorsal fin has a sharp spine and the anal fin is very long. Members of the genera *Schilbe* and *Eutropius* of Africa are important elements in freshwater fisheries and are known as butterfish. The genera *Physailia* and *Paralia* contain species which resemble the Glass catfish in having almost transparent bodies, at least when young, and very long barbels. *Pangasianodon gigas* from Thailand is one of the largest of all the catfishes, reaching 7½ ft (2·2 m) and like the wels has been thought to be responsible for the disappearance of small children.

The Clariidae have the same range as the schilbeids (Asia and Africa). They are naked, often elongated, bottom-living forms with cylindrical bodies and flat heads. Characteristic of this family is the possession of an accessory breathing organ in the form of blind sacs extending along the sides of the vertebral column from the top of the gill cavity or occurring as spongy tissue in the gill cavity (see air-breathing fishes). The dorsal and the anal fins are long and the adipose fin is small or absent. These are very voracious feeders, some growing to a length of 3 ft (90 cm) and forming important elements in fisheries. The genus *Clarias* is widespread and contains species which sometimes migrate overland at night. *Heterobranchus longifilus* from Africa, like several other catfishes, has very sharp spines in the pectoral fin which are capable of injecting poison and causing a most painful wound. *Heteropneustes fossilis* from India is commonly kept in aquaria when small.

The African family Mochokidae contains one of the best known of all the catfishes, the famous Upside-down catfish *Synodontis nigriventris*. The body is naked, an adipose fin is present, and there is a strong spine in both dorsal and pectoral fins. This fish has the habit of swimming on its back, with the belly uppermost, a habit that is, however, shared with a few other members of this genus. In most fishes the back is much darker coloured than the belly, but in *S. nigriventris,* as its Latin name suggests, the belly is darker than the back. This reversal of the normal pattern of counter-shading is a clear indication that this type of camouflage is of value to the fish. This species, which reaches 12 in (30 cm) in the wild, does well in an aquarium, remaining small, but it is liable to uproot the vegetation. Species of *Synodontis,* like certain other catfishes, have an ingenious mechanism whereby the spines of the dorsal and pectoral fins can be locked when erect and in some the spines can inflict a painful, stinging wound. *Synodontis angelicus* from West Africa is one of the prettiest species, with round white spots on an intense red-violet background.

The family Chacidae from India and Burma contains only a few species. *Chaca chaca* grows to about 8 in (20 cm) in length and has an extremely flat body and a large head. It lives on the bottom and is beautifully camouflaged with blotchy dark browns and small protuberances to break the outline of the fish. So confident is it in its camouflage that it rarely moves even if touched, lying on the bottom like a piece of dead wood.

The South American family Pimelodidae is related to the rather similar Bagridae of the Old World. *Pimelodus clarias* has a grey-blue body with dark spots but should be handled with care since the dorsal and pectoral spines are capable of causing blood poisoning. *Sorubim lima* from the Amazon has a very flat head and a spatulate snout which overhangs the mouth. This lengthening of the snout is taken a step further in the Tiger catfish *Pseudoplatystoma fasciatum,* found from Venezuela to Uruguay, in which there is a very long, flat snout with three pairs of barbels round the mouth. This family also contains, like the Bagridae, species which are referred to as Bumblebee catfishes, for example species of *Microglanis* which are covered in yellow markings. *Typhlobagrus kronei* is a blind, cave-dwelling species from the Caverna das Areias, São Paolo, Brazil. Living at the surface in this same area is a normal species, *Pimelodella transitoria,* from which the blind form may have evolved.

Perhaps the most curious of the South American catfish families is the Trichomycteridae which contains the parasitic forms. One of these, the *candiru, is the only vertebrate parasite of man. *Stegophilus insidiosus* is a small, worm-like catfish that lives in the gill chambers of armoured catfishes. A second rather unpleasant South American family is the Cetopsidae which contains the genus *Cetopsis*. These repulsive, flaccid catfishes live in the upper reaches of the Amazon and feed on offal. They have a naked, slimy body and small eyes.

The family Aspredinidae contains the Banjo catfishes (*Bunocephalus*) the large round head and slender body of which has earned it its common name. Some members of this nocturnal family have developed ingenious methods of egg protection and incubation. In *Aspredinichthys tibicen* from the Guianas the female develops spongy tentacles on the belly during the breeding season, to which the eggs become attached. Most members of this family are from freshwater but a few species of *Aspredinichthys* venture into the sea.

Two of the South American families of armoured catfishes are very well known to aquarists. These are the Callichthyidae and the Loricariidae. The first is found throughout the tropical part of South America and in Trinidad. In these fishes the flanks are covered by two rows of bony plates and the adipose fin is preceded by a spine. They live in small shoals in slow-flowing water and grub around for food. The pectoral fins are provided with strong spines which are used in some species to help them move overland when the ground is moist and the air humid. Since the water in which they live is often foul and depleted of oxygen, the ability to breath air by taking it into the intestine enables the fishes both to survive the dry seasons and to make overland journeys. These are hardy fishes, well suited to life in an aquarium, where they undertake the important task of clearing up food from the bottom of the tank. The genus *Corydoras* is probably the best known of this family. *Corydoras paleatus* was one of the first of these catfishes to be imported into Europe, not later than 1878. It reaches about 3 in (7·5 cm) in length and has a brown to olive green body with darker spots and marblings. The Bronze catfish *C. aeneus* has a bronze-green body with a dark patch on the shoulder. *C. melanostictus* goes under a variety of common names (Pepper catfish, Leopard catfish, etc.) which refer to the many small brown spots on the pinkish flanks. Also called the Leopard catfish is *C. julii*. These and the many other species of *Corydoras* grow to about 3 in (7·5 cm) long, but the Dwarf corydoras *C. hastatus* is minute, reaching only 1 in (2·5 cm). Unlike the others it swims in midwater and rests on leaves of water plants. *Callichthys callichthys* is much larger, reaching 6 in (16 cm) in length. This species builds a kind of bubble nest under the leaves of floating plants and the male guards the eggs, grunting if disturbed. Species of *Hoplosternum* build similar nests, which may be strengthened with pieces of plants.

The distribution of the family Loricariidae is similar to that of the callichthyids. The loricariids are depressed, flattened forms with sucking mouths and three or four rows of plates along the flanks. Some species pass into brackish water, while the powerful sucking mouth enables others to live in mountain torrents, where they cling to stones with their sucker mouths while rasping away at algae with their jaws. The genera *Plecostomus*, *Otocinclus* and *Loricaria* are kept by aquarists primarily to keep down algal growth on the sides of the tank. In *Xenocara* the body is very depressed and there are twig-like processes on the snout and shorter spine-like processes on the cheeks. *Plecostomus plecostomus* and *P. commersoni* have the same flattened shape but lack the outgrowths on the snout and cheeks and have large, flag-like dorsal fins. Rarely growing to more than 6 in (15 cm) in aquaria, they reach 2 ft (60 cm) in the wild and are valued for food by the local people, who shoot at the fish with bows and arrows as they browse in shallow water. Large museum specimens of *Plecostomus* often bear telltale arrow holes. Members of the genus *Farlowella* have extremely thin bodies with long, slender snouts, giving them a passing resemblance to small twigs in the water. The whip-tail *Loricaria filamentosa* has the uppermost ray of the tailfin elongated into a filament. Members of this genus are flattened, bottom-living forms with bony plates not only on the flanks but also on the belly. This would appear to provide protection, but the author once made the mistake of keeping a 6 in (15 cm) whip-tail in an aquarium with two small piranhas of only 1½ in (4 cm) long. On one occasion the food for

the piranhas was forgotten and the following morning only the tail of the whip-tail remained! Species of *Otocinclus,* and especially *O. affinis,* grow to 2–3 in (5–7 cm) and are placid, long-lived aquarium fishes.

Closely related to the loricariids is the family Astroblepidae, the members of which have lost their bony armour. The capitane *Astroblepus chotae* from the Andes has a sucker formed from the pelvic fins in addition to that formed by the mouth. These two suckers are used alternately to enable the fish to climb the vertical rock walls of waterfalls or potholes. Although progress is slow, the fish is able to live under conditions which would be impossible for other fishes. Since there are no predators to feed on it, the armour of the capitane has been lost.

The Doradidae, yet another family of armoured catfishes from South America, includes *Acanthodoras spinosissimus,* a sluggish creature that spends most of the day buried in the sand with only its eyes visible. When removed from the water, the fish is reported to make a grunting noise but one that the author, as a boy, kept for three years, was almost dried out in that time with attempts to make it communicate, but never was a fish more silent.

In addition to their astonishing success in freshwater, there are two families of catfishes that are adapted to life in the sea. The Plotosidae contains *Plotosus anguillaris,* a colourful fish with longitudinal black stripes interspersed with thin bright yellow stripes set on a pale pinkish background. It is just as well that this species is conspicuous since it is one of the most poisonous fishes of the entire Indo-Pacific area. Reaching 20 in (51 cm) in length, it has sharp dorsal and pectoral spines that can cause exceedingly painful wounds even from a slight scratch. A curious feature of this fish is a small bush-like process near to the vent which is joined to the vertebrae by a ligament. The function of this organ is not yet known. The second marine family is the Ariidae containing shoaling catfishes from tropical and subtropical seas. The females lay very large eggs, ¾ in (2 cm) in diameter, which are incubated in the mouth of the male for over a month, the fish being unable to eat during this period. These fishes are important in certain fisheries and the cleaned skulls are sold as religious and tourist curios under the name of *crucifixfish.

The family Malapteruridae from Africa only contains the Electric catfish a species which is described under Electric fishes.

If diversity is a mark of evolutionary success, then the catfishes can be considered a most successful group. Over 2,000 species are known, adapted to a vast range of ecological niches and displaying such curious habits as cave-dwelling and parasitism. ORDER: Siluriformes, CLASS: Pisces.

CAT SHARKS, small and often colourful inshore sharks found chiefly in the Indo-Pacific region but with species in the temperate and tropical parts of the Atlantic. The Cat sharks resemble the Carpet sharks in having the tail straight and not bent upwards, as in most sharks. They can be distinguished from them by the absence of fleshy barbels near the nostrils. There are two dorsal fins, without a spine in front of each, and one anal fin. The body is usually slender and graceful. A spiracle is present and, as in other sharks, this is correlated with the absence of a nictitating membrane or 'third eyelid' (see article on sharks). This family contains the species familiarly known as dogfishes, which are described elsewhere. It also includes the curious Swell sharks of the genus *Cephaloscyllium* found commonly in the Indo-Pacific region but absent from the Atlantic. These sharks swallow water or air when alarmed and are able to inflate their body to twice its normal diameter, presumably as a method of defence against predators (see also pufferfishes). When lifted from the water, a Swell shark will fill the stomach with air and if thrown back will float until the air is released. Some of the Cat sharks are brightly coloured, for sharks, and the skaamoog *Holohalaelurus regani* of South Africa has a particularly striking pattern of markings on the body. Almost all the Cat sharks lay eggs which are contained in rectangular egg cases with a tendril at each corner. It is remarkable, however, that whereas *Galeus melastoma* lays eggs, the very similar and closely related *G. polli* is ovoviviparous, giving birth to live young. FAMILY: Scyliorhinidae, ORDER: Pleurotremata, CLASS: Chondrichthyes. (Ill. p. 56, 57.)

CAVE FISHES, species adapted to a life in underground waters, usually caves but also artesian wells. Some 32 troglobiotic (cave-living) species are known, of which 18 belong to the large superorder Ostariophysi (carps, characins, catfishes, etc.), 11 being members of the order Siluriformes (catfishes). The remaining 14 belong to the families Synbranchidae, Amblyopsidae, Brotulidae, Eleotridae and Gobiidae. In most of these families, the cave-living forms represent only a small proportion of known species, but in the family Amblyopsidae six out of the nine species are troglobiotic. In the Brotulidae, three freshwater cave species are most closely related to certain deep-water marine species, many of which are blind. It is noteworthy that cave fishes are found amongst the less highly evolved and not amongst the more advanced orders.

In most cave fishes there is at least some degeneration of the eyes, but in the extreme forms the eyes are no longer visible superficially. In the Mexican characin every gradation from 'eyed' to 'eyeless' forms is found, apparently depending on the degree to which the particular cave is isolated. Other features of cave fishes are reduction or loss of pigment on the body (which thus is pink or white), a rather small size (the largest, the Cuban brotulid *Stygicola dentatus* and the Kentucky blindfish *Amblyopsis spelaeus* reaching 6 and 8 in (15 and 20 cm) respectively), reduction or loss of scales (some come from scaleless families, however) and a tendency towards constant and active swimming. The sensory system of the lateral line is often, but not always, better developed than that in related surface-living forms, nor are the senses of taste, smell and hearing particularly acute. The basal metabolism, however, is much lower than in surface forms.

Cave fishes are concentrated mostly in the tropics: 21 in the New World, five in Africa and the remainder in the Middle East, Japan, India and Australia. No true cave fishes are found in Europe although partial cave forms (*Paraphoxinus* sp) are known which spend only a part of their adult lives below ground.

Most troglobiotic species are quite closely related to surface-living forms; the three brotulid species are an exception. It has been found, however, that the presumed stock from which the cave forms have evolved usually comprises species that already show some pre-adaptation to underground living. Such species are often reticent, preferring dark places, and have reduced eyes but well developed organs of taste and touch.

The evolution of cave fishes poses interesting problems, particularly that of eye loss. It has been suggested that since the eye in fishes develops relatively more quickly than any other part of the body, in an environment where poor growth results from scarcity of food it will be the eye that is most affected and will be most inhibited in its development. Other workers favour mutation as the agent leading to eye loss and it is thought this might be a positive advantage from the point of saving energy. See Blind fishes.

CEPHALASPIDS, primitive, extinct fishes belonging to the class Agnatha. Their nearest living relatives are the lampreys, but unlike them the cephalaspids had an extensive, bony exoskeleton consisting of a broad, flattened head-shield and thick, bony scales. The paired eyes were set close together on the upper surface of the head and between them lay the pineal organ and a single nasal opening; three depressions probably contained organs sensitive to vibrations. On the lower surface were a small, jawless mouth and ten pairs of gill openings. The trunk was roughly triangular in cross section. There were one or two dorsal fins and an asymmetrical, heterocercal tail. Paired fins were absent in some, but others had peculiar flaps attached to the head-shield.

Cephalaspids were not very large, about 6–24 in (15–60 cm) in length, and are thought to have been poor swimmers spending much of their time on the bottom where they fed by filtering the water. They are first recorded from the Upper Ordovician and seem to have died out before the end of the Devonian, a time-range of roughly 90 million years.

CHARACINS or tetras, small fairly primitive, freshwater fishes. The term characin is not easy to define because of its frequent use and loose application in non-scientific literature. Not all members of the family Characidae are termed characins while the names characin and tetra are used, sometimes interchangeably, for members of other families. The name characin is here used for the members of the family Characidae, while the wider term characoid is used for all members of the 16 families making up the suborder Characoidei.

The characoid fishes typically have well developed jaw teeth, a non-protrusile mouth, a single dorsal and anal fin and usually an adipose fin. They are allied to the carp-like fishes (suborder Cyprinoidei), but the latter lack teeth in the jaws, have a protrusile mouth and no adipose fin. The characoids are found in South America and in Africa and this distribution has been taken as evidence that the two continents were once joined but later drifted apart (Continental drift theory). The carp-like fishes are believed to have evolved from the characoid line. (Ill. p. 52, 60.)

CHEIROLEPIS, one of the earliest known genera of actinopterygian fishes. Two species have been described: *Cheirolepis trailli* from the Middle Devonian of Scotland and *Cheirolepis canadensis* from the Upper Devonian of Canada. An unusual feature of this genus is the covering of very small, diamond-shaped scales unlike those of other actinopterygians but similar to the scales of acanthodians. SUBCLASS: Actinopterygii, CLASS: Pisces.

CHIMAERAS or ratfishes (sometimes also called rabbitfishes), members of a subclass of cartilaginous fishes related to sharks and termed the Bradyodonti (or Holocephali). The chimaeras are characterized by the presence of a curious appendage or 'clasper' on the head in front of the eyes. It is found only in the males, which suggests that it may serve some function in copulation. Like sharks, these fishes have a skeleton of cartilage and the males have one pair of claspers or more modified from the pelvic fins which are used for internal fertilization. They differ from sharks, however, in that the gill openings are covered by an operculum (resembling the gill cover of bony fishes) the primary upper jaw elements are fused to the skull (free from the skull in sharks but fused in the lungfishes); the anus does not discharge into a cloaca together with the urinary and genital products but has a distinct opening of its own (as in the bony fishes). Highly characteristic are the teeth of chimaeras, which are formed of three pairs of large flat plates, two above and one below, armed with hard points or 'tritors' in some species but remaining beak-like in others. The majority of species belong to the genera *Chimaera* and *Hydrolagus* in which the snout is fairly blunt, the mouth ventral, the tail elongated and rat-like, and the first dorsal fin provided with a serrated spine capable of injecting a painful venom into wounds. *Chimaera monstrosa* is found along European shores and in the Mediterranean and grows to a length of 5 ft (1·5 m). Its scientific name aptly recalls the chimaera of Greek myth, one of Echidne's dreadful brood, a fire-breathing goat with a lion's head and a serpent's body which was finally slain by Bellerophon. Members of the genera *Harriotta* and *Rhinochimaera,* placed in a separate family Rhinochimaeridae, have a long pointed snout and only a single pair of claspers (there are two or three pairs in other species). Members of this family are found in both the Atlantic and the Indo-Pacific region and occur at depths of about 2,000–8,500 ft (600–2,550 m). The most monstrous of all the chimaeras are the members of the genus *Callorhinchus* (family Callorhinchidae) in which the snout is not only long but curls down and back towards the mouth. They are found in the cold and temperate waters of the southern hemisphere at depths of about 600 ft (180 m) off the coasts of South Africa, South America and Australasia but they also enter shallow water. They grow to about $3\frac{1}{2}$ ft (just over 1 m) in length. The earliest known members of this subclass were found in deposits of the Devonian period and are chiefly recognized by their highly characteristic tooth plates. The 20 or so modern species are the survivors of a once widespread and successful group. FAMILIES: Chimaeridae, Rhinochimaeridae, Callorhinchidae, ORDER: Chimaeriformes, SUBCLASS: Bradyodonti, CLASS: Chondrichthyes.

CHONDROSTEI, a subclass containing the earliest and most primitive fishes of the class Actinopterygii. The group, which has a time-range from the Middle Devonian to the present day (roughly 370 million years), contains many extinct forms as well as the living sturgeons, paddlefishes and snakefishes. Characteristic features are: the primitive skull structure, the presence of a spiracle, thick bony scales, an asymmetrical (heterocercal) tail and numerous, closely jointed fin-rays. SUBCLASS: Actinopterygii, CLASS: Pisces.

CHUB *Leuciscus cephalus,* a carp-like fish

found in England, central and southern Europe and as far east as Asia Minor. It grows to about 2 ft (60 cm) in length and is a great sporting fish although practically inedible (the flesh has been described as tasting like cottonwool full of needles). It shoals when small, usually near the surface, but the larger adults become solitary and very voracious. The young appear to have remarkably little preference for the type of food taken, although cherries are particularly popular. Anglers have caught chub with almost anything that can be placed on a hook as bait. FAMILY: Cyprinidae, ORDER: Cypriniformes, CLASS: Pisces.

CICHLIDS, a family of perch-like fishes found chiefly in freshwaters (rarely brackish waters) in Africa and South America, but with one genus in India and Ceylon. There are over 600 species and more are being discovered every year. Typically, the cichlids have a fairly deep and compressed body, a single long dorsal fin (the first part having spines) and a shorter anal fin beginning with one spine or more. The body bears fairly large scales which in some genera are smooth (cycloid) but in others are rough-edged (ctenoid). The cichlids have a single nostril on each side (paired nostrils are usual in other perch-like fishes).

Cichlid fishes are usually found in lakes or sluggish waters although some are adapted to life in rivers and streams. Many are carnivorous and all have a set of teeth in the throat, the pharyngeal teeth which are adapted to particular diets. In those that feed on fishes or large invertebrates, the pharyngeal teeth are fairly large and coarse, but in species which are filter-feeders and live on algae or other small organisms, the teeth are fine and close-set. In the mollusc-eaters, the teeth of the pharyngeal tooth pads are flat for crushing and grinding. In many species, and not only the filter-feeders, there is a microscopic series of little spines on the inner faces of all but the first gill arch. Each spine bears minute teeth. As the gills move over each other during breathing, the teeth probably comb out the single-cell organisms that collect on the mucus of the gills. A few species feed on higher plants and there are also some that have teeth adapted for eating the scales of other fishes.

Most of the cichlids exhibit territorial behaviour connected with the guarding of a nest in which the eggs are laid. In the nest-building forms, such as the species of *Tilapia,* the male usually excavates a circular hollow in the sandy or muddy bottom and goes through a fairly elaborate display of fin movements and swimming antics when a female arrives. When the female has deposited the eggs the male sheds his sperm and in the mouth-brooding species the female (occasionally the male) sucks the eggs into

her mouth where they remain for the incubation period and even after they hatch the fry remain there until they are able to fend for themselves. In other species the eggs may stay where they are laid or be scooped up and deposited at another site where they are aerated by fanning movements of the fins by one or both parents. In most species the male develops a characteristic breeding colouration and this is thought to help keep the species separate when several are found on the same breeding ground.

Many cichlids are prettily coloured and because of this and their interesting breeding habits they are popular with aquarists.

The angelfishes (*Pterophyllum* sp.) from the Amazon are graceful, deep-bodied fishes with elongated fins and, like many other cichlids, are easy to keep although occasionally pugnacious when large.

The Fire-mouth cichlid *Cichlasoma meeki* from Central America grows to about 6 in (15 cm) and takes its name from the brilliant red colour of the inside of the mouth. This is an excellent aquarium fish, usually being peaceful and fairly easily bred. The genus *Cichlasoma* contains many South American species of interest to the aquarist, including the Jack Dempsey *C. biocellatum,* the Flag cichlid *C. festivum,* the Chameleon cichlid *C. facetum* (a bad-tempered species but one which shows remarkable colour changes), the Banded cichlid *C. severum,* and Cutter's cichlid *C. cutteri.* The last named is notable for having eggs that have stalks. These fishes are fairly deep-bodied, but members of the genus *Crenichla* from South America are known as pike-cichlids because of their elongated bodies and heads. Other South American cichlids are the discusfish and the acaras (both discussed separately).

The Orange chromide *Etroplus maculatus* belongs to the single genus found in India and Ceylon. It grows to about 3 in (8 cm) in length and has a gold to grey body with rows of red spots. If kept in captivity it benefits from the addition of a little sea salt to the water since it is often found in brackish waters in the wild. In this species, as in the discusfish, the young often attach themselves to the body of the parent.

The African genus *Haplochromis* (and some related genera) are of great interest to zoologists because they provide some insight into the speed at which evolution has occurred. Where it has been possible to date the age of a lake the time taken for species endemic to that lake to evolve is thus known. One case is Lake Nabugabo in Uganda, a small arm of Lake Victoria that was cut off from the main lake only 4,000 years ago. Of the seven species of *Haplochromis* in Lake Nabugabo, five are endemic to the lake and must therefore have evolved, not in millions of years, but in only a few thousand. Each of the large lakes in Africa has its own 'flock' of

cichlid fishes, a large percentage of which are endemic to that lake and found nowhere else. The evolution of these flocks has often involved specialization of feeding habits coupled with distinctive breeding habits, colours and behaviour. Many of the species of *Haplochromis* are attractively coloured and the most commonly kept aquarium species is the Egyptian mouthbrooder *H. multicolor.*

The jewelfish *Hemichromis bimaculata* is one of the most colourful of African cichlids. The underparts are a brilliant red, the top of the head and the back are olive green with a red sheen and there are rows of blue spots between dark bars on the flanks. The dorsal fin is of two shades of red separated by brilliant blue spots.

The Blockhead cichlid *Steatocranus casuarius* is so called because of the fatty hump that forms with age on the forehead. It is found in the rapids of the Congo and grows to $3\frac{1}{2}$ in (9 cm).

The tilapias are dealt with separately. They form one of the most important food fishes in Africa and through their introduction as pond fishes in Asia and many other parts of the world have become as popular as some of the carp-like fishes in fish culture work. FAMILY: Cichlidae, ORDER: Perciformes, CLASS: Pisces. (Ill. p. 56.)

CICHLID IMITATES ITS EGGS. The female cichlid's habit of brooding the eggs in her mouth has led to an unusual method of fertilization. The females of *Haplochromis burtoni* and a few related species snap up their eggs before the male has fertilized them. However, the males have a row of red egg-sized spots on the anal fin. When the female has taken all the eggs into her mouth he sheds his sperm and spreads his fin. The female then makes the same engulfing movements with her mouth towards the spots on the fin as she did to the eggs and, as a result, the sperm is taken into her mouth and the eggs are there fertilized.

CISCO, a name used in the United States for certain species of whitefish and particularly for *Coregonus artedii* of the Great Lakes. FAMILY: Salmonidae, ORDER: Salmoniformes, CLASS: Pisces.

CLADOSELACHIANS, an order of fossil sharks from the Upper Devonian deposits of Ohio. The best known genus is *Cladoselache,* represented by fishes of 2–6 ft (60–200 cm) in length. They resemble modern sharks, but have no claspers (modified appendages of the pelvic fins used in copulation) and have terminal mouths (the mouth is on the underside of the head in almost all modern sharks, the Whale shark being a notable exception).

Cladoselache is one of the most primitive of sharks yet discovered. ORDER: Cladoselachii, SUBCLASS: Elasmobranchii, CLASS: Chondrichthyes.

CLEANER FISHES, small fishes that feed on parasitic organisms growing on larger fishes, particularly in the gill region. The cleaner fishes belong to several different families and are found mainly in marine tropical waters. Most of the species have pointed snouts with the teeth at the front of the jaws so that they can feed as though gently plucking off the parasites with a pair of tweezers. They are usually very brightly coloured fishes and they tend to frequent particular areas which are well known to the larger fishes. The latter visit the cleaners and by some particular behaviour pattern indicate that it is safe for them to begin feeding. The cleaner fishes are permitted to wander unmolested in and out of the mouth or gill chamber of large fishes, including species that normally feed on small fishes. The customer will obligingly open its mouth or gill covers to allow the cleaner to enter.

The Rainbow wrasse *Labroides phthirophagus* from the Pacific region is a cleaner. The back has a long black stripe and there is another one on each flank. The belly is violet and the area between the two black bands is white at the front and violet at the tail. Neon gobies *Elecatinus oceanops* from the Gulf of Mexico are also cleaners. They have two longitudinal black bands on the body, separated by a pale blue stripe. Such colours presumably help to advertise their profession and ensure that they are safe from larger predacious fishes. The cleaners also have their mimics, small fishes which have evolved similar colour-patterns thus being afforded the same immunity as the cleaners while undertaking no cleaning duties. (Such mimicry is a well known phenomenon amongst butterflies, the original species usually being unpalatable). Most of the cleaners are small fishes and remain cleaners throughout their lives, but certain species, such as the bluehead *Thalassoma bifasciatum,* only undertake cleaning when young.

The cleaning habit is clearly of benefit to both parties and it is not difficult to see how it arose. Certain crustaceans fulfil the same role, the Red shrimp *Hippolysmata mordax.*

CLIMBING PERCH *Anabas testudinosus,* a labyrinthfish reputedly able to climb trees and suck their juices. It is found in Southeast Asia and the first specimen to be seen by someone from the West, at the end of the 18th century, was found in a crack in a tree. Recent research has shown, however, that the tree-climbing legend is untrue, these fishes being most unwilling tree-tenants, having usually arrived there after being dropped struggling by birds. The Climbing perch has an accessory breathing organ in the form of a series of plates in the upper part of the gill chamber richly supplied with blood vessels (see Air-breathing fishes). The fish frequently moves from one pool to another and it is probably during these overland journeys that it is seized by birds and later dropped. The gill covers are used as an extra pair of 'legs' while it is moving overland. They are spiny and are spread out to anchor the fish while the pectoral fins and tail push forward. The Climbing perch can survive out of water for some time and these fishes are carried about by local people as a fresh fish supply. FAMILY: Anabantidae, ORDER: Perciformes, CLASS: Pisces. (Ill. p. 52.)

CLINGFISHES, small, mainly marine, fishes found in tropical and subtropical seas and distantly related to the toadfishes and the anglerfishes. The common name stems from their ability to hold onto rocks in the weedy intertidal zones in which they live. They cling by means of a sucker on the chest formed partly by the pelvic fins. All the clingfishes lack scales, have large heads and a body that tapers evenly to the tail. In Central America a few species have found their way into freshwater streams.

One of the largest of the clingfishes is *Chorisocismus dentex,* a mottled green and brown species from South Africa that reaches about 12 in (30 cm) in length and has a sucker so powerful that when hooked the line will usually break before the fish relinquishes its hold. This species is often left behind by the receding tide but does not seem to suffer and will survive out of water for several days if kept moist. Another South African clingfish, *Eckloniaichthys scylliorhiniceps,* is highly unusual in that fertilization is internal and yet eggs are laid. Normally, internal fertilization is found only in Bony fishes that are viviparous, giving birth to live young (see Live-bearing fishes).

Clingfishes of the genus *Lepadogaster* are common in the Mediterranean and some are not infrequently caught off the coast of southwest England. The Cornish sucker *L. gouanii* and the Two-spot sucker *L. bimaculatus* are the commonest of the species found in England. The Cornish sucker is the larger of the two and reaches 4 in (10 cm) in length. These fishes spawn in June or July and lay elongated eggs which are attached lengthwise to the sea bed. The young take about a month to hatch. These fishes migrate into deeper water during the winter, returning to the shores in summer. FAMILY: Gobiesocidae, ORDER: Gobiesociformes, CLASS: Pisces. (Ill. p. 52, 60.)

CLOWNFISHES, small damselfishes from the Indo-Pacific region which have a remarkable association with species of Sea anemone and for this reason are often called anemone-fishes. About 12 species are known, all very brightly coloured. *Amphiprion percula* grows to a few inches and has a bright orange body with three intensely white vertical bars, the fins being edged in black. Similar patterns are found in the other species of *Amphiprion.* They spend their lives amongst the waving tentacles of large Sea anemones, which eat fish caught by means of the many hundreds of thousands of stinging cells along the tentacles, and the question arises how the clownfish manages to escape being stung. At first it was thought that the clownfish was agile enough to avoid the tentacles, but closer observation of members of the Australian clownfish genus *Stoichactis* has shown that these fishes actually rub against the tentacles to encourage the Sea anemone to open. When inside, the fish often rests with its head poking out of the Sea anemone's mouth. If danger threatens, the clownfish dives back into the Sea anemone and will remain there even if the latter is removed from the water.

If the clownfish is deprived of its host it usually falls an easy prey to predators. It is difficult to see what the anemone gains from this curious association since the fish not only takes shelter but may feed on the tentacles and on any food that the anemone traps. The anemone can, in fact, live quite well without its guest but it has been suggested that the fish may have a beneficial aerating effect from entering the anemone's stomach and one species of clownfish, *Amphiprion polymnus,* actually feeds the anemone by placing on its tentacles pieces of food from the sea floor.

The immunity of the clownfish to the anemone's stinging cells is not yet understood. The newly hatched clownfishes live for a time at the surface feeding on plankton, but later take up their association with the anemone. Recent work has suggested that either by biting the tentacles or rubbing against them the clownfish immunizes to its particular host but that it may not be immune to the stinging cells of another species of anemone. Another suggestion is that the clownfish has a mucous coating which affords protection. Some of the clownfishes will associate only with a single species of anemone but others can associate with several. Conversely, in many clownfishes only a male and a female will colonize an anemone, while in others, such as *A. percula,* up to seven fishes can be found in one host. This association with anemones seems to be an extension of the common behaviour of many species of damselfishes, which live around coral heads and dive into the interstices of the coral when danger threatens. FAMILY: Pomacentridae, ORDER: Perciformes, CLASS: Pisces. (Ill. p. 49, 56.)

COALFISH *Pollachius virens,* also known

as the coley or saithe, a cod-like fish found from the Arctic to the Mediterranean. It resembles the cod but has only a rudimentary barbel under the chin, no speckling on the body and a dark green or almost black upper surface. It is a fairly deep-water fish usually found at 300–600 ft (100–200 m). One of the largest rod-caught specimens weighed nearly 24 lb (11 kg). Like many of the cod-like fishes it undergoes extensive migrations. FAMILY: Gadidae, ORDER: Gadiformes, CLASS: Pisces.

CODS, a family of almost exclusively marine fishes typified by the Atlantic cod *Gadus morhua* but also including the coalfish, pollack, haddock, ling, pouting and whiting, as well as the rocklings and the freshwater burbot. These fishes have softrayed fins, either one, two or three dorsal fins and one or two anal fins, the scales are small, the pelvic fins are set far forward in front of the pectoral fin base and under the throat, and there is a large and oily liver. The cod-like fishes are one of the largest and most important of all the commercially exploited groups of fishes. The origin of the name 'cod' is unknown.

The Atlantic cod is an olive green to brown with darker spots on the flanks and a silvery belly. It can be recognized by the small barbel under the chin, the pointed snout, the white lateral line and the presence of three dorsal fins. In the North Sea, cod grow to 8 in (20 cm) in their first year and a really large cod can reach 5 ft (1·5 m) in length and weigh up to 210 lb (95 kg). The cod is tolerant of a wide range of temperatures and is found in both temperate waters and in the Arctic. It is omnivorous and voracious, feeding chiefly on crustaceans (especially Norway lobster *Nephrops* in European waters), molluscs, echinoderms, worms and fishes. The feeding of cod has been compared with the action of a vacuum cleaner and amongst the curiosities recorded from their stomachs are a hare, a turnip and a bottle of whiskey! Cod are extremely prolific and a large female may produce up to 7 million eggs, although only a very small percentage ever reach maturity. The eggs and the newly hatched larvae are at first pelagic but after about ten weeks migrate to the bottom and for the remainder of the summer and autumn the young fishes remain in shoals.

The cod is one of the most important of all food fishes in the Atlantic. Cod bones have been found in archaeological sites and certainly by the 16th century cod fishing was practised by Basque, French, Spanish and English fishermen. The major cod fisheries are off the Lofoeten Islands, near Bear Island and on the Newfoundland Banks but large numbers of cod are also trawled elsewhere. Most cod are caught on, or near, the bottom between 60 and 300 ft (20–100 m). They are caught commercially both by trawling and by long-lining with lines with up to 1,500 baited hooks. The bait used is squid (a favourite food of the cod), worms, herrings and mussels. In addition to the high food value of the flesh, the oil from the liver has long been an important source of vitamins A and D. It has been estimated that some 400 million cod are caught annually and since the stocks appear relatively unaffected the actual population must be enormous. Large populations of a few species is a characteristic of temperate fishes; in tropical waters the number of different species is very much greater but the populations of each are correspondingly smaller.

There are three other families closely related to the cods and together they form the suborder Gadoidei.

The Merlucciidae includes the hake and the torsk, the first with two dorsal fins and the second with only one. These are deeperwater forms than the cods. Members of the family Moridae are also deep-water forms, occurring down to 10,000 ft (3,000 m) in parts of the North Pacific. *Mora mediterranea* occasionally penetrates into northern latitudes. The Bregmacerotidae contains the genus *Bregmaceros* from the Indo-Pacific region. Members of this genus are elongated, cylindrical fishes of fairly deep water, reaching a length of about 5 in (13 cm). The first dorsal fin is reduced to a single ray originating from the back of the head and the pelvic fins also have elongated rays. *Bregmaceros mcclellandi* is occasionally washed up on South African beaches after storms. FAMILY: Gadidae, ORDER: Gadiformes, CLASS: Pisces. (Ill. p. 52.)

COD AND RICKETS. Cod has long been a staple food in Europe but the fishery really developed in the 16th century with the discovery of the Grand Banks of Newfoundland. The Basques and Portuguese were the first to make the voyage across the Atlantic to catch cod on long lines bearing up to 5,000 hooks. The cod were split down the middle, salted and brought home to be sold in the protein-hungry Mediterranean countries. Later English and American fishing fleets exploited the fishing grounds and trawling replaced long-lining. Dried or salt cod fed the growing cities of Europe and was used to provision ships and armies. Few parts of the fish were wasted, the swimbladders being turned into isinglass to clear beer and wine and the heads being boiled up for glue. The liver is rich in oil and it became the most important part of the fish when it was used to combat rickets, a condition caused by vitamin D deficiency. In rickets the patient's bones are weakened and it became common in large, smoky towns where the usual process of vitamin D formation by the action of sunlight on substances in the skin was inhibited. As early as 1820 it was found that cod liver was an antidote but a century passed before its use was generally accepted and the importance of vitamin D was demonstrated.

COELACANTHS, primitive fishes belonging to the order Crossopterygii (Fossil fishes), once thought to be long extinct but now known to be represented by a single living species *Latimeria chalumnae*. They are related to the rhipidistian fishes, a group which gave rise to the first land vertebrates. Coelacanths first appear in the rocks of the Devonian period 400 million years ago and the group finally disappears from the fossil record in the chalk of the Cretaceous period 90 million years ago. During all that time they altered remarkably little. They had heavily-built bodies covered by thick, rough scales made up of four distinct layers and known as cosmoid scales (as found also in the fossil lungfishes). The vertebral column was poorly ossified and represented only by the cartilaginous notochord and the fin spines were also hollow cartilage, hence the name 'coelacanth' or 'hollow spine'. One of the most striking features of these fishes were the leg-like lobes that supported the pectoral, anal, pelvic and second dorsal fins and the curious central lobe in the tail. The skull was hinged in the middle as in the earliest of the land vertebrates. In some coelacanths the swimbladder was ossified, for example in *Undina,* a feature not found in other fishes and difficult to account for.

Some of the fossil coelacanths were well preserved and since they stood close to the line that led to the evolution of amphibians, reptiles, birds and mammals they were of great interest to students of evolution. Nothing was known, however, of the soft anatomy and many problems remained concerning the structure of the heart, the possible presence of the primitive spiral valve in the intestine, the presence or absence of lungs and the manner in which the lobed fins were used. As with the dinosaurs, it was assumed that such questions would never be fully answered. The discovery of a living coelacanth hardly seemed possible.

On 22 December 1938 however, Miss Courtney Latimer of the East London Museum in South Africa, went down to the quayside to inspect the fishes brought back by the trawlers. She recognized most of them, but lying on the pile was a large, heavily scaled fish which was 5 ft (1·5 m) long, and weighed 127 lb (58 kg). It was deep blue in colour and had curious fleshy lobes at the bases of the fins, and a central lobe in the tail. Miss Latimer made a sketch of the fish and sent it to Dr J. L. B. Smith, one of the most able ichthyologists in South

Africa. Meanwhile the specimen was sent to a taxidermist to be mounted, but the precious internal organs were lost. Dr Smith recognized the importance of the find, which represented a type thought to have been extinct for 90 million years. He named the fish *Latimeria chalumnae* in honour of Miss Latimer and to record its provenance off the mouth of the Chalumna river. Dr Smith then launched a campaign to find more specimens of *Latimeria*. His patience was rewarded 14 years later in 1952, when a second specimen was caught off the Comoro Islands, north of Madagascar. A third coelacanth was caught nine months later and since these exciting early days more have been found off the Comoro Islands and have been studied by French scientists led by Professor J. Millot.

Many of the tantalizing questions have now been answered. The hinge in the skull, for example, is present in this modern form and its movement is limited by strong fibrous tissues. The brain is very small, much smaller than the brain cavity and the olfactory and optic nerves are curved to allow for the movement of the head. In some respects the brain is more similar to that of the lungfishes than to the brain of the ray-finned fishes. Unlike what is found in the fossil *Undina*, the swimbladder is not calcified but is fatty and resembles a lung in that it opens ventrally into the pharynx as do the lungs of mammals. Breathing is carried out by the well-developed gills, however. The heart is a simple linear structure. As in sharks and in primitive bony fishes, there is a spiral valve in the intestine serving to increase the absorbant digestive surface. The 'backbone' is nothing but a tough cartilaginous rod, the notochord, which reaches forward into the skull and connects with the front half of the skull to form the joint between the two halves. From observations on the eighth coelacanth, a specimen of 56 lb (25 kg) which was kept alive for 17 hours in the sunken hull of a boat, it is known that the pectoral fins have surprising mobility and can be turned through an arc of 180°.

The discovery of a living coelacanth has been of the utmost importance, not only in the study of these fishes but also in checking the accuracy of interpretations made from fossil material. Although Professor Millot and many others have carried out extensive research on the coelacanth, this fish will always be linked with the name of the late Professor J. L. B. Smith. ORDER: Crossopterygii, CLASS: Pisces.

COELACANTH'S LATE 'DISCOVERY'.

The discovery of the coelacanth by Miss Courtney Latimer in 1938 was one of the most exciting finds in the history of zoology: an animal that was thought to have become extinct millions of years ago was still flourishing. Yet it must be pointed out that in this case discovery meant 'made known to science'. It appears that the inhabitants of the Madagascan region have been catching coelacanths for a long time, salting or drying their flesh and using their rough skin as sandpaper.

It is not a rare phenomenon for an animal thought rare by scientists to suddenly appear in considerable numbers. Examples are some of the whales (Beaked whales and Pilot whales) and there is the story of a zoologist who was asked to look out for a certain very rare fly while he was visiting Madagascar. He offered a reward of a cigarette for each fly and was awoken the next morning to find, outside his tent, a cow covered with a swarm of the 'rare' fly and surrounded by eager reward-seekers. 'Rarity' and 'abundance' often reflect the effort which has been made to find an animal, rather than the numerical strength of a species.

COELOLEPIDS, or thelodonts, small, poorly known, fossil fishes generally placed in the superclass Agnatha but without any real evidence. Reasonably intact specimens are rare and give very little information. The group has a fairly long time-range, from the Lower Ordovician to the Middle Devonian (roughly 120 million years), mainly established on the occurrence of the characteristic, isolated scales.

CONGER EEL *Conger conger*, a very elongated fish with no pelvic fins. This is a large marine eel widely distributed in the North and South Atlantic, in the Mediterranean and in the Indo-Pacific region. It is not found off the west coast of America. The life history of this eel is discussed in the section devoted to eels, but it can be noted that the conger, like the freshwater eels, makes a spawning migration. The population of the North Atlantic migrates to an area between latitudes 30° and 40° N and spawns at depths of 4,800 ft (1,500 m). The Mediterranean population spawns in the deeper parts of that sea. The eggs float at that depth until the small, ribbon-like leptocephalus or larva hatches. It metamorphoses into the adult form near coasts but remains pinkish in colour until it is about 12 in (30 cm) long, after which it assumes the grey-brown of the adult. A large female may lay up to 8 million eggs.

Both the Conger and the Common freshwater eel lack pelvic fins but in the Conger eel the dorsal fin, which extends to the tip of the body, begins over the pectoral fins whereas in the Common eel the dorsal begins much further back. There are no scales on the body. Congers are large, voracious fishes of nocturnal habits, feeding on molluscs, crabs and fishes and often haunting wrecks.

Females grow larger than the males and may reach a length of 9 ft (2·7 m); one of the largest rod-caught specimens weighed 84 lb. (38 kg). They are exciting and often exasperating fishes to catch on a line, requiring persistent tug-o'-war tactics which at any moment in the struggle may end in the conger managing to wind the line around a rock or other projection. The flesh is considered excellent and was very popular with the Romans, who gave the fish its name.

A related species, *Conger cinereus*, is found off the coasts of South Africa. FAMILY: Congridae, ORDER: Anguilliformes, CLASS: Pisces.

CORB *Umbrina cirrosa*, a deep-bodied fish up to 3 ft (90 cm) long, from the Mediterranean and the Bay of Biscay but not reaching as far north as the English Channel. The back is dark brown, the flanks brown with series of yellow dots forming oblique bands alternating with grey-blue. A strong barbel is present under the chin. In the Mediterranean these fishes form large shoals over fine sand where rocks outcrop. They feed on shrimps, sardines and marine worms. They are considered to be good angling fishes. FAMILY: Sciaenidae, ORDER: Perciformes, CLASS: Pisces.

CORKWING *Crenilabrus melops*, a fish often found in fairly shallow water along Mediterranean and eastern Atlantic coasts and fairly common in British waters. It is very variable in colour, like many of the other wrasses, but can be distinguished from other European species by one or two dark bands along the spiny part of the long dorsal fin and by a series of vertical brown bars on the body. It grows to about 6–8 in (15–20 cm) and is frequently found in rock pools. The corkwing builds a nest amongst seaweed, the eggs lying loosely within it. The species is also known as the gilthead. FAMILY: Labridae, ORDER: Perciformes, CLASS: Pisces.

COWFISH *Lactophrys quadricornis*, one of the trunkfishes found in the warmer parts on both sides of the Atlantic. The body is encased in a stout armour of plates and is triangular in cross-section, with light blue spots and lines on a yellow background. A related species from the Indo-Pacific area, *Lactorra cornutus*, has a pair of long forward-projecting horns above the eyes. FAMILY: Ostraciontidae, ORDER: Tetraodontiformes, CLASS: Pisces.

COW SHARKS, a family of primitive sharks that can be immediately recognized by the presence of six or seven gill slits (there being five gill slits in all other sharks except the Frilled shark and the Saw shark *Pliotrema*, in which there are six, but in the former the first pair are continuous under the head). The Cow sharks are also known as the Comb-toothed sharks in reference to the graduated series of cusps on the teeth (descending on both sides of the centre of the tooth in the upper jaw but from one end of the tooth only in the lower jaw). The Cow sharks are large fishes, some species exceeding 10 ft (3·3 m) in length and occasionally one is reported over twice that length. There is a single dorsal fin and the teeth of the lower jaw tend to form a kind of pavement, with several rows in use at any one time. There are probably only three species in this family, one with six gill slits and two with seven.

The Six-gilled shark *Hexanchus griseus* is a large and bulky fish with a long tail and is found in all the temperate seas, usually in fairly deep water. Large individuals of 15 ft (4·5 m) are often caught and a specimen of 26 ft (7·8 m) was reported from Cornwall, England in the last century. These fishes are caught commercially on long lines off Cuban coasts, sometimes at depths of over 5,000 ft (1,500 m) but they are also known in shallow waters.

The Seven-gilled sharks are represented by the Broad-headed form, *Notorhynchus maculatum,* of the Indo-Pacific region, found chiefly in fairly deep, temperate waters; and the Narrow-headed form, *Heptranchias perlo,* found in the Atlantic, Mediterranean and off Japan and Australia. The first species is the larger of the two, reaching a length of 10 ft (3·3 m) compared with about 7 ft (2·1 m) in the latter.

Members of this family are all ovoviviparous, the young hatching within the uterus of the female and later being born. At birth, the young are fairly small and may be quite numerous, 108 embryos being recorded from one female Six-gilled shark (only nine embryos have been found in a Narrow-headed seven-gill shark, however). FAMILY: Hexanchidae, ORDER: Pleurotremata, CLASS: Chondrichthyes.

CROAKERS, also known as drums, a family of perch-like fishes capable of producing a great range of sounds. There are nearly 200 species of croakers, a few from freshwaters but most are marine. There is a single dorsal fin, the anterior portion spiny and the remainder composed of soft rays. The body is fairly elongated, the scales are easily shed, and the liver is extremely rich in vitamin A. The noises produced by these fishes result from the vibration of muscles that run from the abdomen into the swimbladder. The muscles vibrate rapidly (about 24 times a second) and the swimbladder acts as a resonator (if collapsed by pricking with a pin no sound is produced). In most fishes the swimbladder is a smooth bag-like structure, but in the croakers it branches into arborescent or tree-like processes around its periphery. Possibly these branches determine the kind of sound produced. The function of the drumming noises is not yet fully understood. In some species the noises are most intense during the breeding season and at feeding periods. A species of *Nibea* from Japan forms large shoals of up to a million individuals which appear to be able to synchronize their drumming. Many of the species have large otoliths or ear stones and in the past these were considered useful in curing colic. A few members of the genus *Menticirrhus,* which includes the Atlantic minkfishes, lack a swimbladder and can only produce rather weak noises by grinding their teeth.

The croakers are fairly large fishes, usually with well-flavoured flesh, and some species are important as sport fishes. The American freshwater drum *Aplodinotus grunniens,* found particularly in the freshwaters of the southern states, also occurs in the Great Lakes where it is known as the sheepshead. A large specimen may weigh 60 lb (28 kg) but archaeologists have found the bones of drums in Indian camp sites which show that fishes of 200 lb (90 kg) were once caught. The average size of fishes caught nowadays is only 5 lb (2·5 kg).

Of the three European species, the meagre, the Brown meagre and the corb, the first is the largest, reaching 6 ft (1·8 m) in length and providing considerable sport.

The croakers are usually rather dull coloured, but the Striped drum *Equetus pulcher* from tropical regions has longitudinal bands of black and white on the flanks and the dorsal fin is enlarged resembling a black flag. The largest of the croakers is the totuva *Cynoscion macdonaldi* from the Gulf of California which reaches weights of 220 lb (100 kg). In South Africa, the croaker *Atractoscion aequidens* is considered a great delicacy and is known as salmon or geelbek. It is not common and when caught it is usually cured, but a certain sharp practice exists amongst the local fishermen who cure the much more common but inferiorly flavoured croaker *Johnius hololepidotus*. As the cured fishes greatly resemble each other in appearance except for the shape of the tail, the latter is cut off by the fishermen to complete the deception. The drums are important commercial fishes in many areas and in India they are used to provide a source of low quality isinglass from their swimbladders, as well as for food. FAMILY: Sciaenidae, ORDER: Perciformes, CLASS: Pisces. (Ill. p. 57.)

CRUCIFIX FISH, a fanciful name given to certain marine catfishes of the genus *Arius* in parts of South America and the West Indies because of the resemblance of the underparts of the cleaned skull to a figure with outstretched arms. The body is formed from the parasphenoid bone, the two lateral processes resembling arms, while the Weberian ossicles form a halo. The upper side of the skull can be seen as a monk or Roman soldier, the dorsal spine being the spear and the ear-stones or otoliths rattling like the proverbial dice with which the soldiers cast lots for Christ's garments. When appropriately painted, the skull gives a satisfying blend of the fortuitous and the contrived. FAMILY: Ariidae, ORDER: Cypriniformes, CLASS: Pisces.

CUCUMBERFISHES, also known as pearlfishes, elongated marine fishes, related to the cods that live inside Sea cucumbers. In England they are often called fierasfers, derived from their former scientific name meaning 'shining beasts'. The most striking feature of these fishes is their habit of entering any small crevice tail first. Some species are very particular and *Carapus bermudensis* will only live in one species of Sea cucumber, while others, such as *C. homei,* will live in any shell or Sea cucumber. Although Sea cucumbers are hollow a certain strategy is required in converting the animal into living quarters. When a young cucumberfish finds its host it searches for the anus and pushes its way in. As the fish becomes larger it tends to enter the Sea cucumber tail first. In many other associations between two animals each partner gains something from the relationship and it is because of this advantage that the association has evolved. In the case of the cucumberfishes, the host seems to gain nothing and may even suffer unintentional damage to its organs. Some cucumberfishes are not above nibbling at their hosts while inside. *Carapus apus* from the Mediterranean is believed to spend its entire life inside the Sea cucumber, presumably feeding on its host. This may not do as much damage as might be thought since the Sea cucumbers have great powers of regeneration.

The eggs of the cucumberfish float at the surface and the young fish do not closely resemble their parents. While still young they search for a suitable home. The body of these fishes is naked and in some species the pelvic fins are lacking. One of the largest species *Echiodon drummondi* reaches 12 in (30 cm) in length and is found in British waters. FAMILY: Carapidae, ORDER: Gadiformes, CLASS: Pisces.

CUSKEELS, elongated marine fishes related to the cods and the cucumberfishes. The cuskeels have long bodies with the dorsal and anal fins running the entire length of the body. The pelvic fins are under the head and are reduced to two barbel-like structures on the chin. They probably serve a sensory function since they are trailed along the bottom as the fish swims and may indicate the nature of the substrate, availability of food, etc. Most species are less than 12 in (30 cm) long although the South African kingklip *Genypterus capensis* grows to 5 ft (1·5 m). In spite of its slimy and unprepossessing appearance, this species is considered to be a delicacy. It is caught in trawls from depths of 1,500 ft (500 m). Like their relatives, the cucumberfishes, many of the cuskeels stand on their tails or enter crevices tail first. FAMILY: Ophidiidae, ORDER: Gadiformes, CLASS: Pisces.

CUTLASSFISHES, and their close relatives the hairtails, ribbon-like oceanic fishes related to the swordfish, mackerel and tunas. The elongated, highly compressed body suggests a resemblance to a cutlass. The dorsal fin is long, the anal fin short and there is either a very small tail (cutlassfishes) or the body tapers to a point (hairtails). The jaws are large and have sharp, widely-spaced teeth, some of which may be fang-like. The frostfish *Lepidopus caudatus* is one of the cutlassfishes.

Trichiurus lepturus is a hairtail that reaches 5 ft (1·5 m) in length. It is widely distributed throughout the Atlantic, western Pacific and Indian Oceans and although it normally lives in deep water it is found in shallower waters off Japan and South Africa where cold currents well up. It is silvery in colour with the anal fin consisting of isolated spinelets. There is not much flesh on it but what there is has a good flavour and the species has some importance in fisheries in India. Several common names are used for it, including snakefish, bandfish and ribbonfish. *Aphanopus carbo,* another member of this family, is an elongated black fish caught in the temperate deep waters of the North Atlantic. FAMILY: Trichiuridae, ORDER: Perciformes, CLASS: Pisces.

D

DAB *Limanda limanda,* a small flatfish living in sandy bays along the coasts of northern Europe. The dab, which reaches 17 in (43 cm) in length, can be recognized by the sharp curve of the lateral line near the pectoral fin and the spiny margins of the scales on the eyed side of the fish (these are smooth on the blind side). The general colour of the eyed side is sandy brown, flecked with orange and black, while the blind side is white. Occasionally specimens are found which are coloured on both sides and the scales are spiny on the two sides as well. The dab is common round British shores and reaches as far north as Iceland. These fishes are inactive during the day but feed at night and are more easily caught then. The breeding season is from March to May, the eggs being pelagic and amongst the smallest of any of the European flatfishes (averaging 0·8 mm in diameter).

The Long rough dab *Hippoglossoides platessoides* is a close relative of the halibut. It is a smaller fish and has rough-edged scales on the body but an almost straight lateral line. It is found on both sides of the Atlantic and is common at depths of 120–480 ft (40–160 m). FAMILY: Pleuronectidae, ORDER: Pleuronectiformes, CLASS: Pisces.

DACE *Leuciscus leuciscus,* a small carp-like fish common in the rivers of England and the continent of Europe. The body is silvery with the back dark, the lower fins often having a yellow or orange tinge. The dace grows to 16 in (40 cm) in length and closely resembles a small chub. The dace, however, can be distinguished by the concave edges to the dorsal and anal fins, those of the chub being slightly convex. The dace is a shoaling fish, usually found near the surface of the water where it feeds on flying insects as well as insect larvae, worms and snails. FAMILY: Cyprinidae, ORDER: Cypriniformes, CLASS: Pisces.

DAMSELFISHES, small tropical coral-reef fishes related to the perches. The damselfishes, which are often very brightly coloured, are mostly small and rarely exceed 6 in (15 cm) in length.

One of the few that grows larger, and also one of the few to be found outside the tropics, is the garibaldi *Hypsyops rubicunda* from the Pacific. This fish is a brilliant orange in colour and grows to 12 in (30 cm). The garibaldi is one of the many fishes that are capable of making noises by clicking together the pharyngeal or throat teeth. Many of the damselfishes exhibit a strong territorial behaviour, each fish having its own particular cranny in the coral and guarding this jealously. Members of the genus *Dascyllus* live in shoals and when danger threatens the whole shoal seems to disappear into the coral. Several species of *Dascyllus* are imported into Europe for aquarists.

The remarkable clownfish is discussed elsewhere.

The damselfishes are among the most colourful of the inhabitants of the coral reefs. The Cocoa damselfish *Eupomacentrus variabilis* from Puerto Rico, which does not exceed 3 in (8 cm) in length, is rich blue on the upper-part of the head, shoulders and front of the dorsal fin and a lemon yellow fading to lime green on the edges of the fins. In the Bicolor damselfish *E. partitus* the front half of the body is black and the rear part lemon to white, with a clear-cut division between the two colour zones. The Sergeant major *Abudefduf saxatilis* occurs in all tropical seas. As well as having a wide distribution it also has a very wide dietary range, feeding on anything from algae to fishes. FAMILY: Pomacentridae, ORDER: Perciformes, CLASS: Pisces. (Ill. p. 50, 54, 55, 58, 59.)

DANIOS, small tropical carp-like fishes belonging to the genera *Danio* and *Brachydanio* and very popular with aquarists. The danios are slim, lively fishes, often brightly coloured and usually with two pairs of barbels. They are found in shoals in the rivers of southern India, Burma and the Indo-Malayan Peninsula.

The Pearl danio *Brachydanio albolineatus,* of India and Sumatra, is so called because of the beautiful pearly iridescence of its pink or grey-green body. It grows to 2½ in (6 cm) in length. The zebra-fish *Brachydanio rerio* has horizontal blue and gold stripes along the flanks, reaches less than 2 in (4·5 cm) and is found in eastern India. The Spotted danio *B. nigrofasciatus* of Burma is slightly smaller and has a light brown stripe along the flanks bordered above and below by thin blue stripes, with a number of blue spots on the lower half of the body. One of the largest species is the Giant danio *Danio malabaricus* of Ceylon and western India. It grows to nearly 5 in (12 cm) and has a much deeper but compressed body. The back is a slate blue-grey and there are three or four steel-blue stripes along the flanks which become fainter towards the tail.

Danios are easy to keep in an aquarium

Dace, European freshwater fish, valued as a sports fish, but too small and bony for eating.

and are also easy to breed. Occasionally other species than the four listed here are imported. FAMILY: Cyprinidae, ORDER: Cypriniformes, CLASS: Pisces. (Ill. p. 60.)

DARTERS, small freshwater perch-like fishes found in North America. They derive their common name from their habit of darting between stones. They occur only in the temperate parts of North America to the east of the Rocky Mountains and about 95 species are known. They are bottom-living forms and some have surprisingly bright colours compared with most freshwater fishes of temperate waters. They lack swimbladders and have two dorsal fins, the first spiny and the second soft-rayed. The darters are carnivorous, feeding on small insect larvae and tiny crustaceans. The entire body is scaled in most species. Their spawning habits vary widely: some bury their eggs in sand or gravel, others carefully guard the eggs and still others simply scatter the eggs and leave them. The Johnny darter *Etheostoma nigrum* spawns in the spring, the female depositing the eggs on the underside of stones and the male aerating them and guarding them in a most ferocious manner for a fish of only 2½ in (6·5 cm).

The Eastern sand darter *Ammocrypta pellucida* has a row of scales only along the midline. It is sand-coloured and translucent and like most darters is secretive, burying itself in the sandy beds of streams with only its eyes and snout protruding. It reaches 3 in (7·5 cm) in length. Most darters live in clear shallow streams but *Etheostoma fusiforme* lives in murky, swampy waters and has been found in estuaries. The Log perches are the largest of the darters. *Percina caprodes* grows to 6 in (15 cm) and the flanks are marked by dark vertical bars which gave rise to the alternative name of zebrafish.

Although darters are common and widespread over a large part of the United States, their small size and secretive habits have meant that they are rarely seen unless especially looked for. FAMILY: Percidae, ORDER: Perciformes, CLASS: Pisces.

DEALFISHES, a family of ribbon-like oceanic fishes related to the oarfish and the opah and usually found in deep water in all oceans. Although quite large, dealfishes are very fragile and it is often difficult to determine the exact form of the fins. In some species there are two dorsal fins, the first one consisting of a few elongated rays narrowly separated from the second long dorsal fin; in other species the two dorsal fins are united. The anal fin is missing, the pectoral fins are very small and the pelvic fins are reduced or absent. The most curious feature is the tail. Only the upper half is present and this sticks up like a fan at right angles to the body. The changes that occur in the fins during the

development of the fish have been studied in the vaagmar *Trachipterus arcticus* of the North Atlantic. In the small larvae the first dorsal finrays are elongated into filaments several times the length of the body and the pelvic fins are also filamentous. As the fish grows, these filaments shorten and some of the pelvic finrays are lost so that only two or three are present in the adult. The tail of the young fish has the rays of the lower lobe elongated while the upper lobe is barely developed. Gradually the lower rays shorten and finally disappear while the upper lobe grows into the vertical fan-like structure found in the adult. The young appear to live in deep and calm water where the filaments are not liable to damage and can be used to support the fish by increasing its surface area.

The vaagmar is the dealfish occasionally washed up on European shores. It derives its name from Old Icelandic, meaning 'Sea horse'. It is found everywhere in the Atlantic and has even been recorded from New Zealand. It lives at depths down to 1,800 ft (600 m). The largest specimen washed ashore was 8 ft (2·4 m) in length. Few people have been fortunate enough to see this fish alive, but in 1966 an angler caught a specimen of 4 ft (1·2 m) at Marsden on the northeast coast of England. Another specimen of 6 ft 2 in (1·9 m) was measured and found to have a body depth of 14 in (35 cm) but a body width of only 3¼ in (8 cm). A related species, *T. iris,* is found in the Mediterranean and the tropical southern Atlantic. A small form growing to only 12 in (30 cm) from South Africa and named *T. cristatus* may perhaps merely be the young of a known larger species.

Curious legends have been associated with dealfishes, although some of the stories may have been based in part on the oarfish. Several species in different countries are known as 'King of the herrings' and one species from the Pacific has been called *T. rexsalmonorum,* that is 'King of the salmon'. The Vikings believed that if anyone hurt one of these dealfishes it would drive away that important food fish, the herring (the fish in the legend may, however, have been the oarfish). Some tribes of American Indians on the American Pacific coast had a similar fable concerning *T. rexsalmonorum.* The basis for these legends has never been satisfactorily explained.

The dealfishes, together with the oarfish and opah, were formerly placed in the order Allotriognathi or 'strange jaws', an allusion to the curious method of jaw protrusion shared by these fishes. By depression of the lower jaw, the whole upper jaw is pushed forward, the mechanism being essentially the same in the deep-bodied opah as in the ribbon-like forms.

The dealfishes are all fairly rare and if any

are found washed up on beaches they should be preserved if possible and a museum or other institution notified. FAMILY: Trachipteridae, ORDER: Lampridiformes, CLASS: Pisces.

DEEP-SEA FISHES belong to a number of families which are not necessarily closely related to each other but which have independently evolved highly modified forms suitable to the rather extraordinary conditions of the deeps. Passing from the shallower waters of the continental slope into the deeper waters, one can see a transition in the fishes. Dr Lev Andriashev, the Russian ichthyologist, has suggested that there are, in fact, two distinct kinds of deep-sea fishes. Those in the primary group are highly modified and seem to have evolved within the deeps, while those in the secondary group are less modified and appear to have evolved in shallow water, only later being forced into the deeper water, perhaps as a result of competition with other species. It was originally thought that the deeper waters of the world might harbour primitive relicts from the time when fishes first evolved. This has not proved to be the case, the deep-sea fishes being merely highly modified and specialized versions of quite advanced groups of fishes.

The deeps are usually taken to mean water below about 650 ft (200 m). No light penetrates to this depth and without light plants cannot grow. Animals living at this depth must, therefore, either feed on other animals (carnivorous) or, if small enough, browse on the detritus that filters down from above. A map of the world shows that two thirds of the earth's surface is covered by water of a depth of over 650 ft (200 m), so that the ocean depths represent a huge environment, but one that is very sparsely populated. Some shallow-water fishes, such as the cod *Gadus morhua,* are found below 650 ft but they are merely visitors. Conversely, many of the true deep-sea fishes regularly migrate every night towards the surface, descending again with the dawn.

Many problems confront the deep-sea fishes. Those that migrate vertically each day, sometimes as much as 5,000 ft (1,500 m), must overcome the great difference in pressure. Even cod trawled from a few hundred metres down will 'explode', the gut of the fish forced out of its mouth by the sudden expansion of the swimbladder as the pressure is decreased. Deep-sea fishes overcome this either by releasing air from the swimbladder as they ascend or they are species that lack a swimbladder. Most of the deep-sea fishes are small, with bone and muscle poorly developed, for there is little use in being swimmers in an environment which is almost uniformly cold and dark. Only when food or predators are near is it necessary to swim from one spot to another with any haste. Most of the deep-sea fishes are pelagic and only a few ever see the bottom. Below 2,000 ft (600 m) the fish populations become very sparse and the chances of meeting food or a mate are slender. To overcome this, various specializations have evolved.

The most striking of the modifications found in deep-sea fishes are the light organs. The light may derive from colonies of bacteria contained in special glands (often covered by a transparent scale, sometimes tinted) or it may result from chemical actions under the control of the fish. In the Lantern fishes (family Myctophidae) the light organs are arranged in rows over the body, appearing as pearly spots the pattern of which differs in each species. This suggests that the pattern is used by the fishes as a means of identifying members of their own species, both to avoid preying on their own species and to aid in recognizing a possible mate.

Light is also used by the ceratioid or Deep-sea anglerfishes to provide a luminous lure to attract prey. The first ray of the dorsal fin is enlarged and can be bent forwards so that a fleshy luminous bulb at its tip can be dangled in front of the mouth. Inquisitive fishes are then seized and swallowed. This fishing method is brought to perfection by another fish, *Galatheathauma,* which has a luminous flap actually on the roof of the mouth. It simply waits with its mouth open until a smaller fish swims inside.

In some deep-sea fishes the light organs are used to illuminate the darkness around the fish. A biologist on the research ship *William Scoresby* watched an eel-like stomiatoid fish one night during a cruise in the Antarctic. The fish, which was about 12 in (30 cm) long, had powerful luminous organs that emitted a beam of blue light sufficient to illuminate the water up to 24 in (60 cm) in front. Any small shrimp-like animals caught in the beam were immediately snapped up.

The sparsity of animal life in the depths means that whenever food is encountered the opportunity must not be wasted, even if, in some cases, the prey is larger than the predator. The viperfish *Chauliodus* is unusual amongst fishes in that the head can be thrown upwards to increase the gape of the mouth and thus enable the fish to swallow larger animals. Its long, thin teeth—a common feature of deep-sea fishes—help to prevent the prey from escaping during the act of swallowing. In the Black swallower *Chiasmodon niger* the gape of the jaws is enormous and the stomach is distensible, so that this species can swallow and accommodate fishes that are actually twice as large as the predator itself. The speed with which the jaws are snapped shut is obviously important. In the stomiatoid genus *Malacosteus* much of the walls and floor of the mouth

are missing; presumably this allows the jaws to be snapped shut extremely quickly, the jaw encountering much less resistance to water than if membranes were present.

Deep-sea fishes that migrate into the upper waters tend to have fairly large eyes, while those that remain in the very deep waters have eyes that are reduced or even absent. Vision is important to fishes that recognize their prey or mates by their light organs. In the giant-tails (family Giganturidae) the eyes are tubular and project from both sides of the head, giving the fish binocular vision, a rare feature in fishes. The deep-sea salmonid *Opisthoproctus* has tubular eyes that point upwards. In the family Ipnopidae the eyes in some species are merely enlarged retinas under a greatly flattened cornea, sometimes with luminous patches near the eyes. In the genus *Idiacanthus* the eyes of the young are set on the ends of stalks but are normal in the adults.

The *lateral line organs, sometimes referred to as the organs of distant touch, are normally in canals below the skin, with small pores communicating with the outside. In some deep-sea fishes, such as the Gulper eels, the lateral line organs are on stalks, presumably for greater sensitivity. Other deep-sea fishes have greatly elongated bodies and thus very long lateral line canals down the flanks. This may increase the sensitivity of the organ.

Breeding in deep-sea fishes is obviously extremely difficult to observe and deductions must be made from specimens brought to the surface. Examination of Deep-sea anglerfishes shows that their breeding habits are unique amongst the vertebrates. The specimens brought to the surface were dumpy, with a large mouth fringed with pointed teeth and, depending on the species, ranged in length from a few inches to almost 3 ft (1 m)—and they were females. It was then noticed that some of the larger ones had one or more small tubular and fleshy appendages hanging from the body and on investigation these proved to be the males. The males, which are slim with small mouths and chisel-like teeth at the front, are free-swimming only until they meet a female. They then bite into her skin and eventually their bodies fuse with that of the female and each male becomes parasitic on the female. The male loses its alimentary tract and sense organs and a placenta-like connection keeps him supplied with nourishment from the blood of the female. Eventually, the male degenerates into a sac of testes hanging from the female. The only free-swimming males found have been immature and presumably those that fail to find a female must die. Spawning takes place in summer. The eggs float to the surface but after hatching the larvae slowly sink again to the depths and the sexes begin their different patterns of development.

The deep-sea fishes provide a spectacular example of the way in which animals can become adapted to an apparently adverse environment. The increasing depth at which underwater observations can be made will help to resolve many puzzling features in the biology of these fishes. (Ill. p. 50, 51.)

DEVIL RAYS, a family of large ray-like cartilaginous fishes whose 'devilish' reputation stems rather from their size and curious appearance than from their supposedly ferocious behaviour. They have the wing-like pectoral fins of the ordinary skate or ray and closely resemble the Eagle rays except that the mouth is much wider and is provided with a pair of appendages on either side which are used as scoops in feeding. The Devil rays are surface-living fishes (unlike the majority of bottom-living ray-like fishes) and they feed on small crustaceans and plankton. The mouth, which is terminal in most of the species, is kept open as the fish cruises along and food is collected by fine sieve-like rakers before the water passes to the gills. Some species grow to an enormous size and there is a record of a specimen that measured 22 ft (6·6 m) from tip to tip of the pectoral fins. There are many records of these fishes leaving the water and sailing through the air, the resounding noise of their return to water having been compared with the sound of a cannon. A single species of the genus *Manta* is known from the warmer parts of the Atlantic and it is possible that it is this same species, *M. birostris,* that occurs throughout the Indo-Pacific region. Teeth are present only in the lower jaw, whereas there are teeth in both jaws in the genera *Mobula* (Atlantic and Indo-Pacific) and *Indomanta* (India), but only in the upper jaw in *Ceratobatis* of Jamaican waters. In some species there is a venomous spine on the tail similar to that found in the Sting rays. The Devil rays are all ovoviviparous and give birth to live young. One observation on a harpooned female off the coast of Florida records that an embryo was ejected into the air for a distance of about 4 ft (1·2 m), the embryo emerging tail first and instantly unfolding its large pectoral fins, which were more than 3 ft (90 cm) from tip to tip. However, this is probably not the normal method of birth. The Devil rays are very graceful swimmers and are favourite subjects for underwater films with an 'intrepid' skin-diver bravely swimming beside these huge but mostly harmless giants. FAMILY: Mobulidae, ORDER: Hypotremata, CLASS: Chondrichthyes.

DISCUSFISHES, flattened disc-shaped fishes of the cichlid genus *Symphysodon* from fresh waters in South America. Their common name aptly describes their shape but much more striking is their magnificent

Clownfish *Amphiprion percula* lives in symbiosis with Sea anemones, protected from predators by tentacles, the anemones profiting from food the fish wastes.

The Three-striped damselfish *Dascyllus aruanus* of the Indo-Pacific.

The West Indian damselfish *Chromis coerulens*.

Deep-sea fishes live in water below 650 ft (200 m) where no light penetrates. Without light plants cannot grow and these animals must therefore feed on other animals. Opposite: One of the Snaggle-toothed fishes *Astronesthes*; top left: Deep-sea angler; bottom left, a juvenile Deep-sea angler; top right: *Anoplogaster*; bottom right: viperfish.

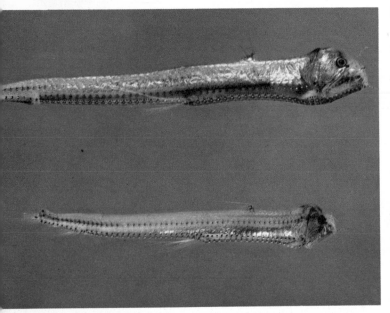

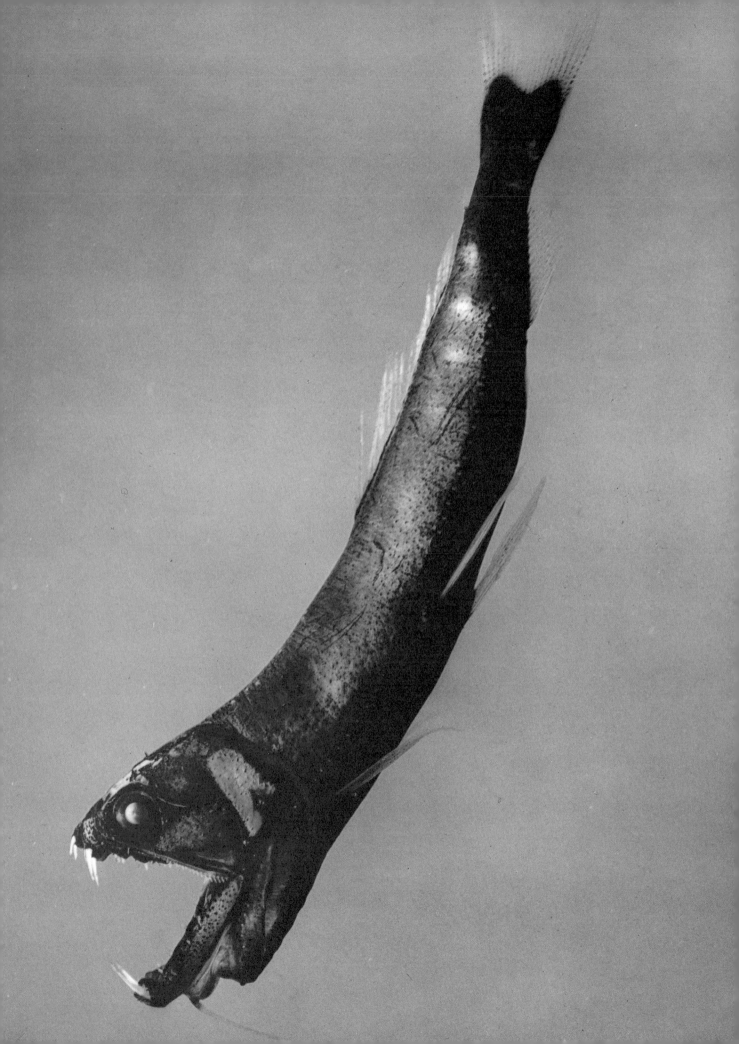

Blind cave characin of Mexico.

Male African lyretails *Aphyosemion batesi* have larger fins and brighter colours than the females.

The Green discus or Pompadour fish, of the Rio Negro and Amazon basins.

Climbing perch, fish that does not climb.

Cardinalfish *Apogon nematopleris*.

Connemara clingfish *Lepadogaster candollei* using its sucker to fix itself (above).

Cardinal tetra is distinguished from its relatives by the red band over the full length of the body.

Atlantic cod, one of the most important food fishes in the North Atlantic.

Armoured catfish showing the six barbels and the spine on the pectorals.

Common carp of Europe.

Crucian carp.

A remarkable association exists between some Sea anemones and fishes known as Anemone fishes. These are able to take shelter among the tentacles of the anemone without being stung.

Jewel cichlid or jewelfish spawning, laying its eggs in a neat circle.

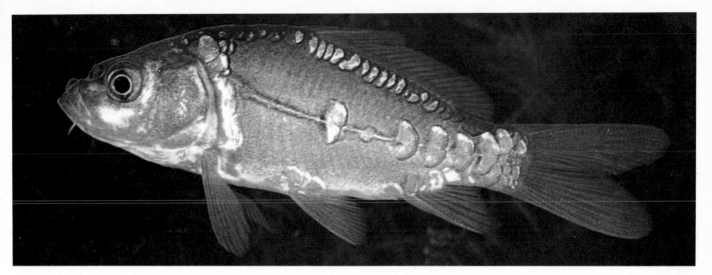

The Mirror carp, a domesticated variety of the Common carp, is named for the large scales on its flanks.

Upside-down catfish, of Africa, lacks the silver belly usual in fishes that swim the right way up.

The Striped drum *Equetus pulcher*, one of the croakers, a fish living in the seas around Florida and the Lesser Antilles which makes sounds, presumably to communicate with its fellows.

Glass catfish or Ghost fish hovering among plants.

Variola louti.

Anthia anthias.

A shoal of coral fish.

The Emperor fish.

Japanese Hi-goi or Golden carp.

Danio aequipinnatus of southeast Asia.

South American Jewel tetra *Hyphessobrycon callistus*.

The Cornish sucker, another clingfish, with eggs which it is guarding (right).

colour. There are four forms of the discus which appear to be referable to two species. The Common discus *Symphysodon discus* grows to 8 in (20 cm) and occurs in the Amazon, the Rio Negro and connected rivers. It is rare and expensive and is greatly prized by aquarists. The Green discus *S. aequifasciata* grows to 6 in (15 cm) and comes from the Amazon; the Brown discus *S. a. axelrodi* is slightly smaller and is also from the Amazon as well as the Rio Urubu; and the Blue discus *S. a. heraldi* is again smaller and from the Amazon.

As in most of the Cichlidae, the parents lavish considerable care on the eggs and young. The eggs are guarded, fanned and mouthed by the parents. When hatched, the fry are picked up in the mouths of the parents and transferred to various surfaces where they remain attached by a short thread. (Ill. p. 53.)

DOGFISHES, small sharks of four quite distinct families.

The true dogfishes belong to the Cat sharks (Scyliorhinidae) and are characterized by having two dorsal fins, which lack a spine in front, and one anal fin. A spiracle is present but there is no nictitating membrane or 'third eyelid'. The two most common European species are the Greater spotted dogfish *Scyliorhinus stellaris* and the Lesser spotted dogfish *S. caniculus*. The former, which is also known as the nursehound or bullhuss, can be distinguished by the fact that its nostrils are farther apart and the nasal lobes or flaps of skin leading from the nostrils back towards the mouth are distinctly lobed. In both species the body is generally light brown with a fine speckling of black on the upper surfaces, the spots being larger in the Greater spotted dogfish. The two are very common along all European coasts. They feed on worms, molluscs, crustaceans and echinoderms, and can be fished for by boat

---

DOGFISHES, are standard animals for dissection in biology classes. The usual dissections are to show the organs of digestion, excretion and reproduction, the gills and their blood supply and the cranial nerves. The advantage for classroom work lies in the dogfishes' simple anatomy and in their abundance. 'The dogfish' which is so familiar as a formalin-reeking carcase to so many students may be one of several species. In British classrooms it is the Lesser spotted dogfish, while on the Pacific coast of the United States students are supplied with Spiny dogfishes. In Britain and the United States dogfish are now marketed for human consumption as 'Rock salmon' and 'grayfish' respectively.

over sandy bottoms using lugworms (*Arenicola*) or small pieces of fish. There is an angling record of just over 20 lb (9 kg) for a Larger spotted dogfish caught in British waters. The dogfishes are oviparous and produce rectangular egg cases with a spiralling tendril at each corner. The embryo is well supplied with yolk and does not hatch for seven months after fertilization. FAMILY: Scyliorhinidae, ORDER: Pleurotremata, CLASS: Chondrichthyes.

DOLPHINS, marine fishes of tropical and subtropical oceans. The head is large and the body tapers gracefully to the tail, which is strongly forked. The long dorsal fin and the back are a superb green and the flanks and tail have an orange band. Young dolphins are marked with a series of black vertical bars. The Common dolphin *Coryphaena hippurus* grows to 5 ft (1·5 m), the males being larger than the females. It can swim at 37 mph (59 kph) and is well able to catch Flying fishes, on which it feeds voraciously. Other fish are also eaten. The only other member of this family is the Pompano dolphin *C. equiselis,* a smaller fish which only reaches 30 in (75 cm). The Common dolphin has a fast growth rate and a specimen weighing about $1\frac{1}{2}$ lb (0·6 kg) kept at the Florida Marine Studios grew to $37\frac{1}{2}$ lb (16·8 kg) in only $7\frac{1}{2}$ months. FAMILY: Coryphaenidae, ORDER: Perciformes, CLASS: Pisces.

DRAGONETS, flattened, bottom-living fishes, members of *Callionymus* and related genera found along coasts in temperate regions. The name *dracunculus* or 'little dragon' was used by Pliny nearly 2,000 years ago and is an appropriate description of these curious little fishes. The dragonets rarely grow to more than 12 in (30 cm) in length. They have flat, depressed heads and slender bodies, but many are so beautifully coloured that they resemble some of the tropical reef fishes. There are no scales on the body. There is a sharp spine on the preopercular bone of the gill cover and there

Lesser spotted dogfish swimming in the aquarium at the Plymouth Biological Station.

Egg of the Lesser spotted dogfish fixed to Sea fan *Eunicella verrucosa* by the long tendrils from each corner of the capsule.

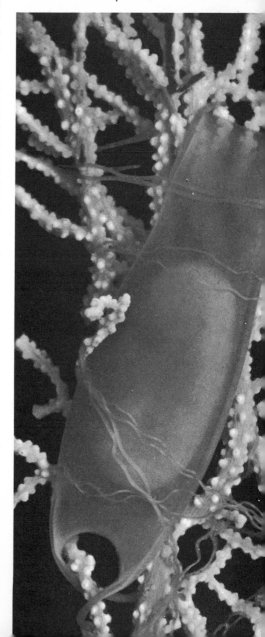

are two dorsal fins of which the anterior is greatly elongated in the male.

Two species of dragonet are found along European shores, the Common dragonet

Callionymus lyra and the Spotted dragonet *C. maculatus*. The former is common in the Mediterranean and reaches northwards to Norway, often being found along British shores. The female is rather dull coloured, but the male is a splendid fish, especially in the breeding season. His back is red-yellow with blue markings and the flanks and lower part of the head are orange, again with blue spots and marks. There are two blue bands along the body and the fins are marked with blue, yellow and green. The differences between the sexes are so striking that they were once thought to be quite different species, the 'sordid' and the 'gemmeous' dragonets. Spawning takes place in spring and summer, the male swimming around the female and displaying with gill covers and fins until the

female is sufficiently stimulated. The two then swim together to the surface, close together and with the anal fins forming a gutter into which eggs and sperm are shed. The eggs have honeycomb markings on their surfaces.

The Spotted dragonet is a smaller fish and can be distinguished by the three or four rows of ocellated spots instead of bands along the dorsal fin. The sexes also differ, the male being much more gaudy than the female. Once thought to be quite rare, recent work now suggests that this species has merely been overlooked.

There is a deep water genus *Draconetta* found in the North Atlantic. FAMILY: Callionymidae, ORDER: Perciformes, CLASS: Pisces.

DRUMFISHES, an alternative name for croakers.

EAGLE RAYS, a family of ray-like cartilaginous fishes with a whip-like tail usually with a venomous spine at its base. The expanded pectoral fins are used to propel the fish through the water with considerable grace, the tail being held stiffly behind. The Eagle ray *Myliobatis aquila* of the Mediterranean and eastern Atlantic can be distinguished from similar Sting rays of these coasts by its prominent head, which is raised well above the level of the pectoral wings. The back is smooth and brown, the undersides a rather dirty white and the tail black. It grows to about 4 ft (1·2 m) in length and feeds chiefly on molluscs which are crushed with the powerful pavement of teeth in the jaws.

As in all members of this family, the young are born alive, having hatched previously within the uterus of the female. At least in the American Pacific coast species, *M. californicus,* the young are born tail first, the poison spine being soft and sheathed in tissue until after birth. In certain areas, such as San Francisco Bay, Eagle rays are a considerable pest of commercial clam and oyster beds, which must be protected with fences of stakes.

Members of the genus *Rhinoptera* are sometimes placed in a separate family, the Rhinopteridae or Cow-nosed rays. They resemble the Eagle rays in having a curious fleshy fold or lobe below the eyes but it is better developed and is split in the middle to give left and right portions looking like the horns of a cow. These fishes can measure up to 7 ft (2·1 m) from tip to tip of the pectoral 'wings'.

The Duck-billed rays (*Aetobatus, Aetomylaeus*) differ from the two previous groups in having only a single but broad band of molar-like teeth in the jaws (there being seven to nine bands in the other species). FAMILY: Myliobatidae, ORDER: Hypotremata, CLASS: Chondrichthyes.

EELPOUTS, a family of blenny-like marine fishes related to the Wolf eels. They are found in the cold northern waters at all depths ranging from the low-tide mark to more than 5,000 ft (1,650 m). Their common

name is derived from their eel-like shape coupled with the word pout, possibly a derivative of the Old Dutch *putt* or toad, a reference to their toad-like head. The dorsal and anal fins and the tail are continuous to form one fin round the body. The pelvic fins are greatly reduced and lie in front of the bases of the pectoral fins. Many species of eelpouts give birth to live young.

The eelpout or Viviparous blenny *Zoarces viviparus* of European shores is frequently found hiding under stones or weeds on the shore when the tide has receded. Like the butterfish or gunnel, this species has only a single ovary instead of the paired ovaries found in most fishes. Fertilization is internal and the eggs are attached by small processes to the ovary walls. They hatch in about 20 days but remain for a further three months inside the mother and the fry are $1\frac{1}{2}$ in (4 cm) long when they are finally released. During that time they receive nourishment from secretions from the walls of the ovary. A female of 8 in (20 cm) may bear 20–40

young, while a large fish may bear up to 300. The eelpout grows to about 16 in (40 cm) in length.

The largest of the eelpouts is an American Atlantic species, *Macrozoarces americanus* which reaches $3\frac{1}{2}$ ft (105 cm) in length. This species is not viviparous but lays large eggs, $\frac{1}{4}$ in (6 mm) in diameter, which are guarded by one or both parents. FAMILY: Zoarcidae, ORDER: Gadiformes, CLASS: Pisces.

EELS, elongated fishes belonging to two suborders of the large order Anguilliformes, namely the Saccopharyngoidei or Gulper eels and the Anguilloidei, which contains all other families of eels. Eels lack pelvic fins and were formerly placed in a large group, the Apodes (meaning 'no feet') which, however, contained a number of non-eel-like fishes included because of the absence of pelvic fins. Characteristic of the eels is the long body and the long dorsal and anal fins which are joined to the tail fin to form a single long fin. Pectoral fins are usually

Elvers 'roping' up rocks. Even adult eels show remarkable dexterity in climbing.

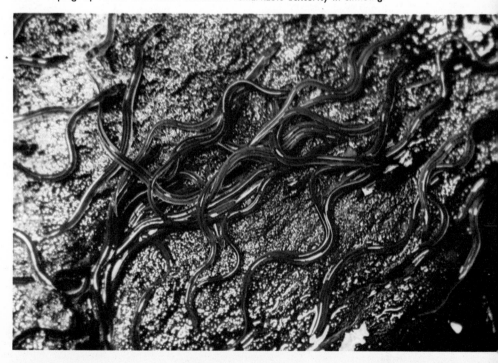

Conger eel, large marine eel, sometimes swims at the surface, on its side, its body undulating.

Colourful Moray eels resting in a drainpipe.

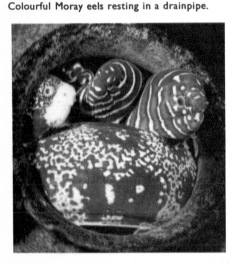

present but the bones supporting them have lost the connection with the skull usually found in the bony fishes. As a result, the pectorals are often distant from the head and the gill apparatus and branchial region of the head are elongated. The long and narrow branchial or gill chamber is used as a pump to force water over the gills and out of the sometimes small gill opening. Some species have smooth, naked bodies while in others there are small but deep-set and irregularly scattered scales. There are very many vertebrae, normally 1–200 but sometimes as many as 5–600, and the sinuous body is extremely flexible. This eel-like form, which is found in certain other bony fishes not related to the eels, is nearly always associ-

ated with a bottom-living, burrowing or crevice-dwelling mode of life. In most of the burrowing eels the fins are reduced or lost and the tail may become hardened to become a digging tool. Eels are often rapacious feeders and the jaws and teeth are well developed. Common to all the eels is a thin, leaf-like larval form, the leptocephalus stage, from which the eel metamorphoses into the adult after a few months or even after two or three years. The muscle segments or myomeres of the leptocephalus not only remain constant in number when the adult form is attained, but also equal the number of vertebrae. The muscle segments are easily counted in the leptocephalus, while the vertebrae can be counted by dissection or X-ray in the adult. Since the numbers of vertebrae are often characteristic of the species, this provides a most useful clue to identifying the leptocephalus larvae of different species.

The eels are clearly a highly successful group. Modern classifications recognize 23 families of eels together with three families of Gulper eels. There are over a hundred genera and several hundred species. The best known family is the Anguillidae, which contains the freshwater eels, but the three largest families are the Congridae (Conger eels), the Ophichthidae (Worm eels) and the Muraenidae (Moray eels), the two latter essentially tropical in distribution and characteristic of coral reefs. Eels are essentially warm water species with a distribution that coincides with that of the tropical, shallow-water corals (i.e. bounded by the 68°F (20°C) isotherm). Some species have, however, penetrated into subtropical and temperate waters but return to warmer waters to breed. Probably all eels require a temperature of at least 65°F (18°C) and a salinity of 35 parts per 1000 in order to spawn, even though the adults may live in colder and less saline waters.

Members of the Congridae, the Conger eels, are like the anguillids in that they have colonized temperate waters but must return to warmer waters to breed. The Conger eel is described elsewhere.

The Garden eels, of the family Heterocongridae, are plankton-feeders. They live in colonies in fine coral sand, excavating a tube in the sediment by means of the tail and sinking out of sight if danger threatens. A colony of these fishes resembles a garden of waving spindly plants.

The Moray eels (family Muraenidae) from the Mediterranean and tropical oceans are large naked eels with mottled bodies that often live in holes in coral or rocks. One species, *Thyrsoidea macrura,* is reported to reach 13 ft (4 m) in length. These fishes are very voracious and were much admired by the Romans; Vedius Pollio was said to have kept a pond of morays into which recalcitrant slaves were thrown. Morays,

Two Common European eels among seaweed. Male eels stay nearer the coast than females.

which are good to eat except for a few extremely poisonous species, are much more colourful than the anguillids. The American Atlantic moray *Gymnothorax funebris* is a beautiful yellow-green in colour; *Muraena helena* from the Mediterranean and the Atlantic is brownish with yellow-ringed irregular brown blotches. The genus *Echidna* from the Indo-Pacific region contains eels that have flattened, grinding teeth instead of the more usual biting teeth and many species are highly coloured.

The family Cyemidae contains deep-sea Snipe eels. *Cyema atrum* is found in all tropical and temperate oceans at depths below 6,000 ft (2,000 m). The jaws are slender and elongated like the beak of an avocet and the dorsal and anal fins are separated at the tail. This species, which grows to 6 in (15 cm), has a short and deep-bodied leptocephalus.

The Snipe eels (Nemichthyidae) are elongated, deep sea eels with long and slender jaws that curve away from each other at the tips. The body tapers to a point.

The deep-sea eels of the family Serrivomeridae also have long jaws that cannot be closed at the tips.

The Snake eels (family Ophichthyidae) are tail-burrowers with sharp and spike-like tails and most species lack pelvic fins so that the body is a simple unimpeded cylinder. About 200 species are known, mostly small, less than 3 ft (90 cm), and many are brilliantly coloured.

The Worm eels (family Moringuidae) are also burrowers but appear to enter the sand head first. These species are worm-like, with one lip (usually the upper) often overlapping the other.

The eels are an example of a group of animals that have exploited the possibilities of a particular body feature (elongation) and have successfully used it in conquering a wide range of habitats. The fossil history of the group is fairly well known. One fossil is a moderately elongated eel-like fish in which the pelvic fins are still present (absent in all modern eels). Another fossil, from 60 million year old beds at Monte Bolca in Italy, is so well preserved that the brown pigmentation is still clearly visible.

One feature of eel behaviour which arises directly from the elongated form, and the powerful muscle system associated with it, is their skill in climbing. This has been noted in the freshwater eels. They will climb banks of rivers to travel overland, so can find their way from rivers to lakes, thereby widening the range of water they can use. Even dams are no obstacle, whether these include a sloping face of concrete or a brick wall. An eel, migrating upriver, will swim at such an obstruction, lunge at its face and, half-jumping, half-wriggling, pull itself up. If unsuccessful at the first attempt it will persist,

Moray eel *Rhinomuraeana amboinensis*.

trying again and again until it has achieved this first step. When the obstruction is made of bricks, the eel will exploit every crack, crevice or hole, using the head and tail alternately to scale the wall. ORDER: Anguilliformes, CLASS: Pisces.

ELECTRIC FISHES occur in several groups of quite unrelated fishes which have independently evolved the ability to discharge an electric current. The two principal uses to which this is put are to incapacitate other creatures (for defence or feeding purposes) or to receive information about the environment in the manner of radar. At first sight,

the ability of an animal to generate electricity seems strange. In fact, it is merely an extension of the normal operation of muscles and nerves. Every time an impulse passes down a nerve to stimulate the contraction of a muscle a tiny electric current is involved. In the electric fishes some of the muscles have lost their power to contract but have increased their electrical power. The size and number of nerve endings, where the electricity is normally released, are increased while the electrical units are arranged to multiply the discharge from unit to unit so that a battery effect is achieved. The electrical discharge does not affect the fish itself, largely because of the great insulation around the nerves. The discharge of the organ is controlled by the brain.

Amongst the cartilaginous fishes, the best known species are the Electric rays (*Torpedo* spp). These are Mediterranean and subtropical Atlantic fishes with a round, disc-shaped body and short tail, found over sandy or muddy bottoms. The largest is the Black electric ray *Torpedo nobiliana*, which may reach 5 ft (1·5 m) and weigh 100 lb (45 kg). The electric organs are in the wing-like pectoral fins. They can produce a current of 200 volts, quite enough to stun small crustaceans and fishes on which they feed.

The best known of the bony fishes is the Electric eel *Electrophorus* found in the Amazon basin. It is not a true eel, in spite of its eel-like appearance, but is related to the carps and characins. This fish can grow to more than 6 ft (1·8 m). The body is elongated but about $\frac{7}{8}$ of the total length is tail, the alimentary canal, heart, liver, kidneys and gonads being crowded into the first $\frac{1}{8}$.

Undersea photograph of the Black electric ray of the Mediterranean.

The 'tail' part is largely occupied by the electric organs. These fishes are able to emit two kinds of discharge, a high voltage (over 500 volts) for stunning prey and a much weaker regular pulse used as a direction finder and indicator for locating objects in the vicinity.

The Electric catfish *Malapterurus electricus* is a rather repulsive looking fish found in the Nile system, the Zambesi and certain of the African lakes. It has the Arabic name of *raad* which means 'thunder'. The electric organs are in the muscles over much of the body. These fishes grow to about 4 ft (120 cm) in length and can discharge 350 volts.

The electric organs found in the mormyrids or Elephant-snout fishes are located in the caudal peduncle, the muscular base to the tail. In these fishes a continuous stream of electrical impulses is discharged from the organ, at a variable frequency (lowest when the fish is resting but rising to 80–100 impulses per minute if the fish is disturbed). The fish thus surrounds itself with an electromagnetic field and any electrical conductor that enters the field will bring a response. In this way, fishes living in muddy waters can detect the presence of prey or of predators. The Elephant-snout fishes are remarkable for the relatively enormous size of their brains, the brain weight equalling $\frac{1}{52}-\frac{1}{82}$ of the total body weight. Since the largest part of the brain in these fishes is the cerebellum and the areas of the hind brain associated with the hearing and lateral line systems, it seems possible that the large brain has evolved in conjunction with the electric organs to process information received from the 'radar system'.

The Knife fish *Gymnarchus niloticus,* related to the Elephant-snout fishes, is shaped rather like a compressed eel and also uses its electric organs for detection of prey and predators. It has rather poor sight and lives in muddy waters.

There is only one group of marine electric bony fishes and this is the stargazers. Members of the genera *Astroscopus* and *Uranoscopus* are bottom-living fishes in which the electric organs are located in deep pits behind the eyes. These organs generate currents of up to 50 volts and this may be used both for defence and for stunning prey.

ELFIN SHARK, *Mitsukurina owstoni,* also known as the Goblin shark, a grotesque shark with a long and pointed snout separated from the upper jaw by a deep cleft to give the appearance of a horn. As in the Frilled shark, the tail continues the line of the body and is not bent upwards as in other sharks. There are two dorsal fins and five gill slits. The teeth are awl-shaped but split into two basal lobes, the blade of the tooth becoming shorter at the edges of the jaws. This species was first discovered in deep water off Japan in 1898 and it created considerable interest because members of this family had previously only been known from the fossil genus *Scapanorhynchus* of the Upper Cretaceous rocks. The Elfin shark, which can reach a length of 14 ft (4·2 m), is now known from Indian waters and from Portugal. FAMILY: Scapanorhynchidae, ORDER: Pleurotremata, CLASS: Chondrichthyes.

F

FATHER LASHER *Cottus scorpius,* a shore fish of the eastern Atlantic belonging to the family of sculpins which includes the Miller's thumb. The common name is of dubious origin but is supposed to refer to the fish's habit of lashing its tail to drive away intruders. It is also known as the bullhead. It occurs over a wide range, from Greenland to the Bay of Biscay, and is commonly found in rock pools and shallow water round British coasts. It is sometimes taken in shrimpnets and is said to grunt when removed from the water. The head is broad and flattened and bears a number of spines. There are two dorsal fins and the pectoral fins are large and fan-shaped. The general colour is green-brown with darker markings. Large speci-

mens may be up to 3 ft (90 cm) in length. FAMILY: Cottidae, ORDER: Scorpaeniformes, CLASS: Pisces.

FIERASFERS, an alternative name for cucumberfishes or pearlfishes.

FIGHTING FISHES, species of fishes belonging to the genus *Betta* and members of a family of labyrinthfishes. The Siamese fighting fish *Betta splendens* is chiefly found in Thailand but occurs also throughout the Malayan Peninsula. Because of the pugnacity of the male, these fishes have been 'domesticated' for a considerable time in Thailand and used for sport, wagers being laid on the outcome of a fight between two contestants.

Wounds from a Father lasher's spines often turn septic.

Two male Siamese fighting fish.

In the wild, the dorsal and anal fins are short and the colour of the body is variable but dull. As in the case of the goldfish and many other fishes kept in captivity, however, special varieties have been bred that have long fins and vivid colours. The males are always more spectacular than the females.

During a fight between two males, the fins are spread as far as possible and the mouth and gill covers are opened wide. This fighting is in fact a travesty of the male's normal courting behaviour except that the male does not bite the female unless the latter fails to respond.

A single male fish can be kept fairly well in a community tank. When full grown, these fishes are only 3 in (7·5 cm) in length and are usually peaceable but may occasionally nip another fish. To make a male display, a mirror can be placed against the side of the tank.

There are several other species of Fighting fish, such as the Slim fighting fish *B. bellica* and the Striped fighting fish *B. fasciata,* but these are rather rarely imported. The Fighting fishes construct *bubble nests. FAMILY: Anabantidae, ORDER: Perciformes, CLASS: Pisces.

FILEFISHES, a term rather loosely applied to certain members of the triggerfish family, Balistidae, marine shore fishes of tropical and temperate seas. The filefishes were formerly placed in a separate family, the Monacanthidae (meaning 'one-spine'), a reference to the large spine of the first dorsal fin which lies immediately above the eye. They are mostly small fishes of less than 12 in (30 cm), but *Aleutera scripta* grows to a little over 3 ft (90 cm). Pelvic fins are missing and the highly compressed body is covered with rough scales. See also triggerfishes.

The filefish *Alutera scripta*, of tropical seas.

The lionfish or scorpionfish *Pterois* has elaborate fins used to warn off potential attackers.

FAMILY: Balistidae, ORDER: Tetraodontiformes, CLASS: Pisces.

FINGERFISHES, a group of fishes dealt with under the name Malayan angels.

FINS, characteristic projections from the bodies of fishes, usually composed of hard or soft finrays with a thin membrane between the rays, basically for swimming movements but secondarily adapted for a wide variety of functions (defence, digging, display in courtship, gliding, flying, etc.).

In the earliest fishes it is assumed that a continuous ridge or fold of skin passed down the back and along the belly. If certain areas of this primitive fin-fold were of greater mechanical use than others, then it can be supposed that these would become larger, leaving gaps between, leading to the formation of discrete fins. There is no way of confirming this hypothesis but it is significant that in one experiment using a wax model shaped like the body of a fish, the passage of a fast current of warm water over the body produced a very similar pattern of ridges or fin folds. A continuous fin-fold is also found in the early larval stages of most fishes. In the earliest fossil fishes, however, the fins are already well developed but much can be deduced about the habits of these fishes from a study of the function of each fin and the part that it must have played in swimming.

During swimming, the body of a fish is thrown into a series of sinuous curves which become more pronounced towards the tail or caudal fin. If the tail is cut off, the fish can still swim forward but the tail end of the body vibrates very rapidly from side to side. Clearly, the expanded tail of the fish slows

down these oscillations and makes the swimming smoother and more efficient. A large tail with a rounded margin, as in a pike, gives fast acceleration but its large surface area creates friction or drag so that prolonged swimming is tiring. So a pike habitually lurks among waterplants and darts out swiftly at passing prey. In oceanic fishes such as tuna the tail is crescentic and bound stiffly to the base of the vertebral column so these fishes can be constantly on the move. In long-bodied eel-like fishes the tail is either lost or is often joined to the long dorsal and

Angel fish have slender, filamentous pelvic rays.

Rock goby *Gobius poganellus* showing united pelvic fins which act as a sucker with which the fish clings to rocks.

anal fins. In such fishes, which are not fast swimmers, the body is thrown into a large number of sinuous waves and this is sufficient to propel the fish forwards.

The early bony fishes, as well as the sharks and sturgeons, possessed no organ of buoyancy (swimbladder) so that the fish had to rest on the bottom or swim constantly. To counteract the rather heavy head and body by providing sufficient 'lift', the end of the vertebral column is bent upwards and the tail is developed from its lower edge (heterocercal tail). This condition arose from even more primitive fishes in which the vertebral column is not bent upwards and a lobe of the tail is present both above and below (protocercal tail). In the modern bony fishes the tail appears to be symmetrical but in fact the end of the vertebral column is still bent upwards and a series of bony plates (hypurals) square-off the end of the body and provide the base for the attachment of the rays supporting the usually equal upper and lower lobes of the tail (homocercal tail). The great range in tail shapes found in bony fishes is due to variations in the size, number and shape of the hypurals supporting the tail.

The vertical fins, the dorsal and anal, are basically stabilizers that prevent rolling, especially during turns. The more primitive of the modern fishes, such as the salmon and herring, have the short-based dorsal and anal fins set close behind the centre of gravity. In lurking predators, such as the pike, in which a sudden thrust of speed is required, the dorsal and anal fins are set well back on the body. In the more advanced perch-like fishes the dorsal fin is long-based and often separated into two distinct parts, the first part supported by spiny rays and the second by soft and flexible rays. The spiny rays appear to act as 'cut-waters' and were perhaps only secondarily adapted for defence. In some fishes, for example members of the salmon family, there is a small and fleshy adipose fin behind the main dorsal fin. Its function may be the adjustment of eddies along the back to reduce drag. A similar function can be supposed for the line of small finlets behind the dorsal fin in mackerels and tuna.

In sharks and primitive bony fishes which lack a swimbladder the pectoral fins act as hydrofoils which lift the front half of the body as the fish swims through the water. With the evolution of a swimbladder the pectorals were able to take on other functions. They were then chiefly used as brakes or, if only one pectoral is extended, for steering. In perch-like fishes, which hover in the water, the pectorals are gently back-paddled to prevent the fish moving forward by the force of the stream of water pumped out of the gill chamber. The pelvic fins in primitive fishes are set back on the body somewhere below the dorsal fin (herring,

trout). In the more advanced bony fishes they are brought forward to below or even in front of the pectoral fins. In this position they can work in conjunction with the pectorals in braking and turning, counteracting the lift of the pectorals with a downward drag so that the fish does not tend to shoot upwards every time it stops.

Slow swimming movements are achieved in some fishes by undulations of the dorsal fin (Sea horse, eels, pike when cruising) or by sculling movements of the pectoral fins (Ocean sunfish). The pectoral fins can be adapted for gliding (flyingfishes) or flapping flight (Flying characins), for crawling on the bottom (some gurnards) or for progress on land (mudskippers). The pelvic fins have been adapted as suckers (gobies). The dorsal fin has become a means of defence (spines, sometimes with venom glands), a sucking disc (remoras), a 'sail' (sailfish), a fishing rod (anglerfishes) or a factor in sexual display (Fighting fishes). The anal fin has sometimes become modified into a copulatory organ in those fishes which are live-bearers. The tail may be used for digging (some eels) or may be modified into an extraordinary variety of shapes. In certain groups of fishes some or all of the fins may be reduced and certain fins lost.

The greatest impetus to the evolution of fins was the development of a swimbladder. Once buoyancy was achieved, the fins could be used for functions other than swimming.

FIREMOUTH, a common name for a rather distinctive cichlid fish. See cichlids.

Two Sarcastic fringeheads *Neoclinus blanchardi* 'kissing'. These Californian fishes have unusually large mouths.

The rare scorpionfish *Taenionothus triacanthus* of the Pacific, swims like a piece of seaweed, oscillating from side to side as if swayed by the current.

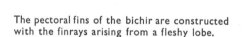
The pectoral fins of the bichir are constructed with the finrays arising from a fleshy lobe.

Conger eel *Conger conger* stranded at low tide.

Mediterranean seahorse *Hippocampus guttulatus*.

FISHES, a large group of cold-blooded aquatic vertebrates that breathe by means of gills, the bodies of which bear a vertical tail fin. Most fishes fall within this definition, but a few breathe atmospheric air by means of a lung or lung-like organ (see air-breathing fishes), some species have a body temperature slightly above that of the surrounding water (see tunas) and in certain fishes the tail may be missing (see Ocean sunfish) or reduced to a filament (see grenadiers). The definition does exclude, however, whales, dolphins, seals and porpoises which are warm-blooded, have lungs and have a tail that is horizontal, not vertical. The question *What is a fish?* is complicated by the fact that there are four classes of fish-like vertebrate, which differ in so many fundamental ways that it is as misleading to lump them together as it would be to place all mammals, birds and reptiles in a single group 'land animals'. For this reason, the jawless fishes (Agnatha), the placoderms (Placodermi) and the cartilaginous fishes (Chondrichthyes) are described under separate headings and only the fourth class, the Pisces Osteichthyes or bony fishes are considered here.

The class of bony fishes includes three rather distinct subclasses. Of these, the extinct Acanthodii are dealt with under fossil fishes and the Sarcopterygii are discussed under the same heading and also under coelacanth and lungfishes. The remaining subclass, the Actinopterygii or ray-finned fishes, contains the chondrosteans (bichirs, sturgeons and one entirely fossil order), the holosteans (bowfins and five fossil orders) and finally the teleosteans. The overwhelming majority of present-day fishes are teleosts. There are at least 20,000 different species of teleosts and countless millions of individuals inhabiting the seas, lakes and

A remarkably colourful tropical marine fish *Gramma hemichrysos*, the second part of its name meaning 'half-golden'.

rivers of the world. The teleosts represent the ultimate stage in the evolution of the Actinopterygii, a group that dates from the Devonian period. The teleosts first appear in Jurassic rocks and for the next 100 million years several evolutionary lines seem to have arisen from the more ancient holostean stock and to have attained what can now be recognized as the teleostean level of organization (form of fins, scales, skeleton, jaws and so on).

The teleosts show an amazing diversity of form. One has only to compare a perch with a frogfish, eel, Sea horse or Flounder flatfish to see the degree to which the teleostean organization has become adapted to particular living conditions. The classification of this huge group has always presented considerable difficulties and many problems still remain. For example, similarity between members of different families or orders may truly reflect a common ancestry; it may, however, be due to convergent evolution, similar features arising to meet similar needs (such as the elongated form in eels and blennies). Again, two or more families may have evolved independently along quite similar lines (parallel evolution). Until fairly recently, it was assumed that whenever a particularly advantageous feature arose radiation of species with this character followed and that it was from one of these that the next advantageous feature would appear (and thus the next radiation). The great radiation of the perch-like fishes (the largest of the teleost orders), for example, seemed to stem from the ability to protrude the jaw. It is now realized, however, that the freeing of the upper jaw to make protrusion possible must have occurred quite independently in a number of lineages. It is better, therefore, to regard some groups of fishes as representing

The parrotfish *Scarus* sp. Note the parrot-like beak with which this fish feeds on corals.

John dory *Zeus faber* seizes small fishes with a sudden protrusion of its telescopic jaws.

a 'level of organization' rather than a homogeneous group descended from a single ancestor. A classification is, however, an essential tool to the study of a group, even if that study results in modifying the classification. The scheme adopted here is essentially that proposed by Dr Greenwood, Dr Rosen, Dr Weitzman and Dr Myers in the *Bulletin of the American Museum of Natural History* (vol 131, pp 339–456). (The interested student should also consult the work of Dr Rosen and Dr Patterson in the same journal—vol 141, article 3—in which certain changes are made.) These two papers have brought up to date the earlier classifications of C. Tate Regan and later L. S. Berg, and they probably mark a new era in our understanding of the way in which the teleost fishes have evolved. It should be stressed, however, that considerable work yet remains to be done before a really satisfactory classification of this difficult group can be achieved.

The diversity of the teleost fishes makes description of a 'typical' member difficult. They range in size from a total length of over 20 ft (6 m) in certain sturgeons and the oarfish and a weight of over 2 tons in the case of the Ocean sunfish, to an adult length of only $\frac{1}{2}$ in (1·2 cm) in a Philippine goby (*Paudaka pygmaea*), the latter qualifying as the smallest of all vertebrates. Typically, the body is streamlined, rising smoothly from the head and tapering gently to the tail, but the body shape clearly reflects the mode of life of the fish. The torpedo-shaped tunas show streamlining taken to extreme lengths for fast and sustained swimming. The disclike body of the Angel fishes (*Pterophyllum*) is an adaptation to a life camouflaged amongst weeds, the fish darting out to catch its food. The spherical or box-like pufferfishes and boxfishes leisurely 'row' themselves about the coral reefs, while the cylindrical pipefishes hide away among the leathery strands of seaweeds. In most fishes swimming is achieved by throwing the body into a series of lateral undulations which travel along the length of the body growing in amplitude towards the tail (marine mammals undulate *vertically,* so that 'sea serpents' can be identified as mammals or fishes from their mode of swimming). The tail provides the final thrust and evens out the oscillations of the body (amputate the tail and the fish can still swim but the body vibrates more rapidly while progress is slower). The tail is stiffened along the upper and lower borders and the larger the tail the greater the thrust but also the greater the turbulence created (and thus the greater the drag). For fast but sustained speeds, fishes such as tunas have a crescentic tail with stiff edges and reduced central rays; its small surface area keeps drag to a minimum, but it also reduces the rate of acceleration. In a pike, on the other hand, the large

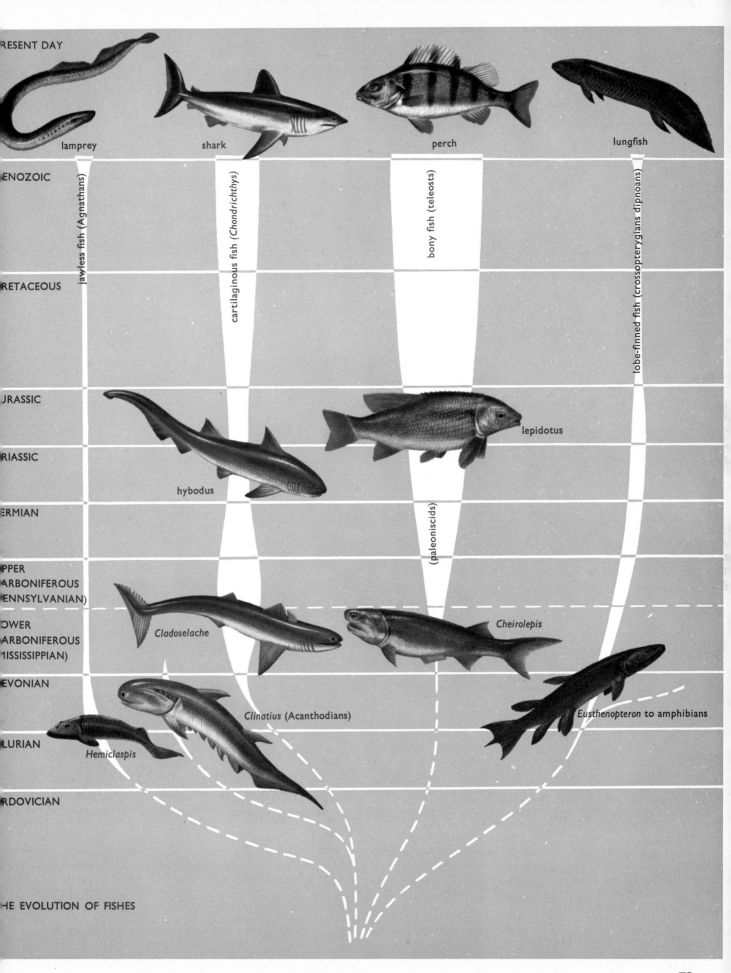

PRESENT DAY

lamprey

shark

perch

lungfish

CENOZOIC

CRETACEOUS

JURASSIC

TRIASSIC

PERMIAN

UPPER
CARBONIFEROUS
(PENNSYLVANIAN)

LOWER
CARBONIFEROUS
(MISSISSIPPIAN)

DEVONIAN

SILURIAN

ORDOVICIAN

jawless fish (Agnathans)

cartilaginous fish (Chondrichthys)

bony fish (teleosts)

lobe-finned fish (crossopterygians dipnoans)

lepidotus

hybodus

(paleoniscids)

Cladoselache

Cheirolepis

Clinatius (Acanthodians)

Eusthenopteron to amphibians

Hemiclaspis

THE EVOLUTION OF FISHES

73

blunt tail can give tremendous thrust for sudden spurts towards a prey but would be exhausting for sustained speeds. The article on fins describes in more detail the modifications of the tail and other fins to various modes of life. In general the fins are used as stabilizers, brakes, hydrofoils, occasionally as paddles or as sensory appendages (see gurnards), as means of defence (see poisonous fishes), rarely as wings or aerofoils (see flight in fishes), and possibly as sails (see sailfish), sometimes as copulatory organs (see live bearers) and in a few fishes to assist in terrestrial locomotion. The variation in shape, number and position of fins provides a useful clue to the identity of a fish and was widely used to classify fishes by early ichthyologists until it was realized that the same pattern had often evolved in quite unrelated groups. Even so, the late Professor J. L. B. Smith devised a useful key to all the marine fishes of southern Africa based simply on the numbers of hard and soft rays in the fins.

The more primitive teleost fishes, such as the tarpon, herring, salmon and Bony tongues, are long-bodied and have soft-rayed fins with the pelvic fins set well back from the pectorals. Although some of these fishes are fairly fast swimmers, they lack the manoeuverability of the more advanced perch-like fishes grouped in the super order Acanthopterygii. One has only to watch the fishes of a coral reef to see that some structural change has occurred to enable these lightning-fast twists and turns around the coral. Typically, the acanthopterygians have rather short and deep, compressed bodies which results in fewer undulations along the body during swimming but gives a much tighter and more direct control of movement. The pectoral fins lie higher on the body and the pelvic fins have now moved forward to lie below the pectorals. The combined effect of the four fins enables the fish to stop or turn with great rapidity and the deeper and more compressed body helps to prevent rolling. The dorsal fin is now much longer and the rays in the anterior part of the fin are no longer soft but spiny. The spiny portion of the fin can be raised and lowered at will and when erected provides a further means of stabilizing the body during sudden turns.

Although all these advanced features are found in the acanthopterygians, it should be remembered that they are essentially adaptations to a life in which manoeuverability is important. In many cases these spiny-finned fishes have adopted a mode of life in which reduction of fin spines or the evolution of a long body has been of greater advantage than the ability to make sudden turns. As shown in the table, a second advanced group of teleost fishes, the Paracanthopterygii, appears to have evolved independently of the acanthopterygians. They share many common features with the latter, as well as a number of features of their own, and they provide a good example of parallel evolution.

One characteristic (but not invariable) feature of fishes is the presence of scales on the body. The smooth *cycloid* scales typical of the more primitive teleosts (tenpounder, tarpon, herring, etc) represent a tremendous reduction from the thick scales of their palaeoniscid ancestors (see fishes, fossil). In the perch-like fishes the hind margin of the scale is often roughened by little comb-like projections, a fact that is immediately apparent if the fish is stroked the 'wrong way'. Such scales are referred to as *ctenoid*. In a number of fishes (anglerfish, some catfishes)

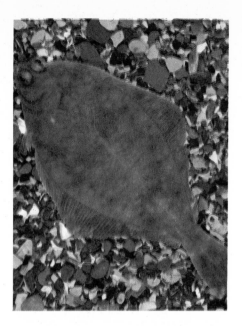

A fossil fish illustrating the fine detail preserved, enabling scientists to reconstruct the anatomy of extinct fishes particularly well.

The dab *Limanda limanda*, which lies on its left side, the left eye moving around the body to lie alongside the right.

A ray, one of the flattened bottom-living fishes related to sharks.

Wreckfish or Stone bass *Polyprion americanum*.

scales are absent or greatly reduced and the skin is leathery. In the pipefishes and Sea horses the body is covered by bony rings, while the trunk- or boxfishes are the tortoises of the fish world with a hard carapace of bony plates. Even in normally scaled fishes, such as the carp, varieties occur with few scales (Mirror carp) or none at all (Leather carp). The scales are essentially a means of protection.

A very great diversity is found in the form and placing of teeth in the mouth of teleosts. In a number of filter-feeding species (e.g. some of the shads) there are no teeth at all. In other teleosts, teeth may be present along the jaws, on the tongue, on various bones that roof the cavity of the mouth, along the gill arches and in the gullet. Unlike mammals, fishes usually have teeth of a similar shape along the jaw, but in the wolf-fish and some Sea breams the teeth in the front of the jaw are canine-like while those behind are grinding molars. The teeth are normally used to hold the prey during swallowing but in the bluefish and the piranha the jaw teeth are actually used to bite chunks out of the prey. Fine comb-like jaw teeth are found in species that browse on algae, while fang-like jaw teeth are characteristic of predators. The teeth are usually kept throughout life but are

occasionally replaced by subsequent rows (some catfishes).

In the more primitive teleosts, the pre-maxillary bones are rather small and most of the upper jaw is made up by the maxilla. In the more advanced members, however, the pre-maxilla elongates and excludes the maxilla from the biting edge of the jaw, the maxilla then playing a part in the complex mechanics of jaw protrusion. The ability to protrude the jaw led to the development of a variety of nibbling, seizing and sucking mouths. The John Dory can protrude the mouth a remarkable distance. In the Elephant-snout fishes the small mouth is at the end of a long tube which can be probed into the mud. The tube-like snouts of the pipefishes and Sea horses are used like a pipette to suck up minute organisms. In the catfishes there are species with expanded lips which act as suckers to attach the fish to rocks while the teeth rasp away at algae. In certain deep-sea fishes the jaws can be un-hinged to allow the entrance of prey much larger than its captor.

The diversity in the form of jaws and teeth is rivalled by the diversity of foods eaten by teleosts. It is, indeed, difficult to think of any organic matter that is not eaten by some teleost fish, including such unlikely diets as

coral (parrotfishes), gill parasites (Cleaner fishes), and the fins and scales of other fishes (certain African cichlid fishes). An equal diversity is found in the methods used to capture food. Usually the food is seized, nibbled or sucked in, but this may follow a long chase, a sudden lunge, a placid filtration process or a cunning use of some form of lure (see anglerfishes). One of the more bizarre methods of capturing prey is the shooting of insects by the archerfish.

The development of the various sense organs in teleosts clearly reflects their way of life. Eyes are well developed in those that rely mainly on sight for feeding and the avoidance of predators, but the eyes are regressed or absent in some deep-sea and cave fishes, such fishes relying more on information from their lateral line system. This system is used for positioning by shoaling fishes in the well-lit surface waters but it is reduced in fishes such as sticklebacks in which sight and smell are of more importance. Smell is particularly important in scavenging fishes and it plays a critical role in the homing of salmon. Hearing is well developed in most fishes and especially in those that produce sound. The echo-location system in electric fishes is without parallel among vertebrates (bats use sound and not electric pulses). Luminous organs are found in many deep-sea fishes and these provide means for species and sex recognition, for producing a form of obliterative shading and for illuminating the environment. Communication between fishes (by sound, light, colour changes, behaviour, etc) is a subject that requires much more study, as do many aspects of the ways in which fishes perceive elements in their surroundings.

The teleosts have evolved a wide range of breeding habits. The vast majority lay eggs. In species that do not exhibit any form of parental care the number of eggs laid by a female may reach several millions (cod, ling, etc), of which an average of only two survive to adulthood if the species is not increasing. Such eggs may float freely at the surface or adhere to stones or plants. Fishes which show some form of parental care usually lay fewer eggs and may build a crude nest (salmon) or a very well constructed nest (sticklebacks) in which the eggs are deposited and hatch. In some species of *Tilapia* the nest is used merely to deposit the eggs, the latter then being picked up by one of the parents and incubated in the mouth, as in the Sea catfishes. In the pipefishes the eggs are incubated by the male in a special pouch on the abdomen and in the Sea horses the eggs are also nourished in a pouch. One characin lays its eggs out of water and keeps them moist by splashing. In the Annual fishes the eggs are drought resistant and will sur-

The fish *Aeoliscus* swims with its head down.

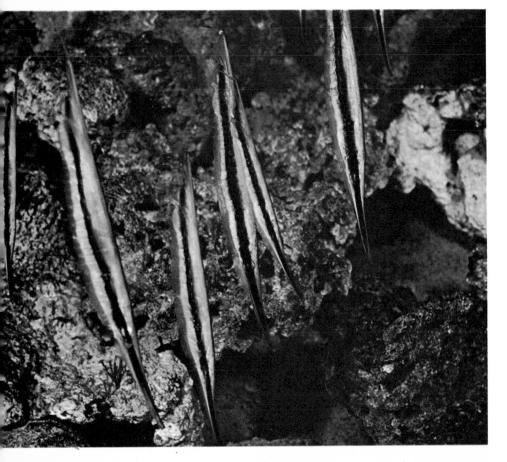

A Triggerfish.

vive desiccation until the next rains. In several groups of teleosts the eggs are retained in the ovary and hatch there, the larvae later being born (redfish and live bearers). In certain of these viviparous fishes the embryos and larvae are nourished by secretions from the mother and some form of connection between the two may develop (a pseudoplacenta). The young may be variously guarded and in the mouth-brooding species of *Tilapia* the fry are taken into the mouth in times of danger. In the discusfish the young feed on a mucous secretion from the body of the parents.

An entire chapter could be written on the ways of teleost fishes and the vast range of habitats into which they have penetrated. They are found in the seas, from the shallows to the abyssal depths, in lakes and rivers, in caves, hot soda springs (some *Tilapia*), artesian wells (some catfishes), in torrential streams (Capitane catfish), in the gill chambers of other fishes (candiru) and in water just above freezing (icefishes). Some tropical lakes support a high density of fishes and will yield a standing crop of 300–500 lb (135–225 kg) per acre (per 0·4 ha). In the deep parts of the oceans food is so scarce that only one fish per cu mile can be supported. Some species are so numerous that several million tons can be caught every year without any appreciable effect on the stocks (see anchovies), while others are so rare (or depleted by man) that only a few hundred individuals are known. One of the most curious modes of existence is that of the adult male deep-sea anglerfish, which becomes totally parasitic on the female, but closer inspection shows that in its way each species is very beautifully adapted to its own living conditions. What appears to be a rather uniform environment—water—is quite as varied as any land surface and has resulted in an extraordinary range of adaptations. The teleost fishes have shown a basic plasticity in their form, physiology and behaviour which has enabled them to conquer habitats denied to their ancestors. The number and diversity of present-day species is an indication of the great evolutionary success of this group.

FLATFISHES, bottom-living fishes characterized by their highly flattened body-form and the extraordinary development which results in both eyes being on the same side of the head. They are grouped in the order Pleuronectiformes, Whereas a skate or an anglerfish is depressed, that is to say flattened from top to bottom, the flatfishes are compressed or flattened from side to side. The larva of a flatfish, however, is a perfectly normal symmetrical animal, much like the

Dab *Limanda limanda* half-hidden under sand it has flipped over itself with its fins.

Plaice *Pleuronectes platessa* swimming. Its normal habit is to lie inconspicuously on the seabed.

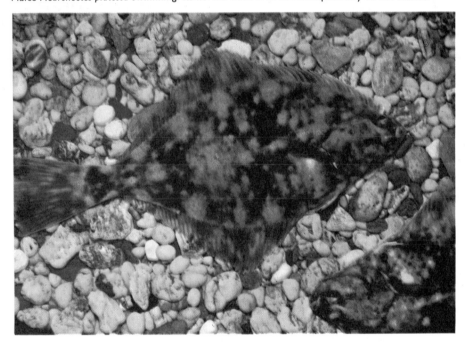

Flounders *Platichthys flesus*, on pebbles, their colours changed to blend with the seabed.

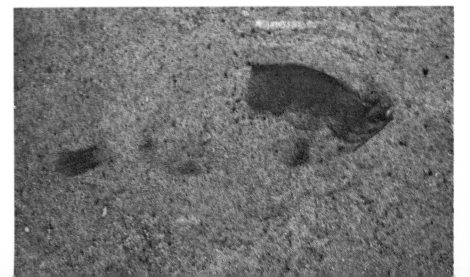

78

Flatfish with its head raised waiting for prey, such as a marine Bristle worm, to show its head above the sand.

larval forms of other fishes, and it swims at the surface. During its development it undergoes a remarkable metamorphosis, the body gradually changing shape and becoming flattened, one eye moving across to the other side of the head and the mouth becoming, to varying degrees, asymmetrical also. By the time that both eyes are on the same side of the head, the small flatfish has settled on the bottom. Flatfishes lie on the 'blind' side, which in some groups is the right and in others is the left. The upper side of the body becomes pigmented but the blind side remains white. Occasionally freaks are found in which the lower surface is partially or even fully pigmented and, conversely, albinos have also been recorded. Normally, all members of a species lie on the same side, but in certain primitive flatfishes, such as the members of the Indian Ocean genus *Psettodes*, equal numbers are found lying on one as on the other side. In all flatfishes, except the primitive family Psettodidae, the dorsal fin is extremely long, extending not only the length of the body but forwards above the head. The anal fin is also very long indeed, the small pelvic fins lying just in front of it. One pectoral fin is on the upper side of the body while the other is on the blind side. In the soles (Soleidae) and the Tongue soles (Cynoglossidae) the pectoral fins are absent. The general body shape of the flatfishes

varies considerably, from being almost disc-like to being quite elongated. Thus, the turbot and its relatives are almost as broad as they are long, while the little Tongue soles, as their name suggests, are rather long and narrow.

Most flatfishes are predators, spending much of their time on the bottom. For most of them, camouflage is important. In some this is achieved by covering the edges or even the whole body, except for the eyes, with sand which they flick over themselves by a wriggling movement of the fins. Most flatfishes are predominantly brown in colour on the dorsal surface and only a few have any very striking colour-patterns, although a few species have strong black bars on the

Dab, enormously abundant European flatfish.

body. If a pattern is present, it is more usually made up of spots and blotches, The Peacock flounder *Bothus lunatus* of the American tropical Atlantic has purple rings and spots on a brown background while the plaice has well-marked orange spots. A number of flatfishes have the ability to change colour to match their background. In some fish, such as the Mediterranean *Bothus podas,* the ability to match a background is carried to such an extent that the fish will make a remarkably good attempt to produce a black and white pattern if layed on a chess board. Some American species of flounders of the genus *Paralichthys* can produce an effective camouflage on coloured backgrounds, although they are not very accurate in matching red backgrounds.

The halibut *Hippoglossus hippoglossus,* one of the largest of the flatfishes, reaching a length of 9 ft (2·7 m), is a very active swimmer that hunts for its prey. Other species make rather elegant flutterings after small crustaceans that come within their reach.

For the most part the flatfishes are marine, but a few species, including the flounder, can live either in the sea or in freshwaters. The small American flatfish *Achirus* is a freshwater species that is often imported into Europe as an aquarium fish. It provides a splendid example of certain uncharacteristic but revealing uses to which the

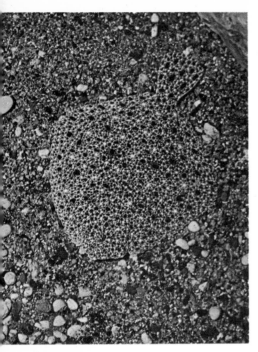

The brill lives on sandy bottoms and is sand-coloured.

flattened body can be put. Small *Achirus,* for example, have such a relatively large surface area to body weight ratio that they can suspend themselves from the surface of the water solely by surface tension. They are also able to form a vacuum with the underside of the body and can then adhere to rocks, leaves, or the glass sides of the tank.

Flatfishes are egg-layers and in most cases the sexes are similar in appearance. In *Bothus podas,* however, the eyes are much further apart in the males than in the females, while in *Arnoglossus imperialis* the first few rays of the dorsal fin in the male are elongated into a plume.

The flatfishes appear to be a very successful group judging from their wide distribution, They are found from the Antarctic Circle to beyond the Arctic Circle and they range from freshwater forms living in a few inches of water to marine species adapted to life at considerable depths. Even the halibut has been caught at depths of 3,000 ft (about 1,000 m). In temperate seas some species are represented by enormous numbers of individuals and the flatfishes rank high amongst the commercially exploited fishes of the world. In the North Atlantic, species such as the plaice have been intensively fished and the demand seems at times to outstrip the natural rate of replacement of stocks. Since the pelagic stage of the larval life is the most vulnerable to predators, large scale experiments have been conducted in an attempt to maintain the larvae in tanks until they have metamorphosed and can safely rely on their camouflage at the bottom of the sea. The young are then transported to areas which are known to provide good growing condi-

tions. The flesh of flatfishes is firm and white and they have long been regarded as amongst the most desirable of table fishes.

Flatfishes are regularly caught by trawl. Normally, a trawl net would merely pass over the fishes as it skims across the bottom, but by means of chains hung from a rope in front of the trawl the fishes are disturbed, swim up and are scooped up into the net.

The flatfishes form a very distinctive group, the characteristic flattened form and complicated metamorphosis apparently having proved sufficiently advantageous for numerous species to have evolved in this manner. The origin of the flatfishes is, however, a little obscure, although they are clearly derived from perch-like ancestors. The primitive genus *Psettodes* has pectoral and pelvic fins which are essentially perch-like in form and it is only the eyes and long dorsal fin that distinguish it superficially from the Sea perches. Certain perch-like fishes tend to rest on the bottom lying on one side, and the advantages that this gives in concealing the fish may have led to the evolution of the true flatfishes. The earliest fossil flatfishes, however, are already just as specialized as the modern forms.

Species of flatfishes are also described elsewhere under their common names. ORDER: Pleuronectiformes, CLASS: Pisces.

FLIGHT IN FISHES has been evolved independently in several groups of bony fishes. The flight may be little more than a prolonged leap from the water in which the fish glides by means of expanded fins, or it may involve active flapping movements of the fins which serve to keep the fish airborne

for half a minute or so. The most likely reason for the evolution of flight in certain groups is as a means of escape from predators.

The term flyingfish is most usually applied to the members of the marine family Exocoetidae. These fishes have streamlined bodies, large pectoral fins which can be spread like wings, and the lower lobe of the tail enlarged to provide the motive power for taxiing at the surface. It is interesting to note that in the related sauries and half-beaks the lower lobe of the tail is also larger than the upper although the pectoral fins are not greatly enlarged. Both the sauries and the half-beaks will skip along the surface, but the flyingfishes have taken this further and, having attained sufficient speed, will spread their 'wings' and glide. The species of *Cypselurus* have both enlarged pectorals and enlarged pelvic fins and they taxi at the surface and reach speeds of 35 mph (56 kph) before lifting themselves into the air. Species of *Exocoetus* have small pelvic fins and launch themselves straight from the water. The flight may last up to half a minute and the fishes can cover $\frac{1}{4}$ mile (400 m). Like some oceanic birds, the flyingfishes probably make use of the updraughts of air in the troughs of waves and in a stiff breeze may be lifted 20–30 ft (6–9 m) sometimes landing on the deck of a ship. Flyingfishes are hunted by the dolphins and many of the tuna-like fishes, and flight offers only temporary safety.

The so-called Flying gurnard *Dactylopterus volitans* also has very large pectoral fins which can be expanded horizontally as in the flyingfishes. It is a bottom-living fish

Profile of a flounder, from left side.

found in the Mediterranean and the warmer parts of the Atlantic. No photographic evidence has been produced to show that this rather heavily-built fish ever flies. When disturbed, however, the Flying gurnard will suddenly spread its colourful pectoral fins and this flash of colour is startling and even a little menacing. It is quite possible that this is the true function of the 'wings'.

There are also certain freshwater flyingfishes. In South American waters the little hatchetfishes belonging to the characin family, Gasteropelecidae, exhibit true flapping flight. Members of the genera *Gasteropelecus* and *Carnegiella* make little leaps out of the water while rapidly vibrating their sickle-shaped pectoral fins (causing a faint humming noise). The anterior part of the body is greatly deepened for the insertion of the relatively large muscles operating the pectoral fins. These fishes can fly for about 15 ft (4·5 m).

In Africa, the freshwater butterflyfish *Pantodon buchholtzi*, a relative of the Bony tongues, is also able to flap its large pectoral fins during flight. This species appears to require a short run before becoming airborne.

FLOUNDER *Platichthys flesus*, one of the best known of European flatfishes. It can be distinguished from other inshore flatfishes by the opaque, mother-of-pearl whiteness of the underside. The upperside (right) is brownish-green with some faint orange marks which are similar to those found in the plaice, but soon disappear once the fish is out of water. The body is lozenge-shaped, there is a strong spine in front of the anal fin and the scales are small and embedded except along the bases of the dorsal and anal fins, behind the eyes and behind the gill cover, where they are firmly attached and rough.

Most flatfishes live their entire lives in the sea, but the flounder migrates up rivers to feed. Anglers are sometimes surprised to catch flounders 40 miles (65 km) or so from the coast. They spend most of the summer in rivers feeding and then in late autumn they make their way down the rivers, without feeding, to spawn in fairly deep water off the coast. Unlike the salmon, the flounder does not necessarily go back to the same river when it returns to feed in the spring. When in the sea, moderate migrations of several miles

take place and one marked individual was found to have travelled 70 miles (112 km) in 18 days.

The flounder is common in the Mediterranean and is found in the eastern Atlantic as far north as Iceland. These fishes, the flesh of which is not particularly pleasing, reach 12–15 in (30–38 cm) and a weight of 6 lb (2·7 kg) although a 2 lb (0·9 kg) fish is considered a fair size. FAMILY: Pleuronectidae, ORDER: Pleuronectiformes, CLASS: Pisces.

FLYINGFISHES, a term usually reserved for a family of marine fishes (Exocoetidae) with large pectoral fins adapted for gliding out of water. These fishes are discussed under flight in fishes.

FOUR-EYED FISHES, freshwater toothcarps of the family Anablepidae found in Central America and characterized by appearing to have four eyes. The eyes are in fact divided horizontally into two distinct parts, the upper half for vision in air and the lower for vision under water.

A different kind of lens is required in air than in water and although these fishes have a single lens it is through the thickest part of it that underwater objects are viewed. The Four-eyed fish *Anableps* spends its time cruising along at the surface with the upper part of the eyes exposed. This enables the fish to search for food and at the same time to keep an eye out, so to speak, for predators.

In most of the land-living animals there is a tear duct which keeps the eye moist but such a duct has never been evolved in fishes and the Four-eyed fish must constantly duck its head under water to prevent the eyes from drying out.

Like many toothcarps, the Four-eyed fishes are live-bearers and fertilization is internal, involving an act of copulation. In other toothcarps, the intromittent organ or gonopodium of the male, a hollow tube formed from the anal finrays and used to channel the sperm to the female, can be moved both to the left and to the right. In the Four-eyed fishes the gonopodium of the male can be moved either to the left or to the right but not both.

The situation is complicated, however, by the fact that in the females there is a scale on one or other side of the genital opening. The

result is that a 'right-handed' male can only mate with a 'left-handed' female, and *vice versa*. Fortunately, the numbers of left-handed and right-handed individuals in natural populations appear to be about equal. FAMILY: Anablepidae, ORDER: Atheriniformes, CLASS: Pisces.

FRILLED SHARK *Chlamydoselachus anguineus,* a primitive shark with six gill slits (there being five in most other sharks) of which the first slit is continued right across the throat. Characteristic of this species are the partitions between the gill slits, each of which is enlarged to cover the slit behind, thus forming a frilled collar. The body is slender and elongated, with the tail continuing the line of the body (not bent upwards as in most other sharks). The mouth is large and terminal, with well-developed teeth, giving the head a reptilian appearance. This species reaches a maximum recorded length of 6½ ft (2 m). It is a rather rare species that was first caught off Japan in 1884 but has since been found in the Atlantic (Portugal to Norway) and off the coast of California. It is essentially a deep-water species that feeds on octopuses and squids. It is an ovoviviparous form, the young hatching within the female and later being born, but little is known of its biology. FAMILY: Chlamydoselachidae, ORDER: Pleurotremata, CLASS: Chondrichthyes.

FROGFISHES, or antennariids, a group of fishes closely related to the anglerfishes.

FROSTFISH *Lepidopus caudatus,* a long and compressed, scaleless fish belonging to the family of cutlassfishes. It is world-wide in its distribution but is especially common off New Zealand and in the Mediterranean and eastern Atlantic. Its common name comes from New Zealand and is more often used than the European name of scabbardfish. The New Zealand name derives from the great sensitivity shown by these fishes to sudden drops in temperature, the fishes swimming ashore in thousands on cold nights. Members of the related genus *Trichiurus* have been reported in a comatose condition off the coast of Florida during a cold spell. FAMILY: Trichiuridae, ORDER: Perciformes, CLASS: Pisces.

GARFISHES, or needlefishes as they are often called in the United States, elongated, long-jawed fishes related to both the flying-fishes and the sauries. The body is long and slender and slightly compressed. The most striking features are the jaws which are as long or longer than the head and bear needle-like teeth. The dorsal and anal fins are set far back on the body and the lower lobe of the tail is larger than the upper.

The garfish *Belone belone* of Europe is found in the Mediterranean and Black Sea but reaches as far north as Trondheim and the Baltic. It has an electric-blue back, silvery belly and flanks, rosy pectoral fins and a yellow eye encircled with red. Hunted by tunas, they themselves feed on herring, sardines and crustaceans and are sometimes caught by fishermen on spinners intended for mackerel. The bones of this fish are a surprising green. Several other members of this family have green bones but this does not detract from their flavour, for the flesh is delicious.

Most of the garfishes are marine but at least two species enter freshwater. *Xenetodon cancila* is found in the rivers of Southeast Asia and India. The young fishes are frequently imported for aquarists but it must be remembered that the adults reach 12 in (30 cm) in length. They require live food, especially fishes, and should be kept in a tank of their own. They are graceful, fast-swimming fishes that are capable of leaping almost vertically out of the water. The tank should be kept well covered. *Potamorhaphis guianensis* is another freshwater species and is found in the Amazon. Most garfishes grow to about 2 ft (61 cm) in length but a few reach 4 ft (1·2 m). FAMILY: Belonidae, ORDER: Atheriniformes, CLASS: Pisces.

GARPIKES, primitive fishes from the fresh waters of the southeastern states of North America (see fishes and bowfins). There are several species belonging to the genus *Lepisosteus*. All have long thin bodies covered with thick, shiny scales which are diamond-shaped and, unlike the overlapping scales of other fishes, fit together like a mosaic. The scales can be fairly easily removed and have

been used in jewellery. The dorsal and anal fins are short-based and far back on the long body. This positioning of the fins is typical of fishes that need to accelerate rapidly towards their prey, all the thrust-receiving surfaces being at the rear of the fish. The gars are usually rather lazy fishes living in weedy water and it is only when lunging forward towards their prey that they move swiftly. The jaws in some species, for example in the Allligator gars, are elongated and have rows of long, sharp teeth. In spite of the heavy covering of scales the gars are surprisingly flexible fishes.

They are of considerable scientific interest in the study of the evolution of the higher fishes. Amongst their primitive anatomical features are the large number of bones in the head, the heavy armour of scales and the end of the vertebral column which turns upwards to support an asymmetrical tail.

The largest gar is *Lepisosteus spatula* found in the southern states of the USA. It reaches 10 ft (3·3 m) in length. FAMILY: Lepisosteidae, ORDER: Amiiformes, CLASS: Pisces. (Ill. p. 97.)

GHOST PIPEFISHES, a family of marine fishes of the Indo-Pacific region, related to the pipefishes, Sea horses and flute-mouths. They are small fishes, only growing to 6 in (15 cm) and having a rather bizarre appearance. There is a single genus, *Solenostomus,* with about four species. All are rather similar, having a compressed body that is greatly constricted between the first and second dorsal fins. The snout is elongated but deep and the mouth opens vertically. The first dorsal fin consists of only a few rays but is elongated, as also are the pelvic fins. The second dorsal fin and the anal fins are rounded and opposite to each other and the tail is long but rounded. The body is covered in a lattice of stellate bony plates.

Although widespread, these fishes are not commonly found in large numbers, and their secretive life amongst weeds and their excellent camouflage have probably meant that they have often been overlooked. As in the pipefishes, there is a considerable amount of

parental care. In this case the pelvic fins of the female become attached to the walls of the body to form an open bag, into which the eggs are placed after fertilization. They are held in place by small branches which develop from the rays of the pelvic fin (absent in males). FAMILY: Solenostomidae, ORDER: Gasterosteiformes, CLASS: Pisces.

GIGANTURIDS, deep-sea fishes of the family Giganturidae for which no common name exists, except perhaps 'Telescope fishes' in reference to the tubular, forward-looking eyes. The two genera of giganturids, *Bathyleptus* and *Gigantura,* inhabit open oceanic waters, living at depths of 1,500–6,000 ft (500–2,000 m). Like many deep-sea fishes, *Bathyleptus* from the Pacific is known from only a few specimens and *Gigantura* from the Atlantic and Indian Ocean is also rare in collections. In spite of their name, giganturids are small, slim-bodied fishes. They lack scales, pelvic fins and luminous organs but are distinctive in having the lower few rays of the caudal fin elongated into a filament. The mouth is armed with large teeth and as a testimony to their carnivorous habits there is a record of a 2½ in (6 cm) specimen of *Gigantura vorax* with its stomach crammed with the remains of a viperfish *Chauliodus* of 5 in (12·5 cm). FAMILY: Giganturidae, ORDER: Cetomimiformes, CLASS: Pisces.

GILLS, the organs of breathing in aquatic animals, the principle being to bring the animals' oxygen transport system (usually oxygen carrying pigments in the blood) into as close contact with the water as possible so that oxygen can diffuse into the animal and carbon dioxide and other waste products can diffuse out. The gills provide the greatest surface area possible for these processes to take place. Usually, the gills are concerned with the exchange of oxygen and carbon dioxide but they may also be used for osmotic control through the exchange of salts across their membranes.

The gills of fishes lie in the pharynx or gill cavity behind the mouth. Typically, they consist of bony or cartilaginous bars fringed behind with soft tissue, the gill filaments where the exchange of gases takes place. Originally, there were six pairs of gills but in modern fishes this number has usually been reduced to four or less, the remaining gill bars fulfilling other functions (the fifth often being modified into a set of tooth-bearing bones for the mastication of food). The gill filaments, which are arranged in a double row (the anterior and posterior hemibranchs), bear small lamellae and these are richly supplied with blood capillaries (hence the normal red colour of the gills). Blood from the heart passes forward in a single artery which branches into a series of paired vessels, one for each gill. Within the gills these vessels divide and subdivide to form the capillaries. The flow of blood through the gill filaments is against the flow of the water over the gills, so that oxygen-rich blood leaving the gills meets water from which the oxygen has not yet been extracted, while blood deficient in oxygen and entering the gills meets water from which much of the oxygen has already been extracted. In this way there is always more oxygen in the water than in the blood it meets, so oxygen continues to pass into the blood throughout its passage through the gill.

The efficiency of such a counter current can be judged by the fact that if the water current over the gills is reversed experimentally, the intake of oxygen from the water can fall from 50% to only 9%. Fishes can, in fact, utilize up to 80% of the oxygen from the water passing over the gills (about 25% of atmospheric oxygen is actually used by man in breathing). The surface area of the gills in fishes is very large and may be up to ten times the surface area of the body. Once the blood has passed through the gill system it passes into a single vessel in the roof of the throat and from there oxygen is supplied to the rest of the body.

In bony fishes the gills lie in a single cavity, the gill cavity, covered by a bony flap, the operculum. Typically, the mouth cavity and the gill cavity operate as two pumps, slightly out of phase with each other, so that there is a continuous stream of water in through the mouth, over the gills and out through the gill opening. A fleshy flap, the oral breathing valve, at the entrance to the mouth prevents water escaping and membranes round the hind margin to the operculum fulfil the same function. Modifications to this system include the abandonment of the pumping system in favour of swimming with the mouth open (typical of some tuna-like fishes) and the development of a muscular gill cavity which both draws in water and expels it, not through the mouth, but from the gill opening behind the operculum, for example in some eels.

In the cartilaginous fishes (sharks and rays) the gills are contained in a series of pouches which open individually to the outside as gill clefts. Usually there are five such clefts, but in some sharks (Cow sharks and Frilled shark) there may be six or seven. Because of the presence of the gill pouches, the pumping system works in three stages and not two. The first gill cleft in sharks and rays often remains open and is termed the 'spiracle'. In the bottom-living rays it is on top of the head behind the eye and water is drawn in through the spiracle not through the mouth to avoid inhaling sand or silt.

In the jawless fishes or cyclostomes (lampreys and hagfishes), the gills are in muscular pouches, each separate from the next. In lampreys the pouches open to the exterior through seven small apertures but are joined internally to a canal that opens near the mouth. In the hagfishes, the reverse occurs, there being a single exterior opening, the individual pouches each having its own interior opening.

In some fishes, e.g. the lungfishes, the gills are external in the young and project from the gill cavity but later retract, a situation found also in amphibians.

The water drawn into the mouth often contains particles that would clog the gill lamellae. Some fishes have developed a series of fine projections or gillrakers along the leading edge of the gill bars which both prevent silt from covering the gills and extract food from the incoming water. The gillrakers are long and slender in the herring, which filters small crustaceans from the water, but are much more numerous and complex in the Grey mullets, which filter algae and vegetable matter from silt. In some fishes that feed on micro-organisms, for example certain species of *Tilapia,* the gillrakers are fairly large and widely spaced and unicellular organisms are collected by trapping them in a film of mucus. The gill arches in many fishes are modified to bear teeth, usually where the gill bars reach forward on the floor of the mouth or at the back where the fifth arch is modified into a set of pharyngeal teeth.

The form and number of the gill arches are of value in determining the relationships of families and genera of fishes. The form and number of the gillrakers are of even greater value because they reflect both the relationships of fishes and their feeding habits. The numbers of gillrakers can be used to determine the species as well as the geographical race. (Ill. p. 97.)

GILTHEAD *Chrysophrys aurata,* an eastern Atlantic and Mediterranean fish and a member of the family of Sea breams. It becomes rarer towards the English Channel but there are occasional records from the south coasts of Britain. The top of the head has a golden band running between the eyes, from which the fish derives its name. Spelt *gilthedde,* this name was used as long ago as 1613 by Ulysses Aldrovandi, one of the great naturalists of the Renaissance. The body is deep, with the upper profile arched, and is a metallic grey with greenish reflections along the back and a bright orange spot on the gill cover. There are three enlarged and pointed teeth on both sides of the jaws, followed by flat molar teeth which become larger towards the angle of the jaw. The gilthead is found over sandy and gravel bottoms and also enters ports and estuaries in spring. It grows to about 2 ft (60 cm) in length. FAMILY: Sparidae, ORDER: Perciformes, CLASS: Pisces.

GLASSFISH *Chanda ranga,* a fish of fresh and brackish waters of India, Burma and Thailand, formerly known as *Ambassis lala.* The glassfish is a small stocky fish growing to 3 in (7 cm) with two dorsal fins, the first being spiny. Its most remarkable feature is the transparent, glass-like body, which is so clear that not only can the vertebrae and bones supporting the fins be seen but objects behind the fish can be viewed through the body. The abdominal cavity, however, is obscured by silvery tissue, possibly preventing the growth of algae inside the gut. The head is opaque. The transparency of this fish is probably an adaptation rendering the fish less conspicuous in water; transparency is found in other groups such as certain catfishes. The glassfish is easily kept in an aquarium but is shy and prefers quiet companions. Various other species of *Chanda* are imported for aquarists but they are usually less transparent and lack the iridescent lights that filter across the body of the glassfish. This species is so common in parts of India that it is used as a fertilizer. FAMILY: Centropomidae, ORDER: Perciformes, CLASS: Pisces. (Ill. p. 98.)

GOATFISH, an alternative name for the Red Mullets, presumably in reference to the two barbels that hang from the chin.

GOBIES, small fishes found in coastal waters in almost every part of the globe except the polar regions. Although the majority are marine a few species live permanently in freshwater and others are able to pass from one environment to the other. The name *Gobius* was first used by Pliny the Elder nearly 2,000 years ago. Gobies are stocky little fishes with slightly depressed bodies, having two dorsal fins (the first rather flag-like) and pelvic fins which are united partially or fully to form a sucking disc. As a group, the gobies present great problems in classification and identification and there are undoubtedly many species awaiting discovery. Although there is a basic similarity between all gobies, so that a goby can be very easily recognized as such, there is considerable diversity in their habits and in the ecological niches that they have exploited.

Gobies have the distinction of numbering amongst their species the smallest known vertebrate in the world. This is *Pandaka pygmaea* from the fresh waters of the Philippines. It grows to just under ½ in (1·2 cm) when fully mature. A close rival for the title is *Mystichthys luzonensis,* also from the Philippines, the adults of which are only slightly larger.

The Transparent goby *Latrunculus pellucidus* is one of the *annual fishes, completing its entire life-cycle during a single wet season. Several species of goby are blind, even though they live in shallow waters. The Blind goby of California *Typhlogobius californiensis* resembles many other *blind fishes in being a fleshy-pink colour. It inhabits burrows in sand and gravel that have been excavated by a species of shrimp, sharing the burrow with the shrimp and one or two other species of goby but never leaving the burrow. The eyes in this species are functional in the young but become covered by skin in the adults. It is localized in its distribution and is probably descended from forms that lived in crevices in rocks.

Species of the genus *Evermannichthys* are small enough to inhabit sponges. The scales of these fishes are restricted to just a few rows which have developed into long spines and these may enable the fish to clamber round inside the sponge.

Indo-Pacific gobies of the genus *Smilogobius* have a living arrangement with Snapping shrimps. The gobies perch outside the burrow while the shrimp excavates but when danger threatens the fishes dive back into the burrow thus giving warning to the shrimp, which does not emerge until the goby is once more perched on the edge of the burrow.

Some gobies are very well camouflaged and do not have special hideaways. This is the case with the British gobies. Other species are very highly coloured. The Neon goby *Elacatinus oceanops* has a striking colour-pattern which identifies it to other species as one of the cleaner fishes which remove parasites from other and larger fishes. The Blue-banded goby *Lythryphus dalli* from California is another brightly coloured species, having a brilliant red body with several vertical purple bars.

Most gobies are small, but the Tank goby *Glossogobius giuris* from Indo-Pacific coastal waters reaches 20 in (51 cm) and is an important food fish. This species is tolerant not only of freshwater but also of foul conditions, a healthy specimen having been found some distance up a Durban sewer. In the Philippines a fishery exists for goby fry of about ½ in (1·2 cm) in length which moves into fresh waters in vast shoals.

Gobies lay elongated eggs which are attached to little pedestals in protected places and are usually guarded by the parents.

Some gobies can be kept in freshwater aquaria. These include the Bumblebee fish and the Sleeper gobies (Eleotridae) from Australia. All are liable to become pugnacious and their companions should be chosen with care. FAMILY: Gobiidae, ORDER: Perciformes, CLASS: Pisces. (Ill. p. 101.)

GOLDEN ORFE *Leuciscus idus,* a golden variety of the orfe, a cultivated form that has been bred in much the same way as the goldfish. The orfe is a European fish which reaches 2 ft (60 cm) in length but does not occur naturally in Great Britain.
FAMILY: Cyprinidae, ORDER: Cypriniformes, CLASS: Pisces. (Ill. p. 99.)

GOLDFISH *Carassius auratus,* a carp-like fish native to rivers and streams of China. In the wild state, the goldfish is a dull brown in colour. In many carp-like species a form of albinism is known in which all the colour pigments are missing except the reds. These erythritic varieties, occur as a result of a chance mutation. Some 2,000 years or more ago the Chinese appear to have kept such mutants or sports and found that they bred true. They were easy to keep in tanks and were popular pets. Different varieties were bred to produce forms with telescopic eyes, long or split fins and knobbly heads. The various forms of goldfishes are frequently found in Chinese art, where they are used as motifs for pottery and china decoration, paintings and jade and ivory carvings. When China was visited by merchants from the West in the 16th and 17th centuries some goldfishes were brought back to Europe and became extremely popular. Amongst others, Samuel Pepys mentions goldfishes that he had seen and when the Duchess of Portland wanted to impress a distinguished visitor from Sweden, she presented him with 100 live goldfish.

The standard colour is now red-gold, but varieties have been bred from pure white through yellow to brown, orange, red and black and individuals with mottlings of these colours are known. Much of the breeding of varieties of goldfish has been done by the Japanese. The Veiltail goldfish has a characteristic three-lobed tail, the Blackmoor is velvety black and has not only the veiled tail but bulbous eyes. In the Celestial, the eyes are telescopic and point upwards while the dorsal fin is missing. The Lionhead goldfishes also lack the dorsal fin and the head is knobbly. Producing and stabilizing such varieties has been the result of much patient work and fanciers pay considerable sums for perfect specimens. The goldfish is now probably the most widely cultivated of all fish species, both in aquaria and in ornamental ponds.

When goldfishes are released into streams and rivers they usually revert to their wild colouration. Escapees into natural waters can interfere with local species, as has happened in Madagascar. In Lake Erie in North America, goldfish have now crossed with carp to produce hybrids although hybridization is unknown where the natural ranges of the two species overlap in Asia. FAMILY: Cyprinidae, ORDER: Cypriniformes, CLASS: Pisces. (Ill. p. 99.)

GOLDFISH REFINED. The first book on goldfish culture was written by Chang Ch'ien-te (1577–1643). His method of improving his stock was a demonstration of artificial selection that was perfectly simple and required only time and money. 'Every year in the summer one must buy several thousands and distribute them in several tens of bowls to feed and keep them, daily removing the inferior ones, and when only one or two of every hundred are left, put them together to be reared in two or three bowls; ... a complete set of the peculiar varieties will be the natural result.'

GOLDLINE *Sarpa salpa,* a member of the family of Sea breams and a common fish in the Mediterranean, where it grows to 18 in (45 cm) in length. It is quite distinctive in its colouration, having alternating gold and blue horizontal lines along the body and a black mark at the base of the pectoral fin. FAMILY: Sparidae, ORDER: Perciformes, CLASS: Pisces.

GOURAMIS, tropical freshwater fishes found from India to Malaya, and members of the family of labyrinthfishes. They have moderately deep and compressed bodies, long dorsal and anal fins and one ray of the pelvic fin is elongated and filamentous. These fishes are highly popular with aquarists, as much for their colours as for certain of their curious habits. The name gourami should strictly be applied only to *Osphronemus goramy,* a food fish that reaches 2 ft (60 cm) in length and has now been introduced from the East Indies to India, Thailand, the Philippines and China. The name gourami has now been applied, however, to a number of fairly similar fishes which have in common the filamentous pelvic ray.

The Dwarf gourami *Colisa lalia* is a small fish of 2 in (5 cm) from India. It is a pretty fish with two rows of blue-green spots on the flanks on a red background. One of the best known species is the Kissing gourami *Helostoma temmincki* from the Malay Peninsula and Thailand, a species that reaches 10 in (25 cm) in length and is a food fish in Malaya. In this species the broad-lipped mouths are applied to those of another individual so that the two fishes appear to be kissing. This apparent gesture of affection is more likely to be a threat in the exercise of territorial rights or mate selection. A single specimen can be induced to kiss a mirror. The Lake gourami *Trichogaster leeri,* known also as the Pearl or Mosaic gourami, is found in Malaya, Thailand and Borneo. The general colour is bluish with a fine lacework of white spots over the body. The bases of the fins are red or yellowish. In Croaking gourami *Trichopsis vitattus* the males make a croaking noise when they come to the surface at night for air, for like other species, there is an accessory air-breathing organ in the gill chamber (see air-breathing fishes). FAMILY: Anabantidae, ORDER: Perciformes, CLASS: Pisces.

GRASS CARP *Ctenopharygodon idellus,* a large carp-like fish from China. The Grass carp will crop almost any vegetation, either in the water or along the banks. Because of its rapid growth and the ease with which it can be fed on grass cuttings or the waste leafage of crops, it is highly valued as a pond fish in the Far East. The fishes breed in rivers and the fry are collected and transported to the growing ponds, where they can grow at the rate of 1 lb (0·45 kg) per month. Because of their ability to eat weeds, their introduction in to such areas as the Danube delta has been considered. FAMILY: Cyprinidae, ORDER: Cypriniformes, CLASS: Pisces.

GRAYLING *Thymallus thymallus,* a beautiful salmon-like fish found in the arctic and temperate regions of the Old World; a related species *T. arcticus* being found in the New World. The scientific name records the slight smell of thyme exuded from the flesh of these fishes. The graylings resemble a trout in general body form but the dorsal fin is very large. The colour varies somewhat, the back being a greenish, bluish or ashy grey (hence its common name) with the flanks silver or brassy-yellow and irregularly scattered with black spots and dark yellow longitudinal streaks. In the breeding season the body has a green-gold shimmer and the dorsal and anal fins and the tail become deep purple. The juveniles shoal but the adults become solitary. The grayling is essentially a river fish and avoids lakes and large ponds. It feeds on insects, worms and snails and grows to about 20 in (50 cm). It is a shy fish with a soft mouth and is not easy to catch. FAMILY: Salmonidae, ORDER: Salmoniformes, CLASS: Pisces. (Ill. p. 97.)

GREAT WHITE SHARK *Carcharodon carcharias,* also known as the man-eater or White pointer, the largest of all carnivorous fishes and probably the most dangerous of all man-eating sharks, certainly the most dreaded. It is found in all warm seas and

grows to over 20 ft (6 m) in length; the largest specimen on record was one from Port Fairey (Australia) that was 36½ ft (11 m) in length and although the weight was not recorded specimens half that length can weigh over 7,000 lb (3,000 kg). The jaws are enormous and are lined with triangular teeth, the edges of which are serrated. The Great white shark has an unpleasant dossier on its feeding habits. The 16th century naturalist, Guillaume Rondelet, recorded that at Marseilles and Nice specimens had been found with an entire soldier in the stomach, complete with armour. Another specimen was recorded with a complete horse in the stomach.

These sharks are chiefly found in open waters and are usually caught near the surface although there is a record of a specimen caught off Cuba at a depth of 4,200 ft (1,260 m). In an underwater encounter with a Great white shark, Captain Cousteau wrote in his book *The Silent World* that the shark's reaction on sighting the author and his companion was to deposit a cloud of excrement in sheer fright and depart at great speed. Often, however, a lone individual 'bull' will appear off a popular bathing coast and cause a series of tragic deaths before being caught or moving on. So far, no effective shark repellent has been developed and protection from this and other species is best gained from shark nets surrounding bathing beaches.

An even larger and more formidable shark seems to have existed in former times. Teeth very similar to those of the Great white shark are thought to have belonged to the extinct species *Carcharodon megalodon* and since the teeth are 6 in (15 cm) in length these monsters must have achieved an overall length of at least 90 ft (27 m). FAMILY: Isuridae, ORDER: Pleurotremata, CLASS: Chondrichthyes.

GRENADIERS, or rat-tails as they are sometimes called, marine fishes found at moderate depths and related to the cods. The head is usually large, with a pointed snout that overhangs the mouth. The most striking feature is the long tapering tail, from which the group derives its alternative name. There is a small dorsal fin immediately behind the head, but the second dorsal fin and the anal and caudal fins have fused to form a continuous fin round the posterior half of the body. The pelvic fins are immediately below the pectorals. In rat-tails from the deeper waters the eyes tend to be smaller than in those from inshore waters. Rat-tails are occasionally caught in large numbers by trawlers off the edge of the continental shelf. Most species are small and rather flabby, but *Macrourus berglax* reaches a length of 3 ft (90 cm).

In many species there is a gland near the

anus that produces a luminous slime. The author recalls his pleasure at first encountering this in fishes hauled aboard a trawler on a dark night off the west coast of Ireland. As the fishes slithered onto the deck, streaks of brilliant blue light could be seen and, being his first experience of luminous fishes, the author wrote his initials in glowing letters across the deck. The luminosity stayed for two or three hours before gradually fading. In the daylight, the luminous secretion was black in colour. FAMILY: Macrouridae, ORDER: Gadiformes, CLASS: Pisces.

GREY MULLETS, members of the order Perciformes or perch-like fishes, but superficially bearing little resemblance to others in the order having long, sturdy bodies, almost cylindrical in cross section, and a weakly spinous first dorsal fin followed by a soft-rayed second dorsal fin. The mouth is soft and weak and is directed downwards since these fishes feed on algae growing on sand, mud or rocks. A certain amount of sand or mud is sucked in while feeding and to prevent this being swallowed, and to sift out the food particles, the Grey mullets have evolved an elaborate sieving mechanism. The gill-rakers on the hind part of each gill arch are very numerous and closely packed, each small raker being lined with tiny processes that further increase the filtration surface. The stream of water passing over the gills probably helps to concentrate the food particles and to push them as a mass back towards the throat. Like most herbivorous animals, the Grey mullet has a very long intestine, a fish of 13 in (33 cm) having an intestine of 7 ft (2·1 m). The stomach is very muscular and is divided into two parts.

Grey mullets are almost world-wide in their distribution in coastal and estuarine waters. The classification of the Grey mullets is not easy but there appear to be three species found in British waters, the Thick-lipped grey mullet *Crenimugil labrosus,* the Thin-lipped grey mullet *Liza ramada* and the Golden mullet *Liza auratus.* One of the commonest of the European species, *Mugil cephalus,* extends as far south as South Africa.

Mullets are shoaling fishes but are shy and difficult to catch on rod and line. Only the finest tackle should be used because of the delicacy of their mouths. The agility of Grey mullets is well known to fishermen, who often see a whole shoal of these fishes calmly leap over the net as it is dragged in. To prevent this, it was once the practice to spread straw near the net, the leapers apparently mistaking this for the net itself. Grey mullets are commonly used in pond culture since they are tolerant of fresh water. Mullet boiled in red wine is greatly recommended.

Grey mullets should not be confused with the Red mullets, to which they are only distantly related. FAMILY: Mugilidae, ORDER: Perciformes, CLASS: Pisces. (Ill. p. 101.)

GREY SHARKS, a large family containing over 60 species of fairly 'typical' sharks with five gill slits, two dorsal and one anal fin, the upper lobe of the tail larger than the lower and the mouth underneath the head. Members of this family are essentially tropical fishes but some stray into temperate waters. The largest group of species are those belonging to the genus *Carcharinus*, which includes the Cub or Bull shark *C. leucas*, the White-tipped oceanic shark *C. longimanus*, the Black tipped reef shark *C. melanopterus*, the Brown shark *C. milberti* and the Dusky shark *C. obscurus*. The identification of these Grey sharks is not easy and the presence of white or black tips to the fins may be misleading since there is a species of each in the Atlantic and Indo-Pacific regions. Members of this genus are also found in freshwaters. One of the best known is the Ganges shark *C. gangeticus*, common in the Ganges and in the Hooghly River at Calcutta, which is known to be aggressive. Another well-known species is the Lake Nicaragua shark, formerly thought to represent a distinct species but now known to be merely a freshwater form of the Bull shark. It grows to about 8 ft (2·4 m) and has been reported to be dangerous to man. Elsewhere, the Bull shark has been found to enter freshwaters. It is this species that is known as the Zambesi shark and it probably accounts for many other records of sharks in freshwaters throughout the tropical regions of the world.

The Grey sharks are of some commercial importance in many parts of the Indo-Pacific, the flesh often being sun-dried and spiced. During the last war these and other sharks provided an important source of vitamin A in the rich oils of their livers. Large fisheries were established but with the synthetic manufacture of vitamin A these fisheries have declined. The Soupfin shark *Galeorhinus zygopterus* was not only an important species during the hey-day of the shark-liver industry but is still caught for the high quality of the fins for the preparation of shark-fin soup in oriental countries. After removing the skin of the fin and teasing away the muscle, the fine cartilaginous finrays or ceratotrichia are removed and pressed into discs somewhat resembling pale yellow, matted coconut fibres. It is these elastoidine fibres that are used for shark-fin soup.

Another member of this large family is the Tiger shark *Galeocerdo cuvieri*, named after the great French zoologist, Georges Cuvier. The Tiger shark, a tropical species, has dark vertical bars along the grey-brown flanks. It is both dangerous to man and a notorious scavenger, swallowing all manner of refuse dumped by ships. It was a Tiger shark of 14 ft (4·2 m) that regurgitated a tattooed human arm in an Australian aquarium and led to the famous Shark Arm Murder Case, the rather characteristic tattoo marks enabling the police to identify the victim, thus considerably helping in their search for the culprit.

The Lemon shark *Negaprion brevirostris* of the American Atlantic, which has a yellowish tinge to the body, is one of the most common species and a favourite subject for behavioural and physiological experiments. It reaches up to 11 ft (3·3 m) in length, but specimens of at least 6 ft (1·8 m) have successfully lived in large shark pens and many valuable observations have been made on them by Dr Eugenie Clark and her colleagues.

The Great blue shark *Prionace glauca* is a large species that reaches a length of 12 ft (3·6 m) and is coloured dark blue on the back fading to white on the belly. Although this shark is found mainly in deeper tropical waters it wanders into temperate regions, possibly to breed, and is there found near the surface in summer. It is found in the Atlantic, the Mediterranean and in the Indo-Pacific region. Its distribution appears to be closely correlated with water temperatures. The European angling record was for a fish of 218 lb (98·7 kg).

The Grey sharks are all live-bearers, the young hatching within the uterus of the female. Some species can be termed ovoviviparous, the young merely being sustained by the yolk, but others approach true viviparity in their development of a connection similar to the umbilicus of mammals between the embryo and the lining of the uterus, the young then being nourished by secretions from the mother.

Members of this family are also known as Requiem sharks. This appears to be a corruption of the French *requin* meaning a 'shark' and is not an oblique reference to their man-eating reputation. The Grey sharks evolved fairly recently and are in fact the only family of sharks that does not contain genera found as fossils in Cretaceous rocks. FAMILY: Carcharhinidae, ORDER: Pleurotremata, CLASS: Chondrichthyes.

GROUPERS, or epinephelids, large perch-like marine fishes of temperate and tropical seas. The family Serranidae contains some of the most generalized perch-like fishes and it was from forms of this degree of primitiveness that all the more specialized perch-like fishes evolved. Groupers are usually large, bulky fishes with slightly compressed bodies and enormous mouths. Many have remarkable colour-patterns, often made up of regular spots or mottlings but usually involving rather sombre colours. Colour variations between adults and juveniles, or between adults of the same species from different regions, are sometimes so great that identification is difficult. Some species, such as the Nassau grouper *Epinephelus striatus*, can change colour with chameleon-like rapidity. The Estuary rock cod *E. tauvina* is found throughout the Indo-Pacific region. So variable is its colouration that what were formerly described as 24 distinct species are now all recognized as one. Like most groupers, this species lives amongst coral reefs, but it also enters estuaries. It is a large species, reaching a length of 7 ft (2·1 m) and a weight of 500 lb (220 kg). It has a reputation for being dangerous. An Australian grouper *E. lanceolatus* attains 10 ft (3·5 m) and has been known to stalk divers. Pearl fishermen in the Torres Straits are occasionally killed by these fishes. The Dusky perch *E. gigas* is found in the Mediterranean but sometimes comes as far north as the English Channel. It is eagerly sought by underwater spear-fishermen. All groupers are considered valuable food-fishes. FAMILY: Serranidae, ORDER: Perciformes, CLASS: Pisces.

GRUNION *Leuresthes tenuis*, a fish with remarkable breeding habits related to the silversides and described under that name.

GRUNTS, perch-like fishes of tropical and subtropical seas, related to the drums. They have a single long dorsal fin, the front part of which is spiny. The grunts, as their name suggests, are vocal fishes and produce a variety of noises by grinding their throat or pharyngeal teeth together, the sound being amplified by the swimbladder. Several species of grunts indulge in a curious form of 'kissing' in which two individuals approach each other with their mouths wide open and touch lips. This behaviour, which is reminiscent of the Kissing gouramis, has not yet been properly investigated but may play a part in courtship. Some of the grunts from South African and Australian waters are referred to as sweetlips and the larger species, such as the Painted sweetlips *Plectorhynchus pictus* are considered to be good food fish. The colour-pattern in these fishes is often very distinctive but changes with age. FAMILY: Pomadasyidae, ORDER: Perciformes, CLASS: Pisces. (Ill. p. 97.)

GUDGEON *Gobio gobio*, a small carp-like fish common in the rivers of Great Britain and northern Europe. Related species are found in the Danube basin and southern Europe. The gudgeon has an almost round body, a blunt snout and two barbels round the mouth. The body is grey-green with darker mottlings merging to silver with a reddish tinge on the belly. It is found in lakes, rivers and streams but prefers clear water with a sandy or gravelly bottom. Gudgeon live in shoals and are best caught by disturbing the river bottom and waiting for the fish to investigate the disturbance. They grow to about 6 in (15 cm) in length and are good to eat. FAMILY: Cyprinidae, ORDER: Cypriniformes, CLASS: Pisces. (Ill. p. 97.)

GUITARFISHES, shark-like fishes whose true affinities lie with the rays, the group that contains the skates and other flattened cartilaginous fishes. Unlike most rays, however, the guitarfishes have rather small pectoral fins which are not used to propel the fish, the motive power deriving from sinuous movements of the body, as in sharks. The gill slits are on the underside of the head and the leading edge of the pectoral fins joins smoothly onto the head, as in the rays. The guitarfishes are found in warm and temperate coastal waters throughout the world and about 40 species are known.

The guitarfish *Rhinobatos rhinobatos* of the eastern Atlantic and Mediterranean is typical of this group. The snout is pointed and the pectoral fins are small, tapering from the head. There are two dorsal fins and the teeth are blunt and formed into a pavement. It is a bottom-feeder that browses chiefly on crustaceans. Like all members of this family, the young are hatched inside the female and are born later.

Most of the guitarfishes are fairly small, only occasionally reaching 6 ft (2 m) in length, but *Rhynchobatis djiddensis* of the Indo-Pacific region (sometimes placed in a separate family, the Rhynchobatidae) has been reported to reach 10 ft (3 m) and to weigh up to 500 lb (227 kg). FAMILY: Rhinobatidae, ORDER: Hypotremata, CLASS: Chondrichthyes. (Ill. p. 98.)

GULPER EELS, fishes belonging to three families of deep-sea eels, the Saccopharyngidae, the Eurypharyngidae and the Monognathidae. All these fishes have thin, elongated bodies, in some species reaching as much as 5 ft (1·7 m) in length. The Gulper eels live in all oceans, usually at depths of between 3,600 and 10,000 ft (1,200–3,300 m). Only three genera are known. The relationships of these fishes was for a long time debatable and they were included in the order Lyomeri. It is now known that they pass through a leaf-like leptocephalus stage and this unites them with the eels, the three families being placed as a suborder of the Anguilliformes.

Saccopharynx has a large bag-like mouth and attenuated body. The jaws are provided with sharp teeth and the stomach is elastic and capable of holding any large prey that has been seized. The brain and the eyes are tiny and are placed at the front of the head. The *lateral line organs, instead of being contained in a canal, are on small stalks which project from the body. In appearance, *Saccopharynx* seems to be adapted for one thing, eating. Only a few specimens are known.

Eurypharynx pelecanoides is the most common of the Gulper eels. It has the largest mouth of any of the species but teeth are absent and the mouth is so fragile that it is probably used only for straining small organisms from the water. The stomach is not distensible. These fishes are caught at depths of 800–20,000 ft (250–7,000 m) with a centre of distribution at about 6,000 ft (2,000 m). The tip of the tail carries a light organ, as in at least one species of *Saccopharynx*. The leptocephalus larval stages are fairly well known and from their size it would appear that the larval form lasts about two years. Compared with the other deep-sea eels, the Gulper eels metamorphose to the adult shape at a small size, $1\frac{1}{4}$–$1\frac{1}{2}$ in (30–35 mm). Even at this size, however, the gape of the mouth is enormous and they can swallow relatively large food items right from the beginning of their deep-sea life. The larvae seem to live in much shallower water, usually at about 300–600 ft (100–200 m).

Monognathus is the least well known of the three genera. Its members are carnivorous but have smaller jaws than the other two. Because these fish are all small, Dr J. Böhlke of the Philadelphia Academy of Sciences has suggested that they possibly represent the young of *Saccopharynx*.

Almost nothing is known of the biology of the Gulper eels since by the time their fragile bodies have been drawn to the surface they are usually damaged. SUBORDER: Saccopharyngoidei, ORDER: Anguilliformes, CLASS: Pisces.

GUPPY *Lebistes reticulatus,* also known as the millionsfish, a small live-bearing toothcarp from the fresh waters of the southern West Indies and parts of northwest South America. Its common name records its discoverer, the Rev Robert Guppy, who found this little fish on Trinidad in 1866. Guppies grow to about $2\frac{1}{2}$ in (6 cm). The female is a rather dull olive, but the males, which are smaller and slimmer, are brightly coloured with all kinds of variable spots and patterns (in orange, blues, green-blues, white, etc). In the male, as in all the live-bearing toothcarps, the anal fin is modified into a copulatory organ or gonopodium, with hooks and spines, for the transfer of sperm to the female. Guppies are surface-feeding forms and this has led to their introduction into tropical countries in order to control mosquito larvae. It is possible, however, that they also eat the eggs and small larvae of other fishes. This has certainly been found to be the case in the related species *Gambusia affinis* (often called guppy but better known as the mosquitofish).

The variants, especially in the shape of the tail and the colours, that appear in aquarium populations of the guppy have been bred into distinct and true-breeding varieties and

clubs have been formed for the culture of this species. FAMILY: Poeciliidae, ORDER: Atheriniformes, CLASS: Pisces. (Ill. p. 100.)

GURNARDS, a family of marine bottom-living fishes with strongly armoured heads bearing spines. They are known as Sea robins in the United States. There are two dorsal fins, the second opposite to the fairly long anal fin. The pectoral fins are large and the first few rays are separate and can be used to support the body when the fish moves slowly along the bottom; they may also be used to probe the substrate. The body is heavily scaled, often with a row of spines at the base of the dorsal fins, and the colours are characteristically reds, yellows and oranges, with areas of blue or green on the fins. The gurnards are found in all tropical and temperate seas in shallow to moderately deep water. They grow to 2–3 ft (60–90 cm) in length and many of them are able to produce noises.

The Northern sea robin *Prionotus carolinus* of the Atlantic coasts of the United States is found most commonly in shoal waters from Cape Cod to Cape Lookout. It is a typical bottom-dweller, showing a preference for smooth sand and often becoming completely buried. It is capable of making noises similar to those of a wet finger drawn across an inflated balloon and is in fact the noisiest fish along the American Atlantic seaboard. The noise is produced from muscular vibrations of the large bilobed swimbladder which occupies no less than half the body cavity; a perforated partition in the left lobe vibrates when gas is forced through and this seems to strengthen the sound waves. The Striped sea robin *P. evolans* is another noisy species found along the western Atlantic coast.

The most common species round British coasts is the Grey gurnard *Trigla gurnardus*, a grey, but occasionally reddish, species that reaches 16 in (40 cm) in length and is found from the Mediterranean northwards to Iceland. The Tub gurnard *T. lucerna* has much larger pectoral fins which are orange and reach as far as the vent. Occasionally species common to more southerly waters wander into the North Sea. One of the most easily recognized is the piper *T. lyra* in which bones from the upper surface of the head project forward as two large serrated plates. FAMILY: Triglidae, ORDER: Scorpaeniformes, CLASS: Pisces. (Ill. p. 99.)

HADDOCK *Melanogrammus aeglefinus,* a cod-like fish of the North Atlantic and economically one of the most important of all the species caught by the countries fishing the North Sea. It resembles the cod in having three dorsal fins and two anal fins but can be easily distinguished by the presence of a black blotch above the pectoral fins, the lack of other spots on the flanks and the black lateral line. There is a small barbel under the chin. The haddock grows to about 24 lb (11 kg) in weight but is generally much smaller than this.

It is found throughout the North Atlantic but is more common off European coasts. It spawns early in the year, the female producing half a million small pelagic eggs. After hatching, the young live in the upper waters for the first year or so and then migrate towards the bottom in shallow waters, finally making for deeper waters. They are shoaling fishes that prefer sandy bottoms where they feed on shellfish, Sea urchins and small fishes. They are often marketed smoked sometimes as Finnan haddies, a name that was originally Findon haddies or haddocks and refers to Findon in Scotland where the smoking of haddock was first practised in the middle of the 18th century. After the head has been removed, the fish is split down the back, gutted, steeped in strong brine for a short time, dried and then spread on sticks to be smoked for five or six hours over a fire of peat and sawdust.

The black spot on the side of the haddock is said to represent the thumb-mark of St Peter left when he held the fish and found the tribute money. The same legend is applied to the black mark on the flank of the John dory. Unfortunately, neither fish is found in Lake Gennesaret where the incident is said to have occurred. FAMILY: Gadidae, ORDER: Gadiformes, CLASS: Pisces.

HAGFISHES, marine eel-shaped fishes which constitute one of the two surviving groups of jawless fishes. There are about 25 species and all are found in colder seas at depths of 60–2,000 ft (20–650 m). Hagfishes have a small and fleshy fin around the tail and barbels round the mouth. The eyes are rudimentary in some species, merely small pigmented cups capable of distinguishing between light and dark but nothing more. Other general features are described under jawless fishes.

Occasionally in the North Atlantic a trawler will find amongst its living catch a dead fish which, when opened up, will be almost hollow except for a hagfish. Hagfishes feed on dead and dying fishes into which they burrow with the aid of their rasping tongue covered with horny teeth. They usually live burrowed in muddy areas and are very sluggish, rarely moving unless they have to. One striking characteristic of the hagfishes is their ability to produce copious secretions of slime. An Atlantic hagfish *Myxine glutinosa,* if dropped into a 2 gallon (9 litres) bucket of sea water, will convert it into slime in a few seconds. This useful means of defence has the drawback of clogging the gills. To overcome this, the hagfish has evolved a flexibility that is unique amongst fishes. The backbone is composed of cartilage (as indeed is the entire skeleton) and the fish is able to tie itself into a knot and then to flow through the knot and thus clean off the slime. It can also use this flexibility to lever itself against the body of another fish in order to get a better grip. The hagfishes have four hearts or simple organs for pumping the blood round the body. One is behind the head, two are behind the gills and about a third of the way along the body, and the fourth is in the tail.

Hagfishes are usually putty coloured and reach 30 in (76 cm) in length. They find their food by smell and there is a single nostril above the mouth. Although both sex organs (ovaries and testes) are present in the same individual, only one of these develops. So far, no larval form comparable to the ammocoete larvae of the lampreys has been found. FAMILY: Myxinidae, ORDER: Cyclostomata, CLASS: Agnatha.

HAKE *Merluccius merluccius,* an elongated deep-water fish of the cod family found in the eastern North Atlantic. It differs from the other cod-like fishes in that the second dorsal fin and the anal fins are single and not split into two. It somewhat resembles the ling but there is no barbel under the chin, the scales are larger and the tail is truncated and not rounded posteriorly. The back is greyish, the belly white and the lateral line scales are black. The hake is found at depths down to 2,400 ft (700 m) and occurs in the Mediterranean and northwards to Trondheim and Iceland. It is a migratory species that appears in the North Sea in summer. Hake are voracious fishes with sharp teeth in the mouth and they feed chiefly on other fishes. Large commercially caught fishes can weigh as much as 40 lb (18 kg) and the European record for a rod-caught fish is a little over 25 lb (11 kg). A large female may produce over 1,000,000 eggs which are small and pelagic. FAMILY: Merlucciidae, ORDER: Gadiformes, CLASS: Pisces.

HALECOSTOMES. In some classifications of the actinopterygian fishes the extinct orders: Pholidophoriformes, Aspidorhynchiformes and Leptolepiformes, are considered to form a major group, the Halecostomi, equal in rank to the Holostei. With the possible exception of the aspidorhynchoids, about which comparatively little is known, the halecostomes closely approach the teleosts (bony fishes) in structure and the pholidophoroids were probably ancestral to them, or at least to some of them. Whether the halecostomes are so distinct from the holosteans to warrant separation in this way is a matter of speculation at present since relatively little is known of the origin and relationships of most of the groups.

HALF-BEAKS, members of the group that includes the flyingfishes and the needlefishes, they are small, rarely attaining more than 12 in (30 cm) and are found in both marine and fresh waters in most of the tropical and temperate regions of the world. They derive their common name from their jaws. The lower jaw is elongated and beak-like, but the upper jaw is much shorter; teeth only occur in the lower jaw where it is in contact with the upper. In the needlefishes the jaws are equal in length, while in the flyingfishes the jaws are normal.

A few species are viviparous, producing live young, including a freshwater species from Thailand, *Dermogenys pusillus.* This species is often imported for aquarists. In Thailand it is used as a fighting fish on which wagers are placed as two individuals lock jaws and wrestle until one gives up. Certain marine Indo-Pacific species are also live-bearers, including members of the genus *Zenarchopterus* which live in creeks and brackish areas. In the males, the rays of the anal fin are prolonged into feather-like processes, presumably to channel or fan the sperm towards the female. In *Z. dispar,* which reaches 6 in (15 cm) in length, the fourth dorsal finray in the male is also elongated and probably plays a part in sexual display. Other species live a pelagic life far out to sea. One such is the Long-finned half-beak *Euleptorhamphus longirostris* of the Indo-Pacific, known from only a few specimens, some of which were found after they had leapt on board yachts. One of the largest species is *Hemirhamphus australis,* which grows to 18 in (45 cm) and is an important food fish. Such Australian species are often called garfishes, a term used elsewhere for the Belonidae or needlefishes.

The half-beaks are surface-living forms, the elongated lower jaw apparently being an adaptation to catching food at the surface. A few species, such as *Arrhamphus sclerolepis* of Queensland, have the jaws almost equal in length. Normally, the lower jaw is slightly wider than the upper, but in the Spatulate 'garfish' *Loligorhamphus normani* the lower jaw is very much wider than the upper.

Half-beaks are clearly closely related to the flyingfishes and the juveniles are often very similar indeed. Like the flyingfishes, the half-beaks have the lower lobe of the caudal fin enlarged and they not only skitter along the surface but sometimes leap into the air. Formerly placed in a family of their own, the Hemirhamphidae, the half-beaks are now recognized as so close to the flyingfishes that they are included in the same family. FAMILY: Exocoetidae, ORDER: Atheriniformes, CLASS: Pisces. (Ill. p. 101.)

HALIBUT *Hippoglossus hippoglossus,* the largest of the North Atlantic flatfishes and one of the largest fish in this order. It is reported to reach 9 ft (2·7 m) and to weigh up to 600 lb (270 kg), while specimens of 7 ft (2·1 m) and 300 lb (135 kg) are by no means rare. The body is fairly elongated, the jaws are symmetrical and the scales are smooth. It is dark olive above and pearly-white below. The halibut is carnivorous, feeding on other fishes (chiefly cod-like fishes) as well as squids, crabs and octopuses.

The Pacific halibut *H. stenolepis* is a slightly smaller fish. The females, which are larger than the males, have been reported to reach a weight of 470 lb (210 kg) in 35 years. These fishes spawn in winter producing over 2 million eggs which float in mid-water, the fry swimming to the surface when they hatch and drifting towards the shores before settling on the bottom. At one time the fishery for the Pacific halibut was sadly depleted, but careful studies of the biology of the fish led to recommendations which restored the fishery to its former prosperity.

The Long rough dab *Hippoglossoides platessoides,* a relative of the halibut that is found on both sides of the North Atlantic, is a much smaller fish usually growing to about 12 in (30 cm). It can be distinguished from a small halibut by its rough scales and almost straight lateral line (the front part curves up towards the dorsal fin in the halibut). FAMILY: Pleuronectidae, ORDER: Pleuronectiformes, CLASS: Pisces.

HAMMERHEAD SHARK, most easily recognized of all shark-like fishes possessing as it does a curious lateral extension of the head, from whence its common name is derived. It was known to early writers as the balancefish because of the resemblance of the head to balance scales. Hammerheads are found in all warm seas throughout the world and show a tendency to move into temperate waters during the summer. In general form they closely resemble the Grey sharks except for the two plate-like outgrowths of the head with the eyes set at their tips. Nine species are known, all placed in the genus *Sphyrna* but separated chiefly on the basis of the shape of the head, into three subgenera. In the Common hammerhead *S. zygaena* the flattened head is almost rectangular. It is virtually world-wide in its distribution, occasionally wandering as far north as Great Britain. It reaches 13 ft (3·9 m) in length and feeds on fishes, but like many other sharks is a scavenger and has also been known to attack men. The Great hammerhead *S. mokarran,* also having a world-wide distribution, is the largest of the nine species, reaching 15 ft (4·5 m). In the Bonnet shark or shovelhead, *S. tiburo,* the head is rounded in front giving the appearance of a shovel. This is a common species of the western Atlantic which grows to about 6 ft (1·8 m). The function of the flattened head is uncertain, and suggestions that it may act as a hydroplane are unconvincing when one considers the difficulties experienced by the Wright brothers in their early aircraft, before they moved the steering vanes from the front to the rear. The hammerheads are probably all live-bearers, the young being hatched within the uterus of the female. It is known that in some cases the young are nourished by the mother while still in the uterus. The hammerheads are known to be aggressive fishes and a number of fatalities have been recorded although the actual species involved is not known. FAMILY: Sphyrnidae, ORDER: Pleurotremata, CLASS: Chondrichthyes. (Ill. also on p. 102.)

HARLEQUINFISH *Rasbora heteromorpha,* an attractive small carp-like fish from the Malay Peninsula and Thailand. It grows to 1¾ in (4·5 cm) and has a rather deeper body than in other species of *Rasbora.* The flanks are pinky-silver with violet tints and there is a distinctive dark triangle on the posterior half of the body. It is a shoaling fish that is popular with aquarists. FAMILY: Cyprinidae, ORDER: Cypriniformes, CLASS: Pisces. (Ill. p. 101.)

Hammerhead shark in a marine aquarium. The value to the fish of this curious head is not known.

HATCHETFISHES, small freshwater South American fishes which are capable of flight. Their common name is a reference to their slim bodies and very deep chests which rise up towards the tail to resemble a hatchet in shape. The anal fin is long and the pectoral fins are large and sickle-shaped. These fishes are quite small, rarely exceeding 4 in (10 cm) in length, and are frequently kept by aquarists who are often unaware that the hatchetfishes are in fact flyingfishes. The chest region contains the greatly enlarged bony supports for the pectoral fins to which very large muscles are attached. These extra large muscles enable the pectoral fins to be flapped during flight and it is this flapping of the fins that produces the buzzing noise made by these fishes when they are in the air. The fishes make a short dash before they take off but they cannot change direction once in flight. As in the true flyingfishes, the evolution of flight was certainly in response to the need to escape from predators.

The Marbled hatchetfish *Carnegiella strigata,* and the related Black-winged hatchetfish *C. marthae,* are two of the smallest species, growing to less than 2 in (4·5 cm) in length. The Silver hatchetfish *Gasteropelecus levis* and the Common hatchetfish *G. sternicla* reach about 3 in (7·5 cm) and are slightly less graceful in build than the two *Carnegiella.*

Occasionally, specimens of the hatchetfish *Thoracocharax stellatus* are imported into Europe. They can be recognized by the black blotch on the first few dorsal rays. Since this species comes from Argentina, it should be kept at a slightly lower temperature than the other 'tropical' species.

Hatchetfishes are splendid members of any community tank but it must be remembered that a covering to the tank is essential. FAMILY: Gasteropelecidae, ORDER: Cypriniformes, CLASS: Pisces. (Ill. p. 101.)

HATCHETFISHES, MARINE, small deep-sea marine fishes equipped with light organs and bearing a superficial resemblance to the freshwater hatchetfishes. The marine hatchetfishes are distantly related to the salmon and like the latter possess a small adipose fin behind the rayed dorsal fin. This is also present in the freshwater hatchetfishes, however. The hatchet-shaped body has the lower part lined with light producing organs, the photophores, which shine a blue or pinkish light downwards. The role of these light organs is still uncertain. They can be of little use to their owner since in many species the eyes are tubular and point upwards. They may, however, serve to identify the owner, although it has also been suggested that at these depths a light-coloured belly would render the fish less visible when viewed from below; in fishes of the upper waters this kind of camouflage is achieved by the belly being white or silvery.

The hatchetfishes are deep-bodied and strongly compressed and when seen from the front little is visible except the large gaping mouth with the corners turned down and the bulbous, tubular eyes. With members of the other stomiatoid families, they form the dominant element of the bathypelagic fish fauna, occurring at depths of 800–1,600 ft (250–500 m). There is still a little light at these depths, so that their eyes are of some use to them. Some species make an active migration to the surface at night, descending again at dawn. Rather surprisingly, the hatchetfishes have well-developed swimbladders, organs which have been lost by many deep-sea fishes, presumably because of the great difficulty in adjusting the pressure of the gas in the swimbladder during the migration to the surface and back. The way in which the hatchetfishes have overcome this is still not understood. FAMILY: Stomiatidae, ORDER: Salmoniformes, CLASS: Pisces.

HAWKFISHES, a family of tropical marine fishes from the Indo-Pacific region. They derive their common name from their habit of perching on coral or rock outcrops and apparently surveying the scene. They grow to about 12 in (30 cm) in length and can be distinguished by the enlarged and slightly elongated first pectoral ray and the rather curious fringe behind the anterior nostril. FAMILY: Cirrhitidae, ORDER: Perciformes, CLASS: Pisces. (Ill. p. 98.)

HEARING IN FISHES, a subject which has only recently, with the development of modern electro-physiological techniques begun to be studied fully. Since many fishes are capable of making noises, however, it seemed reasonable to suppose that fishes could hear and stories of mediaeval monks summoning the carp in their stew-ponds by ringing a bell seemed to confirm this. Recent work has shown that in water the higher frequency vibrations (i.e. sound) are picked up by the hearing apparatus while low frequency vibrations (such as result from a struggling fish) are probably detected by the *lateral line system. Experiments have shown that some fishes can in fact hear extremely well.

The ear of a fish fulfils two functions, hearing and the maintainance of equilibrium. It differs in several respects from the ear of a mammal. In man, the outer part of the ear, the external pinna, serves to concentrate sound waves in the air and channel them into the middle ear where they are converted from compression waves in the air to mechanical impulses. In turn, these are transmitted to the inner ear where the sound is actually 'heard'. Fishes have no external or middle ear since sound is better conducted in water than air and the channelling and con-verting mechanisms are not necessary (they only arose when land-dwelling animals evolved from their fish-like ancestors).

Protected by the skull and lying behind the eye is the fish's inner ear. It consists of a sac almost completely divided horizontally into two parts, an upper chamber or utriculus and a lower chamber or sacculus, the latter with a small outgrowth, the lagena. Associated with the utriculus are three semicircular canals filled with a fluid (endolymph), the canals running at right angles to each other and ending in a small swelling or ampulla (the horizontal canal is missing in the lamprey and a single canal with an ampulla at both ends is found in the hagfish). The cavities of the utriculus, sacculus and lagena are lined by sensitive tissue and each cavity contains a disc-shaped concretion of calcium carbonate, the otolith (respectively, the lapillus, sagitta and asteriscus, the second usually the largest but occasionally the third). The otoliths settle at the bottom of their cavities and their position is registered by the sensitive tissue on which they lie. In this way the fish is aware both of its position in the water and of inertial forces operative during fast turns. An intriguing demonstration of the role of the otoliths in maintaining equilibrium is provided by the substitution of iron filings for the otoliths: a strong magnet placed over the fish will induce it to turn upside down. Movement of the fluid within the canals also plays an important role in maintaining equilibrium.

The lower part of the ear capsule, the cavities of the sacculus and lagena, are the centres of hearing. The frequencies that can be detected by fishes range from 13–7,000 cycles per second, although no single species is sensitive to this entire range. The greatest range is found in the ostariophysins (16–7,000 cps) in which a unique method of amplifying sounds has been evolved. This is the Weberian apparatus which consists of three or four small bones modified from the processes of the anterior vertebrae. These bones are linked together and act as levers to transmit the vibrations of the swimbladder to the ear. The gas-filled swimbladder acts as a receiver for water-borne sound impulses and the sensitivity of the ear is enormously increased. There is a striking functional similarity between this system of amplification and the development of an ear and three little bones (malleus, incus and stipes) in our own ears.

Another method of amplification is found in the herrings, anchovies and Elephant-snout fishes. In these fishes the swimbladder has outgrowths which reach forward into the skull and are closely associated with the utriculus within the ear capsule.

Sound production is now recognized as an important means of communication in many fishes and much more work is required on the way in which fishes detect and interpret the noises that they hear.

HERRINGS, or clupeid fishes, a large family of highly important food fishes of world-wide distribution, the best known member being the herring of North Atlantic and Pacific waters. About 200 species are known, may of them small and confined to tropical waters but often of great importance to fisheries. The herring-like fishes have single soft-rayed dorsal and anal fins, the former usually set near the midpoint of the body and over the pelvic fins. Typically, the belly has a serrated 'keel' made up of a series of sharp scutes running from the throat to the anus. The characteristic herring-like lower jaw is short and deep and the upper jaw is composed of rather plate-like maxillary bones which swing forward when the mouth opens. Scales are always present but may be easily shed when the fish is handled. Only the first two or three scales of the lateral line bear pores but a sensory canal system is greatly developed on the head. An important anatomical feature that unites all the herring- and anchovy-like fishes is the forward extension of the swimbladder as a pair of slender tubes that enter the skull and there form small capsules (bullae) associated very closely with the ear. This system may aid in the detection of sound and other vibrations in the water and may be linked to the shoaling behaviour of these fishes.

The herring *Clupea harengus* is the best known member of this family. It is found throughout the North Atlantic, reaching southwards to Cape Hatteras in the west and the Bay of Biscay in the east. There is a distinct population in the White Sea but this is more closely related to the form found in the northern parts of the Pacific. The Atlantic and Pacific forms are recognized as distinct subspecies. The herring has a cylindrical body with the belly rather smooth and the scutes barely forming a keel. Rather rarely it may reach a length of 17 in (43 cm) but usually the adults are about 12 in (30 cm) in length. The herring is a shoaling species that congregates in enormous numbers for feeding or spawning at certain times of the year. It was once assumed that the successive appearance of the herring shoals down European coasts resulted from a gigantic army of these fishes in the Arctic that spread southwards in spring. It is now known, however, that although the herrings undertake some migrations, the shoals in each area are local phenomena and it is the southward spread of the shoaling behaviour and not the southward spread of the fishes that gives the impression of a vast migration.

Off European coasts there is no time of the year when spawning is not taking place. The eggs may be laid some distance from the shore and down to 600 ft (200 m), or close to the shore in bays, brackish water or in the nearly freshwater of the northern Baltic. The coastal herrings spawn mostly in brackish water during spring and early summer, whereas the sea herrings spawn in the open sea chiefly in late summer and autumn but continuing into winter. Off the North American coasts the more northerly fishes spawn in spring while those to the south spawn in summer and autumn. The herring is unique amongst the commercially important bony fishes of European seas in that the eggs are demersal and not floating. They are laid in enormous numbers at the bottom on stones, shells or weeds, either in irregular layers or clusters and are heavily preyed upon by such fishes as cod, whiting and mackerel. A large female may deposit up to 30,000 eggs, which is not a great number compared with the several millions laid by certain of the cod-like fishes but is made up for by the great numbers of fishes in any one shoal. The larvae hatch at the bottom and later migrate to the surface layers where they feed on members of the plankton (diatoms and other single-celled organisms at first, but later small crustaceans).

The herring is the most important of all the pelagic fishes caught off European coasts. The great shoals may be nine miles across and a herring drifter can catch 100,000 fish daily, the daily landings at some of the East Anglian ports in a good year being as much as 20 or 30 million fishes. The fishes are chiefly caught in driftnets, the herrings actively swimming into the meshes of the net. Before the First World War the British catch was about a million tons a year (almost equal to that of all other European nations) and great quantities of pickled herrings were exported to Russia, Germany and other countries. The British fishery has, however, declined somewhat, while the Russians and Germans catch their own herrings. During the Middle Ages, the Baltic herring fishery was of great importance and Rostock and Lübeck and other cities of the Hanseatic League derived enormous wealth from this fishery. In the middle of the 15th century, however, and for no known reason, the Baltic herrings disappeared and for a time the Dutch mainly handled the herring trade until in Stuart times the Royal Navy gained supremacy on the seas and enabled the English fishery to predominate. The fishery has fluctuated, with a good herring brood born every three years between 1915 and 1927 but thereafter there was less regularity, 1930 being in fact a disastrous year. The Swedish hydrographer Professor Otto Pettersson found evidence for a fluctuation over a period of 1,800 years in certain oceanological factors and he related this to the abundance of herring in the Middle Ages—the Hanseatic fishery—and a possible abundance in about 600–400 BC. At the present time no completely satisfactory cause has been found for the fluctuations in the sizes and distribution of the shoals of herring.

The best known herring product is the kipper, first made in 1843 by John Woodger of Newcastle-upon-Tyne. The fish is sliced down the back, gutted and after half an hour soaking in an 80% brine solution is hung in kilns over a hardwood fire (preferably oak chips and sawdust) for six to 18 hours. The herring is an oily fish and thus highly perishable. An early preserving technique was rough salting or rousing, a method perfected in the 14th century by the Dutchman William Beukels. An even older process was that of smoking or redding, the whole fish being salted for about two days, washed and hung in a smoke-house over small wood fires for about six weeks with intervals when the fires were extinguished and the oil allowed to drip from the fishes. Nowadays, Red herrings are roused in a brine solution for one or two weeks and smoked for a week or less and are no longer dark red but more of a golden colour. Bloaters are less heavily cured, being roused for a single night and smoked for only 12 hours. The buckling is cured in the same way but is hot-smoked and thus cooked and ready to eat after curing.

A single member of the genus *Clupea* occurs in the Southern Hemisphere, *Clupea (Strangomera) bentincki* off Chilean coasts. It closely resembles the herring but is of rather little commercial importance.

The family of herring-like fishes includes six subfamilies, all of which contain members of great value to fisheries. The Round herrings (Dussumieriinae) are cylindrical fishes that lack the keel of scutes along the belly. One species *Etrumeus teres* is the third member of the trio that comprise the Iwashi fisheries of Japan. The subfamily to which the herring belongs (Clupeinae) includes many tropical species of small sardine-like fishes that are caught in great quantities in the Indo-Pacific region as well as in the tropical Atlantic. The *shads (Alosinae) have been discussed elsewhere, together with the Gizzard shads (Dorosomatinae), which are closely related to the shads but have a distinct gizzard and an inferior mouth adapted for feeding on bottom-living organisms. The pellonulines (Pellonulinae) are small fishes found chiefly in the fresh waters of West and Central Africa; surface-living species are found in vast numbers in Lakes Tanganyika and Nyasa where they are known as dagaa and support large local fisheries. The pristigasterines (Pristigasterinae) are rather specialized herring-like fishes with projecting lower jaws and long anal fins. In the South American *Pristigaster cayana* the body is deep and highly compressed and resembles that of the freshwater *hatchetfish.

The herring-like fishes are clearly a successful group that have specialized principally in conquering the shallow coastal waters by sheer force of numbers. In temperate waters the number of species is limited but the number of individuals of each species is often enormous (herring, *menhaden, shads). Conversely, there are many more tropical species of lesser abundance but as a whole these are of equal or greater importance to world fisheries although they cannot all be caught by the same fishing device. The herring-like fishes, together with the *anchovies, form the largest commercially important group, comprising a third of the total world production of fish. FAMILY: Clupeidae, ORDER: Clupeiformes, CLASS: Pisces. (Ill. p. 100.)

HILLSTREAM FISHES, species which are adapted to a life in torrential mountain streams. They occur amongst the naked catfishes (e.g. *Astroblepus*) of the Andes and the cyprinids, loaches, suckers and catfishes of Asia, India and the Malayan Archipelago. In many cases only a few members of a particular family have ventured into this turbulent environment, but in the Himalayan region an entire family of loaches, the Homalopteridae, have become adapted to hillstream conditions. The principal problem facing such fishes is to avoid being swept away. Unable to swim for long against the fast currents encountered, the fishes must develop some method of holding their position against the flow of the water. All species live on the bottom and most are rather flattened and have the undersurface very flat. When pressed against rocks there is little danger of the water flowing under them and prising them loose. To supplement this, various methods of attachment have been evolved. In some of the Asiatic catfishes (*Glyptosternum* and *Pseudecheneis*) the lower part of the body bears ridges which appear to act as frictional devices to prevent the fish from slipping backwards. In the more specialized forms an adhesive disc is found. In some cases the pelvic fins have become joined to form a sucker (Homalopteridae), in others the sucker is formed by folds of skin on the chest (some cyprinids), and in others again the lips form the sucker (loaches and suckers). In the latter case the jaws are still free to rasp at the algae covering the rocks. On the whole predators no longer constitute a problem in hillstreams and defensive armour is therefore not necessary. In the loricariid catfishes, for example, the well-armoured lowland forms are replaced by naked forms in the streams of the Andes. Food in hillstreams is almost entirely confined to insect larvae and algae.

Apart from two remarkable species of suckers (family Catostomidae—see carps) which are deep-bodied and have secondarily become adapted to fast streams, the remaining hillstream fishes are small, with squat bodies and large heads. The species adapted to this life are almost entirely confined to the superorder Ostariophysi. European fishes such as the Miller's thumb and the Common trout, which inhabit fairly swiftly moving streams, could never survive in the torrential conditions of the Himalayan or Andean streams where boulders with a diameter of 4 ft (120 cm) are said to be tossed downstream like pebbles, during severe spates.

Some authors restrict the term hillstream-fishes to the single family Homalopteridae. These are flattened loach-like fishes found in Southeast Asian mountain streams and represented by a number of genera. A curious aspect of their biology is the fact that they seem to breathe irregularly. For a time they will respire at the normal rate and then suddenly they will stop breathing completely. During this time, water is stored in the cavities of the throat and gill chamber. The reason for this unusual method of breathing is not known.

In those species which use the pelvic fins to form a sucker, the degree of fusion between the fins varies considerably and this presumably affects the efficiency of the sucker as an adhesive disc. In the Bornean sucker (*Gastromyzon*) the number of rays supporting both the pelvic and the pectoral fins has been enormously increased (over 20 in each fin) and the pelvic fins are fused to form a large and effective sucker. In *Hemimyzon* the fins are smaller and are not fully fused.

One cyprinid fish, *Gyrinocheilus*, is commonly imported into Europe for aquarists, who refer to it as the Aymonieri loach. It is a small loach-like fish from the swift-flowing streams of Southeast Asia. It has a sucking mouth and feeds on algae. Like the homalopterids, it also has a specialized method of breathing, but in this case involving considerable structural adaptations. In most fishes the flow of water over the gills is maintained by the mouth and gill chambers acting as a pair of pumps, slightly out of phase with each other, the water being drawn in through the mouth and expelled through the gill opening. In *Gyrinocheilus* the mouth is not used at all in breathing. The external opening of the gillchamber is divided into two parts. Water enters the upper part through a kind of siphon and then flows via the throat and over the gills to be expelled through the lower half of the gill opening. In this way the mouth can be used entirely for suction purposes.

In the torrent fauna of the Andes, it is the catfishes that form the most important element. The most spectacular of these is the capitane *Astroblepus cotae* which is able to ascend the vertical walls of waterfalls and potholes by alternate use of a sucker formed by the mouth and one formed by the pelvic fins.

Like the deep-sea fishes, the hillstream fishes offer yet another example of the invasion of an inhospitable environment by representatives of a number of families. Similarly, the adaptations that have been evolved to meet these hostile conditions have been repeated in forms which were originally very different. (Ill. p. 98.)

HOGFISH *Lachnolaimus maximus,* a shore fish of the western Atlantic and a member of the wrasse family. It is known as the capitan or Pex perro in the Spanish-speaking parts of the Caribbean. This species has a fairly deep and compressed body and can be easily recognized by the elongation of the first three dorsal rays. In general colour the hogfish is reddish with a dark spot far back at the base of the dorsal fin. Its common name is said to stem from the profile of the head but the resemblance to a hog is not very convincing. These fishes are most abundant in open areas near reefs, especially where gorgonians are present, but are also found less commonly over mud or broad stretches of sand. Hogfishes feed chiefly on molluscs. It is a highly esteemed food fish although on rare occasions it has been implicated in ciguatera poisoning (see poisonous fishes). FAMILY: Labridae, ORDER: Perciformes, CLASS: Pisces. (Ill. p. 99.)

HORNED POUTS, a family of freshwater North American catfishes. Included in this family are the madtoms which have a long adipose fin, sometimes confluent with the tail. Members of this family are found from Canada to Mexico, some species preferring the slow warm waters of the Southern States while others inhabit the cold trout streams of the north.

One of the best known species is the Channel catfish *Ictalurus punctatus*, originally from the St Lawrence basin but now introduced into almost every American state, and at least four of the Hawaiian islands. This fish is generally pale grey with a few distinct dark spots on the sides, although the general colour may vary with the kind of water in which the fish is living. The Channel catfish reaches over 50 lb (22·7 kg) in weight and makes good eating. The results of marking experiments have shown that in spite of their appearance, these are not really sluggish fishes and in one case an individual travelled 46 miles (74 km) in 45 days. These fishes migrate upstream or into the feeder streams of lakes during May and June in search of breeding places in undercut banks or in hollows. The male cleans the site and the female lays 2–3,000 eggs which stick together in a yellow, jelly-like clump. The male then guards the eggs and constantly aerates them until they hatch. Thereafter his duties are those of a sheep-dog, keeping the shoal of young together until they are old enough to fend for themselves. The Channel catfish is fished commercially and artificial rearing is practised to increase stocks.

The Flathead catfish *Pylodictis olivaris* inhabits sluggish waters chiefly in the central and southern parts of the United States. The wide flat head, coupled with the underslung jaw, make this species easily to identify. It occasionally reaches 100 lb (45 kg) in weight.

The largest member of the family is the Blue catfish *Ictalurus furcatus* which ranges from South Dakota and Iowa to Mexico. Superficially it resembles the Channel catfish but it lacks the spots on the flanks and the body is much bluer. In the last century a fish weighing 150 lb (68 kg) was recorded from the Mississippi at St Louis. The record weight by fair angling is 102 lb (46·2 kg), a fish from Kentucky Lake.

The White catfish *I. catus* is found in the east and central parts of the United States but has been introduced into other waters. It grows to only 12 lb (5·4 kg) and unlike the previous species is also found in estuaries. The Brown, Black and Yellow bullheads *I. nebulosus, I. melas* and *I. natalis* rarely exceed 1 ft (30 cm) in length. They are all amenable to life in aquaria and the Brown bullhead has for some time been imported into England as the Cold-water catfish. FAMILY: Ictaluridae, ORDER: Cypriniformes, CLASS: Pisces.

HORN SHARKS,

also known as Bullhead sharks, primitive fishes found in warm and temperate seas throughout the world except in the Atlantic and Meditterrenean. The head is large and rather blunt and there are two dorsal fins, each preceded by a spine; tissue surrounding the spines secretes a venom capable of causing considerable pain. The suspension of the jaws shows an arrangement intermediate between that found in most sharks and that found in the Cow sharks, the upper jaw fitting into a deep groove in the cranium and thus hinting at the condition found in the chimaeras and lungfishes where the upper jaw is completely fused with the head. An equally important, but more easily seen, characteristic of the Horn sharks is the curious arrangement of the teeth, with sharp cutting teeth in the front of the jaws and blunt molar-like teeth towards the edges. This pattern is virtually unique amongst living sharks but is found in the fossil hybodonts of the Jurassic period. The two best known species are the Port Jackson shark *Heterodontus phillippi* and the Pacific Horn shark *H. californicus,* the first from Australia and the second from the Pacific coast of North America. These fishes feed on molluscs and crustaceans and reach about 4 ft (1·2 m) in length. The Horn sharks are oviparous, laying eggs in cases that are decorated with curious spiral flanges quite unlike those of any other group. About ten species of Horn sharks are known. FAMILY: Heterodontidae, ORDER: Pleurotremata, CLASS: Chondrichthyes,

HORSE MACKERELS,

also known as scads, jacks, cavallas and pompanos, are not true mackerels (Scombridae) and are distinguished from them by two small spines before the anal fin and the absence of small finlets behind the dorsal and anal fins. The Horse mackerels are usually fast-swimming fishes, well streamlined, but in some species deep-bodied and compressed. The body has a line of little keeled scutes along part or the entire length of the flanks. They are found in temperate and tropical waters throughout the world.

The common Horse mackerel *Trachurus trachurus* of the Mediterranean and eastern North Atlantic grows to about 14 in (36 cm) and is found as far north as Trondheim in Norway. Similar forms are found off the coasts of South Africa, China, Australia and western America. It has a short first dorsal fin, with the first spine directed forwards, and a long second dorsal fin with soft rays. The back is grey-blue or green, the flanks silvery and there is a dark spot behind the gill opening. It feeds on fishes and invertebrates. The young take shelter in the bell of the Sombrero jellyfish *Cotylrhiza,* probably for protection. The derbio or glaucus *Trachinotus ovatus* is a more southerly fish, rarely entering British waters. It is deeper-bodied than the Horse mackerel, the scutes are absent and the first dorsal fin is reduced to a number of isolated spines. Similar isolated spines are found in the leerfish *Lichia amia,* another species from the southerly parts of the Atlantic. Another member of this family is the Rainbow runner, described elsewhere. Amberjacks of the genus *Seriola* are large sporting fishes that can reach 5 ft (1·5 m) in length and are highly prized by sport fishermen. The Horse mackerels are of great importance to fisheries in many parts of the world.

Among the less typical members of this family are the thread-fin *Alectis ciliaris* with streaming filaments from the rays of the anterior dorsal and anal fins, the lookdown-fish *Selene vomer* with a curious pointed head and the pilotfish which accompanies sharks. FAMILY: Carangidae, ORDER: Perciformes, CLASS: Pisces. (Ill. p. 100.)

HOUNDS,

also known as Smooth hounds or Smooth dogfishes, a family of small sharks externally resembling the Cat sharks but being distinguished by the arrangement of the teeth, which are in the form of a pavement as in the rays. Most sharks have triangular or pointed teeth used for cutting or grasping their prey, but the flat pavement of teeth in the hounds is used for grinding and crushing food found on the bottom (mostly molluscs and crustaceans). They have a world-wide distribution but the best known species of European coasts is the Smooth hound *Mustelus mustelus.* It has a supple, streamlined body with two dorsal fins and one anal fin and grows to 6 ft (1·8 m) in length. It is extremely abundant, as is its counterpart in the western Atlantic the Smooth dogfish *M. canis.* Both are inshore species that frequent shallow waters and mostly browse on the bottom for food. A more colourful member of this family is the Leopard shark *Triakis semifasciata* of the Pacific coasts of North America with a body marked by dark spots along the back and sides. The hounds are viviparous fishes in which the young are not only hatched within the uterus but are nourished through a placenta-like connection between the embryo and the uterine wall of the mother. There are about 30 species known in this family, none of which grow to more than 6 ft (1·8 m) in length. They are a considerable pest to commercial fishermen because of their predation on lobsters, crabs and other fishes. FAMILY: Triakidae, ORDER: Pleurotremata, CLASS: Chondrichthyes.

HOUTING *Coregonus oxyrhinchus,* a salmon-like fish of northern Europe that spends the larger part of its life at sea. It was formerly common in the North Sea, ascending rivers to spawn, but pollution has made the houting rather scarce. It is silvery and has an adipose fin but can be distinguished from its relatives by the pointed snout. It grows to about 16 in (40 cm) in length. FAMILY: Salmonidae, ORDER: Salmoniformes, CLASS: Pisces.

HUCHEN *Salmo hucho,* the migratory salmon of the Danube basin. This species is only slightly smaller than the Atlantic salmon and in their general biology the two are also similar. Pollution has now made the huchen rather rare and some that were introduced into the Thames in the last century did not become established. FAMILY: Salmonidae, ORDER: Salmoniformes, CLASS: Pisces.

HYBRIDIZATION IN FISHES, the natural or artificial crossing of members of different species, genera or even subfamilies. As a general rule, it has been found that where the parents differ noticeably in any particular character, then the hybrid offspring will be intermediate. This has been recorded for colours, numbers of body parts (fin rays, gillrakers, vertebrae, etc.), and the shape and proportions of the body or individual bones. In many cases, hybridization results in progeny that fail to develop properly. Those that do reach adulthood often

Trout hybrid, result of crossing Brown trout *Salmo trutta* and Brook trout *Salvelinus fontinalis*.

show skewed sex ratios, males or females predominating, sometimes to the complete exclusion of the other. This is a most useful attribute in fast-breeding pond fishes since it prevents overpopulation and thus stunted growth. Few reports are available of hybrid fertility, but total infertility has been recorded in trout × char hybrids, in many toothcarp hybrids and in generic crosses between darters (Percidae). Reduced fertility has occurred in crosses between certain salmon-like fishes. Hybrid vigour may be shown by a faster growth rate or greater tolerance to environmental conditions. Hybridization is rare in natural populations but may result when exotic species are introduced. In Lake Erie, carp and goldfish have hybridized; both are introduced fishes that do not cross where their natural ranges overlap in Asia.

Hybridization has been studied in a number of groups of fishes. Amongst the darters, natural and artificial hybrids between species and between genera have been investigated. In the cichlid fishes a number of hybrids have been recorded between species of *Tilapia,* usually in ponds or lakes where an exotic species has been introduced. In the carp-like fishes hybridization is also fairly common and has been achieved artificially between members of different subfamilies.

In nature, barriers to hybridization are numerous and usually effective. Apart from the geographical separation of different species, there is often a separation of spawning grounds or spawning times. If these coincide, then species may be kept apart by various aspects of breeding behaviour, breeding colouration or, in the case of livebearers, by differences in the structure of the gonopodium, or copulatory organ. Even if mating takes place, the sperm head may not match the size of the micropyle of the egg. Occasionally, however, apparent hybridization has been the result of the sperm triggering off development of the egg without actually joining the female gamete. Finally, the crossing of two species may be prevented by an incompatability of the developmental pattern of the embryo. Since the evolution of new species has involved isolating mechanisms capable of perfecting themselves, it is perhaps not surprising that hybridization is both rare and rarely productive.

I-J

ICEFISHES, or bloodlessfishes, antarctic fishes that appear to lack blood. Reports of these bloodless fishes by men back from whaling expeditions were not believed until about 1930 when scientists examined specimens on the spot. They found that the fishes were not, in fact, without blood but that the blood contained no red cells. This was most noticeable in the gills, which were a pale cream instead of the usual red. The common name icefish is preferred to the older name of bloodlessfishes. A number of genera are included in this group (*Chaenocephalus, Chaenodraco, Cryodraco,* etc.) which is placed in the family of antarctic cods. All are slim-bodied fishes, less than 12 in (30 cm) long, and have large heads and mouths. The shape of the head has given rise to another common name, the crocodilefishes.

The red colour of blood is caused by the presence of haemoglobin, a chemical agent capable of uniting with oxygen, transporting it around the body and releasing it where it is required for muscle action, etc. It is difficult at first to see how the icefishes can survive without any oxygen carrier. Their blood is almost colourless and contains only a few white corpuscles. Experiments have shown that the only oxygen in the blood is the very small amount that is dissolved in the blood plasma, the watery fluid that normally carries the red blood cells. In active fishes in warmer waters this would certainly not be sufficient for the normal body requirements. In the icefishes, however, the environment is very stable, with the water only a little above freezing point, and the fishes themselves are rather sluggish in their habits. In addition, there is an unusually large amount of blood in the body. These seem to be the principal factors that enable the icefishes to survive without red blood cells. FAMILY: Nototheniidae, ORDER: Perciformes, CLASS: Pisces.

IDE, a carp-like fish otherwise known as the orfe.

INDOSTOMID FISHES, a highly specialized family of freshwater fishes containing a single genus and species, *Indostomus paradoxus* known from about 50 specimens dis-covered in Lake Indawgyi of the Myitkyina District of Upper Burma. This tiny species, which reaches only $1\frac{1}{4}$ in (30 mm) in length, is covered in bony plates and when it was first discovered in 1926 it was thought to be intermediate between the pipefishes and the sticklebacks, having the bony plates of the former and the spines along the back of the latter.

Recent studies at the British Museum (Natural History) have shown that the relationships of *Indostomus* are far more complex and cannot be properly understood until the anatomy of many other possible relatives has been examined in much more detail. These studies have also shown that *Indostomus* is highly unusual in being able to move its head both sideways and up and down, actions which are normally impossible in fishes since there is no neck. Not much is known of the biology of these fishes, but a fishery officer in Thailand who kept some in an aquarium, noticed their curious habit of jumping when frightened and sticking to the glass sides of the tank above the water line. FAMILY: Indostomidae, ORDER: Gasterosteiformes, CLASS: Pisces.

JACK DEMPSEY *Cichlasoma biocellatum,* a small freshwater fish of the Middle Amazon. It reaches a length 7 in (18 cm). The body has a general background of mottled brown with bright blue spots anteriorly and pale spots towards the tail. In the larger males a curious bulge develops on the forehead. These fishes are often kept by aquarists but are rather unruly and are not recommended for a community tank unless very small. FAMILY: Cichlidae, ORDER: Perciformes, CLASS: Pisces.

JACKS, a name often used in the United States for members of the family Carangidae, here referred to as mackerels. The name jack is also used in England for small specimens of the unrelated pike.

JAMOYTIUS, a fossil fish *Jamoytius kerwoodi* from Silurian deposits near Lesmahagow, in Lanarkshire, Scotland. It has been variously considered to be either the sole representative of an order, the Euphanerida, of naked primitive, rather amphioxus-like vertebrates, or the ammocoete larva of an ostracoderm and an anaspid. Recent work by Dr A. Ritchie, while confirming both its primitive nature and its anaspid relationships has revealed unexpected lamprey-like features.

Jamoytius was elongated, up to 8 in (20 cm) or more in length. Its head was bluntly rounded and scaleless. The eyes were laterally placed and there was probably a circular mouth. The roughly cylindrical trunk was covered with unusual scales, thin and flexible, only about $\frac{1}{32}$ in (2 mm) wide, but apparently extended all the way from the belly to the back. Each was shaped like a V with the apex pointing forwards. They did not overlap but seem to have been separated from each other by a narrow gap. Dr Ritchie suggests they may have been horny, epidermal structures. Their peculiar shape suggests that they coincided with the underlying muscle blocks or myotomes. There were a number of long, low fin-folds: one along the middle of the back and one low on each flank, with a short anal fin. The tail was asymmetrical but it is not certain which was the upper and which the lower lobe. Internally there was a well developed notochord. The mouth was supported by a circular cartilage and in the branchial region on each side lay two longitudinal cartilages linked at regular intervals by seven or eight shorter, vertical cartilages, the whole forming a simple branchial support reminiscent of the branchial basket of modern lampreys.

Jamoytius was probably marine. There have been many and varied speculations as to its mode of feeding but no firm conclusions. CLASS: Pisces.

JAWFISHES, small, rather elongated marine fishes related to the weeverfishes. They derive their name from their very large mouths. Some species have a backward extension of the upper jaw like that found in some of the tropical anchovies. There is a single, long dorsal fin, the first part supported by spiny rays. The most remarkable feature of this otherwise rather undistinguished group is their habit of constructing burrows. The burrows are very elaborate, with a chamber at the end several times larger than the fish itself and lined with pieces of rock and coral. One or two of the species are mouth-brooders. The Yellowhead jawfish *Opisthognathus aurifrons* from the Virgin Islands, which grows to about 4 in (10 cm), has a beautiful blue body, which becomes darker towards the tail and merges into a striking yellow on the head. It builds its burrows in sand and spends much of its time hovering obliquely over the mouth of the burrow eating small animals and larvae that float past.

Jawfishes also live in shallow waters in the Indo-Pacific region. Their burrowing and territorial habits have been studied, but as yet little is known of these fishes and there are very few specimens in collections. FAMILY: Opisthognathidae, ORDER: Perciformes, CLASS: Pisces.

JAWLESS FISHES, primitive fishes now represented solely by the lampreys and the hagfishes. When the first aquatic vertebrates evolved during the Ordovician period of 450 million years ago, they were fish-like in general shape but had poorly formed fins and lacked jaws. The absence of jaws was clearly not a complete disadvantage since two quite successful jawless groups, the lampreys and the hagfishes, have survived to the present day using an effective combination of a sucking mouth and a horny rasping tongue. The evolution of jaws was, however, one of the several major steps that led to the success of the higher fishes.

The jaws in fishes are thought to have evolved from cartilage that supported the gills. In the earliest vertebrates there was a row of perforations opening from the throat to the outside and these perforations were strengthened with rods of cartilage, the gill bars. With the passage of time the first pair of gill bars was lost. The second pair moved forward as the mouth itself developed from a simple tube to an enlarged cavity. Eventually, this second pair of gill bars came to support the sides of the mouth, which had taken over the area previously occupied by the anterior gills. From supporting the sides of the mouth it was a fairly short step to the gill bars actually forming the bones of a jaw. The third pair of gill bars changed their position and served to join the second pair to the head. In modern sharks, the hemibranch or spiracle is the remnant of the gills attached to the third gill bar. This third gill bar later became the hyomandibular, a bone which continued to change both its position and function throughout the long evolution of the vertebrates. In the reptiles it became involved in hearing and in the mammals it is represented by one of the three tiny bones of the middle ear which transmit the vibrations of the eardrum to the inner ear.

The early jawless fishes are now extinct and the modern forms appear to be somewhat degenerate representatives of what was once a flourishing group. The fossil species show considerable diversity and it is not certain whether they were evolved in marine or freshwaters. Characteristically, they had a median or pineal eye on top of the head. This is vestigial in the hagfishes but is well developed in the lampreys and under the microscope can be seen to have a pair of lenses. One lens is larger than the other and there is a possibility that the pineal eye was in fact a paired structure. This third eye is still sensitive to light in the lampreys. Just in front of the pineal eye is the nostril. In embryo lampreys it is in the normal position on the upper lip but during development it moves round to take up a position on top of the head. In the hagfishes the nostril connects with the mouth but in the lampreys the nostril ends blindly in an expanded sac. This sac, the nasopharyngeal pouch, acts as a pump and lies close to the pituitary gland. During the course of evolution various parts of the nostrils and the sac have become involved in the pituitary gland.

JEWFISHES, large sea-perches of tropical seas otherwise known as groupers. The name is inconsistently applied to various members of the family Serranidae but some authors restrict the name jewfishes to species not belonging to the genus *Epinephelus,* the latter being termed groupers. FAMILY: Serranidae, ORDER: Perciformes, CLASS: Pisces.

JOHN DORIES, rather grotesque fishes of temperate oceans related to the boarfish. Their name has an interesting derivation. John appears to be a nickname bestowed on the fish by fishermen. Dory is derived from the French *dorée* or golden, in turn derived from a Latin word meaning gilded, a reference to the shining yellow of the flanks. However, the John dory is also called the St Peter fish because legend has it that it was in this fish that the apostle found the tribute money, the dark blotch on the flank being St Peter's thumbprint. Yet another name given to the fish, by fishermen in northern Germany, is 'King of the herrings' since it is reputed to shepherd the herring shoals. In reality, the John dory is a fish-eater, feeding on herrings, pilchards and sand-eels.

The John dory *Zeus faber* is an almost oval, compressed fish with the rays of the anterior spiny dorsal fin greatly elongated into filaments. The pelvic fins are also long. The jaws are protrusile and can be thrust out a surprisingly long way. This fish is found in moderate depths down to 600 ft (200 m) and it is widely distributed in the Atlantic, occurring as far north as Scandinavia and as far south as South Africa. It reaches 3 ft (100 cm) in length and although its flesh is delicious its grotesque appearance discourages would-be purchasers. Other species of dories are fishes of deeper water which are infrequently caught. FAMILY: Zeidae, ORDER: Zeiformes, CLASS: Pisces. (Ill. p. 98.)

The grunt *Plectorhynchus albovittatus*.

Garpike, freshwater fish of the United States, has scales which fit together as in a mosaic.

Blood-red gills of the bass *Morone labrax* exposed when the operculum or gill-cover is lifted.

Grayling, a European fish highly sensitive to the slightest environmental changes.

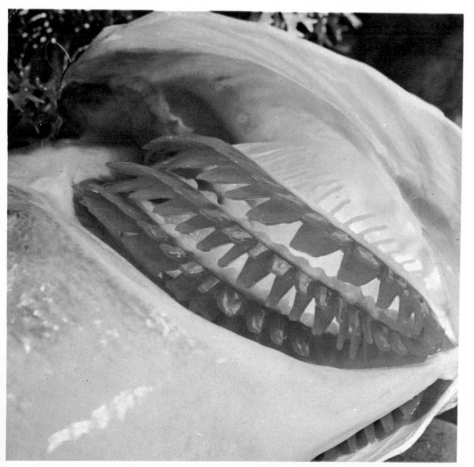

Gudgeon, freshwater fish of Europe, sometimes victim of its own sense of curiosity.

Highly magnified section through the gills of a lamprey showing the numerous filaments.

Head-on view of a John dory.

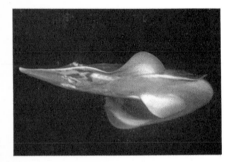

The Californian guitarfish *Rhinobatos productus*.

One of the hillstream-fishes is the Bornean sucker *Gastromyzon*. Its paired fins are joined to form suckers, which are used to cling to the stream bed.

Thick-lipped grey mullet and very young fry.

The hawkfish *Amblycirrhites pinos*.

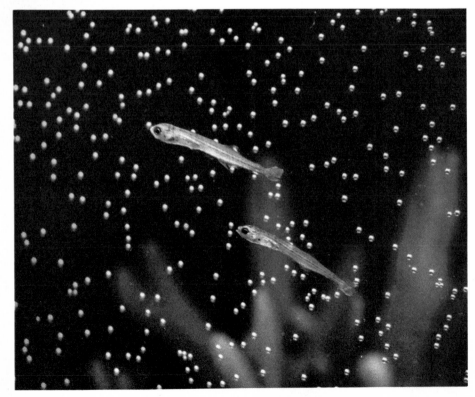

By being transparent the glassfish achieves near invisibility.

The Golden orfe, the counterpart to the goldfish.

A typical goldfish, household pet for the last 2,000 years.

Wild goldfish, progenitor of many fancy varieties.

The hogfish, or Pex perro.

The front rays of the pectoral fins of the gurnard are used to feel for food on the seabed.

A catch of herring, a fish that moulded man's history. No other animal has made so great an impact on the fortunes of Western Europe.

Young of the Common horse mackerel in the Plymouth Aquarium.

One of many colourful varieties of the millionsfish, better known as the guppy, bred by aquarists.

Freshwater half-beak of Thailand, the lower jaw elongated and beak-like, the upper jaw much shorter. Half-beaks are close relatives of the better known flying fishes.

Thick-lipped grey mullet of British waters.

Silver hatchetfishes, freshwater flying fishes, capable of true flight over very short distances.

Harlequinfish under a leaf about to spawn.

Female Rock goby Gobius paganellus of Europe.

Below: Black goby Gobius niger of Europe.

Clown loach.

Bonnet shark, or shovelhead, showing the mouth, the nostrils and one eye.

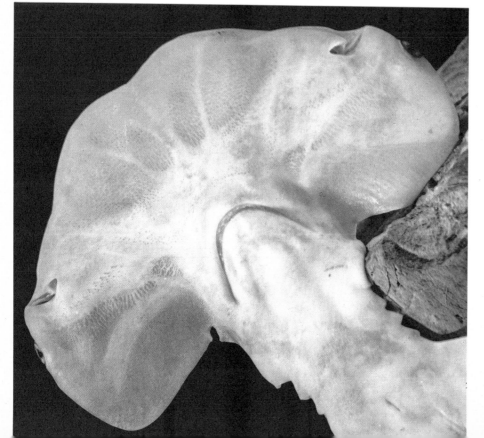

K-L

KNIFEFISHES, three families of South American freshwater fishes related to the Electric eel, family Electrophoridae, the four families being placed as a suborder, Gymnotoidei, of the ostariophysin fishes. The knifefishes have an eel-like body but are in no way related to the eels. There is a very long anal fin and these fishes swim gracefully by passing a series of undulations along the anal fin. The elongated and whip-like tail is in some species used as a probe when the fish is swimming backwards. Often, the tail is bitten off by other fishes, but this does not seem to cause the owner much distress and a new tail is grown. Like the Electric eel, the knifefishes have electric organs along the flanks. Impulses are discharged intermittently at a rate of up to 1,000 per second and this system is used for the location of food or other objects around the fish.

Members of the family Gymnotidae have elongated, compressed bodies with no dorsal, pelvic or tail fins. One well-known species is the Banded knifefish *Gymnotus carapo,* which is often imported for aquarists. The body is light brown with vertical dark bars that coalesce on the back. It reaches 2 ft (60 cm) in length and is peaceful with other species but is liable to attack members of its own. It is best fed on meat and live foods and may eventually take food from the hand of its owner. The Green or Glass knifefish *Eigenmannia virescens* is more ribbon-like than the previous species and the body is semi-transparent with a brown or green tinge to it. Other members of this family are rarely seen in aquarists' shops.

The family Rhamphichthyidae contains one of the largest of knifefishes, *Rhamphichthys rostratus,* a food fish of the Amazon region that reaches 4 ft (1·2 m) in length. Members of this family are similar to the gymnotids but are more elongated and usually have rather long snouts.

In the family Apteronotidae there is a small tail fin and a rather curious filamentous dorsal fin that can be folded into a groove along the middle of the back. *Sternarchus albifrons* has a velvety black body with two off-white vertical bars on the tail

and reaches 18 in (45 cm) in length.

The knifefishes are fairly easy to keep in aquaria provided that plenty of plants are present in which they can hide. Live foods and chopped meat or worms are the best food and all are sensitive to a drop in water temperature below 71·6°F (22°C). FAMILIES: Gymnotidae, Rhamphichthyidae, Apteronotidae, ORDER: Cypriniformes, CLASS: Pisces.

LABYRINTHFISHES, perch-like fishes from the tropical fresh waters of Africa and Southeast Asia. The name refers to an accessory breathing organ, the so-called labyrinth organ, which lies in the upper half of the gill chamber. These are air-breathing fishes, the labyrinth being made up of highly convoluted layers of skin which are richly supplied with blood vessels. Air is taken in through the mouth and forced into the organ where gas exchange takes place, the oxygen diffusing into the blood and the carbon

South American knifefish *Sternopygus macrurus.*

dioxide being eliminated. In many labyrinthfishes the normal breathing by means of the gills is so reduced that if the fish is prevented from reaching the air it will drown. This is clearly an adaptation to adverse conditions in foul streams and in swamps where the oxygen content of the water drops to a very

The labyrinthfish *Ctenopoma ansorgei* from the freshwater of West Africa.

A pair of gouramis 'kissing'.

low figure. Such conditions often arise at the end of the hot season. The labyrinth organ does not develop until the young fishes are some weeks old; presumably the oxygen requirements of the immature fishes can be met by normal exchange at the gills. The evolution of an accessory breathing organ has enabled the labyrinthfish to evolve species like the Climbing perch which can travel overland.

A number of anabantids are now very well known to aquarists (e.g. the fighting-fishes, the gouramis and the leaf-fishes). Most of these fishes are compressed and fairly elongated, but the gouramis have rather deep bodies while the fightingfishes are slender. The anal fin is usually fairly long-based, the first part being spiny, and the dorsal fin may be the same shape or much shorter (e.g. the Lace gourami). Many species have the long feeler-like pelvic fins familiar to aquarists.

There is a strong tendency amongst these fishes for the eggs to be laid in some form of bubble-nest (see separate entry) but in some species, such as the Climbing perch, the eggs float freely in the water.

Apart from the fightingfishes and the Climbing perch, most of the anabantids are reasonably peaceful fishes in aquaria when they are young. Large adults, on the other hand, are liable to become rather fierce and it is best to keep them with fishes of their own size. FAMILY: Anabantidae; ORDER: Perciformes, CLASS: Pisces.

LADYFISHES, rather primitive herring-like fishes found in tropical seas. They are also known as bonefishes because of the large number of tiny bones in their flesh. There are two species, *Albula vulpes* which is widespread in tropical waters and *Dixonina nemoptera* which is found in the West Indies and off the Pacific coasts of Mexico.

These are slightly compressed silvery fishes with the pelvic fins set far back, that is in the primitive position (in the more advanced fishes the pelvic fins approach the pectoral fins and eventually lie beneath them or even in advance). The snout projects beyond the mouth and is used for rooting around the bottom for small invertebrates.

The most surprising thing about these, otherwise rather ordinary-looking fishes, is that the young are totally unlike the adults, being ribbon-like and closely resembling the leptocephalus larvae of eels. This is now considered as strong evidence that the lady-fishes are more closely related to the eels than they are to fishes without this lepto-cephalus larval stage.

The ladyfishes grow to over 3 ft (91 cm)

in length and 20 lb (9 kg) in weight and are considered to be amongst the prime game fishes. FAMILY: Albulidae, ORDER: Elopi-formes, CLASS: Pisces.

LAKE NICARAGUA SHARK, one of the Bull or Cub sharks of the family of Grey sharks, which seems to be equally at home in fresh water and the sea.

LAMPREYS, primitive *jawless fishes found in both fresh water and the sea. The body is eel-like and there is a round, sucking mouth lined with horny teeth with which the lampreys rasp away at their prey. In some parts of England the old name for lamprey is nine-eyes, a reference to the seven external gill openings, the median nostril and the eye. In Britain there are three species of lamprey, the River lamprey *Lampetra fluviatilis*, the Brook or Planer's lamprey *L. planeri* and the Sea lamprey *Petromyzon marinus*, which is found on both sides of the Atlantic. There are ten other species in Europe. Many species of lamprey are parasitic when adult, feeding on the flesh of living fishes. A few fresh water species in North America are non-parasitic and do not feed at all as adults, merely breeding and dying. Lampreys lack paired fins (pectorals and pelvics) but have either one or two dorsal fins and a tailfin.

The gills are contained in muscular pouches which open to the exterior by a series of seven small apertures but are connected internally to a canal which opens in the mouth. The skeleton is of cartilage.

The River lampreys move upstream to breed but the Sea lampreys make a major migration from the sea into fresh waters, using their sucker mouths to ascend rapids and waterfalls. Crude nests are made by both parents, the mouths being used to remove stones to form a hollow of about 2 ft (60 cm) in diameter (*Petromyzon* means 'stone sucker' and *Lampetra* means 'rock licker'). Many thousands of eggs are laid by the female but after they have been fertilized both parents die. From each egg hatches a blind, worm-like larva quite unlike the parents and known as an ammocoete or pride. So different is it from the adult that it was at one time given the scientific name of *Ammocoetes branchialis*. It lacks the sucking mouth of the adult and there is a kind of hood present with structures adapted for filter-feeding. For six, seven or more years the larva lives a burrowing life, blind yet shunning light. At the end of this period a most remarkable metamorphosis occurs, the larva changing into the adult. The eyes appear, the circular sucking mouth develops and part of the former ciliated filter-feeding mechanism becomes associated with the pituitary region of the brain. The Sea lamprey then migrates downstream to the sea where it remains and grows·from 8 in (20 cm) to 3 ft (90 cm). When mature, it makes the return journey to spawn in the rivers. The non-parasitic species become mature almost

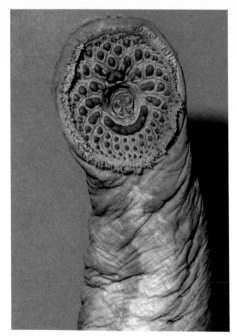

The suctorial mouth of a Sea lamprey.

as soon as they have metamorphosed and thus breed and die without feeding.

The Sea lamprey has wreaked havoc among the fisheries of the American Great Lakes. Originally, they were unknown in all but Lake Ontario. In 1829 the construction of the Welland Canal linked Lake Ontario with Lake Erie but it was not until nearly a century later, when the canal was deepened to accommodate larger ships, that the lampreys began their invasion. The first Sea lamprey was caught in Lake Erie in Nov-

ember, 1921 but apparently this lake was too warm for the lampreys to breed effectively. By 1930, however, the Sea lamprey had reached Lakes Michigan and Huron and had bred most successfully, and by 1946 Lake Superior was reached. The large populations of trout and whitefish seemed to act as an irresistible magnet to the Sea lamprey. In the 1930's some $14\frac{1}{2}$ million lb (6·5 million kg) of trout were taken annually from Lakes Huron, Michigan and Superior. By 1961, less than $\frac{1}{2}$ million lb (0·2 million kg) of these valuable food fishes were caught, mostly from Lake Superior. Commercially at least, the Lake trout of Huron and Michigan were finished and the lampreys now turned avidly to the whitefish. Lampreys rasp a hole in the side of a fish and suck out the blood and body fluids, their saliva containing a chemical that prevents the blood from clotting. Thus, when the lamprey is satiated and drops off the fish, the 'victim' may swim away apparently little harmed but the wound continues to bleed and is thus open to infection. In this way the invasion of the Sea lamprey into the American Great Lakes has cost the country many millions of dollars by ruining a once flourishing fishery. This is a supreme example of the care that should be taken to explore beforehand the possible biological consequences of commercial projects.

Lampreys also occur in the Indo-Pacific region. In Australasia the lamprey *Geotria australis* passes through several phases starting with an ammocoete larva before reaching the adult form. The adult has a large sucker and a pouch behind the eye. This species

The River lamprey, one of the few remaining species of jawless fishes.

ascends rivers to breed. Like European lampreys, the adult and larva are so different that they were at one time considered to be different species. The young stages are beautifully coloured with blues and greens, unlike the brown colours of the adult European lampreys.

Lampreys are now rarely used as food, but in the Middle Ages they were considered to be a great delicacy and the demise of Henry I of England was reputedly caused by a surfeit of lampreys. They are still eaten by the Maoris in New Zealand. FAMILY: Petromyzontidae, ORDER: Cyclostomata, CLASS: Agnatha.

LANCETFISHES, oceanic fishes of moderately deep waters, related to the lanternfishes and the lizardfishes. They have long, thin bodies with large mouths armed with rows of fierce dagger-like teeth. Characteristic of the lancetfishes is the huge, sail-like dorsal fin, behind which is a small adipose fin. They are large fishes, reaching a length of 6 ft (183 cm), and are very voracious, appearing to eat almost anything.

There are two species of lancetfishes. *Alepisaurus ferox* is found in the Atlantic and the closely related *A. borealis* occurs in the Pacific. Off Madeira, *A. ferox* is not infrequently caught by fishermen who have set their long lines for tunas or other species. It was here that the first lancetfish was caught in the early part of the last century. FAMILY: Alepisauridae, ORDER: Salmoniformes, CLASS: Pisces.

LATERAL LINE ORGANS, a system of sensory cells usually embedded in small pits or canals in a line along the side of the body, sometimes centred over the head in fishes and tailed amphibians. These organs probably detect low frequency vibrations in water, such as those made by the movements of another animal (prey, shoaling companion, mate, etc). It is also possible that water movements set up by the fish or amphibian itself may be reflected off distant objects and detected by the lateral line system, the time taken giving an estimate of

the distance. This has been called *Ferntastsinn* or the sense of 'distant touch' and would clearly be of use in dark or turbid waters. Higher frequency vibrations in the water (i.e. sound) are detected by the ears.

In most scaled fishes a series of special scales bearing small pores can be seen running down the length of the body. This is the lateral line series and it provides a useful guide-line for counting the number of scale rows, a feature that often helps to distinguish one species or genus from another. The pores in the scales lead into a small canal in which the actual sense organs lie. The canal is continued over the head, often with branches running above and below the eyes, on the gill cover and along the jaws, sometimes in closed bony canals with pores and sometimes in open channels covered by skin. In some cases the canal is discontinuous and the organs lie in small pits (pit organs). In scaleless fishes the lateral line canals open directly to the surface by small pores.

The individual sensory cells or neuromasts that line the lateral line system are composed of support cells surrounding fine sensory cells, each of which bears small hair-like processes. The 'hairs' are embedded in the base of a long gelatinous rod or cupula that projects above the surface of the skin. Any movements of the liquid in the canal will bend the rod and thus stimulate the sensory hairs which then transmit nerve impulses to the lateral line nerve.

In some deep-sea fishes the lateral line organs are placed on stalks for greater sensitivity, while in others with a greatly elongated tail the canal runs to its tip giving a greater area of receptivity. In sharks and in

The lateral line in this freshwater fish is marked by a row of dark scales.

one bony fish (the Sea catfish *Plotosus anguillaris*) there is, in addition to the normal lateral line system, a series of minute jelly-filled canals on parts of the head, the ampullae of Lorenzini. It is now generally agreed that these are electro-receptors of extraordinary sensitivity. They appear to be able to detect the electrical activity in the muscles of another fish, even if it is lying quietly on the bottom, and they thus provide a very sensitive detector of prey.

LEAF FISHES, a family of tropical freshwater fishes from South America, West Africa and Southeast Asia the members of which, to a greater or lesser degree, resemble floating leaves. The most famous of all is the leaf fish *Monocirrhus polyacanthus* from the Amazon and Rio Negro basins of South America. The body is leaf-shaped and tapers towards the snout where a small barbel increases the camouflage by resembling the stalk of the leaf. The general body colour is a mottled brown, sometimes lighter and sometimes darker, but always matching the dead leaves that subside in the water where the fish lives. It grows to about 4 in (10 cm) and drifts with the current, head usually downwards until it approaches a small fish on which it can feed. The mouth is large and the jaws can be extended to engulf fishes half its own size. It can show a remarkable turn of speed once its prey is within reach.

The African leaf fish *Polycentrus abbreviata* is found in tropical West Africa and a related species *P. schomburgki* occurs in Trinidad and the Guianas. One species from India and Burma, *Badis badis,* shows an extraordinary ability to change colour, often very rapidly, but does not resemble a leaf. FAMILY: Nandidae, ORDER: Perciformes, CLASS: Pisces.

Leaf-fish *Nandus nebulosus* of southeast Asia.

Lionfish.

The colourful and dangerous lionfish.

A black variety of the live-bearing Variegated platy.

LING *Molva molva,* an elongated marine fish of the cod family found in the eastern North Atlantic. The common name is believed to be a corruption of 'long' in reference to its rather long and slender body in comparison with other cod-like fishes. There are two dorsal fins and one anal fin, the scales are small and embedded and there is a barbel on the chin. The general body colour is brownish, sometimes marbled, with the flanks a little lighter and the fins edged with white. The ling is found chiefly over rocks in fairly deep water from 120–300 ft (40–100 m). It occurs from the Bay of Biscay northwards to Scandinavia. It grows to about 6 ft (1·8 m) in length and may weigh up to 70 lb (32 kg). Ling are frequently fished for by trawlers but the mottled brown skin is usually removed before the fishes are placed on sale in shops. It is a most prolific fish, a large female producing up to 50 million eggs.

The Blue or Lesser ling *M. dypterygia* is a smaller species with a similar distribution. The body colour is bluish-brown and it lacks the mottling found in the ling. FAMILY: Gadidae, ORDER: Gadiformes, CLASS: Pisces.

LIONFISH *Pterois volitans,* an extremely colourful and dangerous fish of the tropical Indo-Pacific and a member of the family of scorpionfishes. The body and fins are brilliantly striped in red, reddish brown and white or cream and the pectoral fins and spiny part of the dorsal fin are produced as separate rays, those of the pectorals appearing soft and feathery. When danger threatens, the lionfish will erect the fins and it is then a magnificent sight. Its beautiful appearance, however, is deceptive since the spines are armed with poison glands and the fish has been known actually to attack by jabbing with its dorsal spines. The poison is strong and causes great pain to humans although no fatalities have been recorded. The bright colours of this fish serve as a warning to other species. It should be noted, also, that the poison is still effective when the fish is dead, so that even preserved specimens must be handled with care.

In the United States this species is known as the turkeyfish, a reference to its appearance when the colourful pectoral fins are erected. FAMILY: Scorpaenidae, ORDER: Scorpaeniformes, CLASS: Pisces.

LIVE-BEARING FISHES, viviparous species in which the eggs are fertilized and hatch internally. This involves an act of copulation and some structure by which the sperm can be transferred to the female. In sharks and rays the copulatory organs in the male are modified appendages from the pelvic fins, known as claspers or mixopterygia. They are capable of erection and the sperm is pumped along a groove towards the tip, the latter often bearing horny spines which both engage in the cloaca of the female and also may serve to rupture a membrane analogous to a hymen. In some rays and sawfishes the claspers are too far apart to be introduced simultaneously. In the bony fishes it is usually the anal fin that has become modified for the transference of sperm. In the viviparous toothcarps the anterior rays of the anal fin are greatly modified into small hooks and projections, the particular form being characteristic of the species. The organ is known as an intromittent organ or gonopodium.

Once the eggs are fertilized they may remain in the ovary and derive their nourishment from the yolk after hatching but before birth. This is termed ovoviviparity. A modification of this is the nourishment of the hatched larvae by means of secretions from the walls of the ovary, as in the Viviparous blenny. In that species the young hatch within about 20 days but are not born for another four months. A similar situation is found in the Surf perches, in which the males are born sexually mature. In the cartilaginous fishes, however, there are forms of connection between the walls of the uterus and the developing embryos leading in the most specialized cases to a form of placenta such as is found in mammals. This is sometimes termed placental viviparity. This type of development was first suspected by the great 17th century Danish anatomist Nicholas Steno. Placental viviparity is found, for example, in the Smooth hound *Mustelus canis*, as well as in the Grey sharks and the Hammerhead sharks. In rays of the genus *Pteroplatea* long processes develop from the walls of the uterus which enter the spiracle of the developing embryo and supply nourishment.

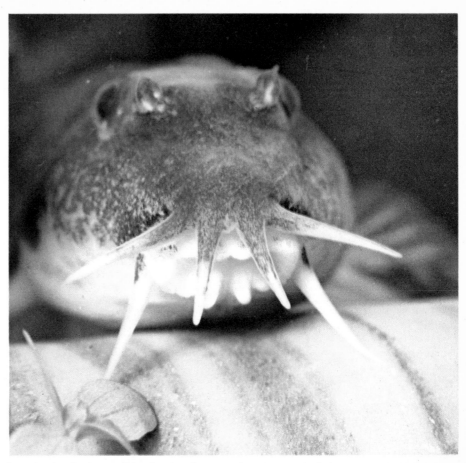

Stone loach, a freshwater fish related to the carps, showing its six barbels.

Amongst the sharks, the Port Jackson sharks and the Whale shark are egg-layers, as also are most of the Carpet sharks but the latter group appears to be transitional. In the Cat sharks (Scyliorhinidae), *Galeus melastomus* lays eggs, whereas the closely related *G. polli* gives birth to live young. In the bony fishes, viviparous species are most common in the toothcarps, that is guppies, swordtails, mollies and platys. The females often have a dark blotch in front of the anal fin during pregnancy. These fishes are ovoviviparous, but in the Four-eyed fish *Anableps tetrophthalmus* a pseudoplacenta is developed for the nourishment of the young.

Like mouthbrooding, that is the incubation of the young in the mouth, viviparity serves to protect the young from predators during the early critical stages. It probably arose through the retention of eggs by the female and the evolution of various methods for nourishing the young. The prior evolution of internal fertilization is more difficult to explain.

LOACHES, fishes related to the carps and living in freshwaters of Asia and Europe, with a few species found in Africa but confined to Ethiopia and Morocco. Loaches are elongated and compressed bottom-living fishes, many being nocturnal in habit. Most species have barbels round the mouth and the dorsal and anal fins are usually short and placed in the rear half of the body. There is no adipose fin and the pelvic fins lie at about the midpoint of the body. They differ from the carp-like fishes (cyprinids) in having the swimbladder reduced and encased, either

One of the best known live-bearing fishes, the Variegated platy *Xiphophorus variatus*.

partially or totally, in bone. Some species of loach use their intestine as an accessory breathing organ.

There are only two species of loach native to England, the Stone loach *Noemachilus barbatulus* and the Spined loach *Cobitis taenia*. The Stone loach is common in most clear brooks and it has a very wide distribution, being found all over Europe and eastwards to China and Japan. It hides in cracks or under stones during the day, coming out to feed at night. Although it only grows to 5 in (13 cm) it makes excellent eating. In bygone days, loaches were caught with small three-pronged spears, as readers of *Lorna Doone* will recall. The Spined loach derives its common name from the presence of a small spine below the eye. Its range also extends across Asia to China, but in England it is much rarer than the Stone loach. Reaching about 4 in (10 cm) in length, it has a light pattern of horizontal rows of spots along the flanks. It is not considered to be edible.

A most interesting European loach is the weatherfish *Misgurnus fossilis*. It has earned its common name from its habit of becoming highly agitated when the atmospheric pressure rises, as for example before a thunderstorm. Under these conditions the fishes constantly come to the surface. This unusual behaviour arises from the great sensitivity of the bone-encased swimbladder. This has a canal filled with a gelatinous substance which passes through the swimbladder capsule and reaches the skin near the pectoral fins. In this way, pressure changes are transmitted to the swimbladder and thence to the Weberian apparatus (see hearing in fishes) and thus to the inner ear. Weatherfishes were formerly kept by country people in tanks as

weather guides. Compared with other loaches, this species is fairly large, reaching 20 in (51 cm) in Europe and Asia.

In colour, the European loaches are not very spectacular but the Southeast Asian genus *Botia* contains several rather pretty species which are kept by aquarists. These fishes are deeper and more compressed than their European relatives. The Clown loach *Botia macracanthus* (Ill. p. 102) reaches 12 in (30 cm) in the wild but remains fairly small in aquaria. The body is a beautiful red-orange, with three vertical wedges of black on the flanks; all the fins are deep red. These are shoaling fishes and while one specimen may tend to hide away a number of them in an aquarium will swim actively. The Coolie loaches of the genus *Acanthophthalmus* from Southeast Asia are active, worm-like fishes. They have salmon-pink to yellow bodies with brown vertical bars or saddle-shaped markings. The extent of the brown markings is characteristic for each species. Rarely growing to more than 4 in (10 cm), they have been aptly described as 'vigorous and rather droll worms'.

Loaches are fairly easy to keep in aquaria. Live food and plenty of shade should be provided and many species will be found to be more active in the daytime than some of the catfishes. FAMILY: Cobitidae, ORDER: Cypriniformes, CLASS: Pisces.

LOUVAR *Luvarus imperialis*, a large pelagic orange and red fish related to the mackerels and tunas. It is common in the Mediterranean and the warmer waters of the Atlantic, and will occasionally stray as far north as the British Isles. The body is powerful, tapering evenly from the rather blunt head to the tail. The pectoral fins are sickle-shaped and the

pelvic fins are minute. The dorsal and anal fins are long and low and are set far back on the body, each consisting of about 12 strong spines connected by a membrane. The caudal fin is deeply forked as in most strong oceanic swimmers. In spite of all this, however, the fish is in fact rather fragile since the skeleton is composed of cartilage and the body is liable to tear under any undue external strain. The small mouth is adapted for feeding on jellyfishes. To obtain the maximum nourishment from these, the intestine is very long and the stomach is lined with numerous internal projections which serve to increase the absorbent surface area.

The louvar is easily identified by its colour. The fins are scarlet and the body is a metallic orange fading to yellow on the belly. Dead fishes, however, tend to turn an indifferent silver. The louvar grows to about 6 ft (180 cm) in length and may weigh as much as 300 lb (136 kg). FAMILY: Luvaridae, ORDER: Perciformes, CLASS: Pisces.

LUMINOUS ORGANS or light organs, specialized structures for the production of 'living light' are found in many different groups of animals. Luminous fishes are found chiefly in the deeper parts of the oceans although a few shore-living forms are also known (*Anomalops keptotron* and *Photoblepharon palpbratus*, both of the Indo-Malayan Archipelago, are perhaps the best known). In the middle regions of the oceans, in the twilight zone where sunlight ceases to penetrate at about 2,000 ft (610 m), about $\frac{2}{4}$ of the 1,000 known species have light organs. These are the bathypelagic species and it is estimated that 80% of the individuals in this zone are luminescent. Light appears to be less important to bottom-living forms and is only found in the rat-tails (Macrouridae) and the Deep-sea cods (Moridae).

The simplest luminous organs are sacs containing luminous bacteria, as in the rat-tails and Deep-sea cods. The light can be 'turned off' by preventing the flow of blood to the sac and thus cutting off the supply of oxygen to the bacteria. It has been suggested that bacteria originally living on the sea floor and in an oxygen-free environment were faced with the problem of getting rid of oxygen once it had permeated the oceans as a result of the evolution of green plants. Their 'solution' was to convert it to water by combination with hydrogen, a reaction from which enough energy is released to excite organic molecules to emit light. Bottom-living fishes must then have evolved methods of using this light.

In most luminous fishes the light is produced by glandular cells in which a chemical reaction occurs leading to the breakdown of luciferin by the enzyme luciferase. Such organs are under the control of the nervous system.

A loach *Botia hymenophysa*, very similar to the Tiger botia or Clown loach, both of southeast Asia.

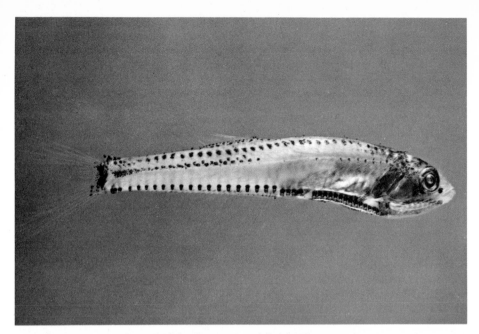

Rows of light organs on the anglerfishes *Bonapartia* and (below) *Ceratias*.

The more advanced light organs may consist of a simple cup backed by a black pigment layer, but in many species a type of lens overlies the cup. There may also be a silvery reflector behind the light, and a plain or coloured diaphragm may adjust the intensity or colour of the light emitted. The light may be white, yellowish, green to blue or reddish and it may merely glow or it may provide sufficient light for the animal to see its immediate surroundings. The light organs or photophores are often in lines, usually on the lower part of the body, and the pattern of lines is characteristic for each species or genus. This suggests that one function of the photophores is to provide identification of the owner. Another function may possibly be to indicate the physiological state of the owner (ready to breed, feed or fight etc.). Those fishes with only a luminous barbel under the chin (members of the Stomiatidae, Melanostomiatidae etc.) and those with a luminous tip to the first or second dorsal ray (viperfish, anglerfishes) use this small light as a lure to entice other fishes near enough to be snapped up. Rat-tails have a long gland near the anus which exudes a luminous slime, an indication perhaps of the way in which luminous organs first arose. In members of the family Alepocephalidae there is a small sac behind the gill cover which can shoot out a stream of glowing sparks. This probably confuses a predator.

Actual observations on luminous fishes at depth have been few and much more work is required before their true biological significance is fully understood.

LUMPSUCKER *Cyclopterus lumpus,* one of the Mail-cheeked fishes, deriving its name from the warty lumps on its body and the presence of a ventral sucker. It is a bulky and ungainly looking fish that is commonly found stranded in rock pools around British and European coasts, especially in spring when it comes into shallow waters to breed. It is also found on the western side of the Atlantic.

The lumpsucker grows to a maximum of 2 ft (60 cm) in length but specimens over 18 in (46 cm) are very rare. The body is rounded and rather flaccid with warty tubercles, the largest arranged in three distinct rows down the flanks. A median soft crest is present in front of the small dorsal fin, the latter set far back and opposite the anal fin. The pectoral fins are large and extend under the head. The pelvic fins are greatly reduced and contribute to the sucker which is formed on the chest. During the breeding season, the time when these fish are most often encountered, the male and female differ somewhat in colour. The male has a dark, almost black back and a red belly, while the female is brown on the back and has a yellow belly. In summer the stomachs of lumpsuckers seem to contain little else but water and as yet there is no

Young lumpsucker in an aquarium.

satisfactory explanation for this.

The lumpsucker has unusual breeding habits. The females produce a very large number of eggs (up to 100,000) and these are laid in a loose ball with gaps between the eggs so that water can percolate through the mass. The eggs are laid just above the low water mark and they are guarded by the male, even though the eggs may be exposed at low tide. The males guard the egg mass. FAMILY: Cyclopteridae, ORDER: Scorpaeniformes, CLASS: Pisces.

LUNGFISHES, primitive bony fishes that were world-wide in their distribution in Devonian and Triassic times but are now restricted to South America, Africa and Australia. They are characterized by the presence of one lung or a pair which are used for breathing air. The early appearance of the lungfishes in the fossil record, and the remarkable survival of a few forms down to the present day, have been commented upon in the article devoted to fishes, fossil. The early lungfishes had large bony scales and the fins were carried on lobe-like bases. Species of *Dipterus* from the Devonian rocks of Scotland, grew to about 2 ft (60 cm) and the median fins were placed far back on the body, suggesting a lurking, predatory life. Two dorsal fins were present and the tail was shark-like (heterocercal), but during the course of the evolution of the group a single continuous median fin gradually appears and the tail becomes reduced and finally lost, being replaced by the union of the upper and lower halves of the median fin. The modern lungfishes have, to varying degrees, retained the primitive form.

The lungfish of Australia, the Burnett salmon *Neoceratodus forsteri,* is confined to a few rivers in Queensland and is both the rarest of the modern lungfishes and the one that has changed least with the passage of time, at least in outward appearance. Large scales are present on the body, the paired fins still retain their fleshy, lobe-like bases, but the dorsal and anal fins form a continuous fin round the hind end of the body. The name 'lungfish' for this species is not entirely apt since in well oxygenated water this species uses its gills for breathing.

The South American lungfish *Lepidosiren paradoxa* and the African lungfishes *Protopterus* spp. are more elongated fishes and share a number of common features. A median fin-fold surrounds the hind end of the body, but the paired pectoral and pelvic fins are reduced to thin fleshy 'feelers' and are filamentous in the African species. In the South American species the pelvic fins grow branching vascular filaments in the breeding season, but the function of these is not known. In both the African and the South American forms the lung is a paired structure lying below the oesophagus (as in man) and these fishes rely to a considerable extent on air breathing. They are thus well equipped to survive in foul conditions and both genera can aestivate in the dry season, the South American species making mud tunnels and the African species forming a hard cocoon in the mud.

These fishes also care for their eggs. Nests have been described for the African lungfish *Protopterus aethiopicus* and *P. annectens.* In some cases these nests comprise holes in the matted roots of the papyrus about 2 ft (60 cm) in diameter and a little deeper, with either a surface entrance or a tunnel. Up to 5,000 eggs are laid in the nest and the young may remain in it for as long as eight weeks.

The South American lungfish was originally caught in various places in the Amazon basin but little is known of its numbers. A recent expedition spent three fruitless months searching foul pools for this species and was about to give up when a local man suggested that a particular sewer serving a nearby city be tried; to their surprise, they caught about 12 specimens almost immediately.

The African lungfishes are widespread and much more common, in certain areas providing a useful source of food. The most elongated of the African species is *P. dolloi,* a species from the Congo basin that reaches 33 in (85 cm) in length. A rather similar West African species is *P. annectens,* which has a deeper body. The most widespread is *P. aethiopicus,* found from the eastern Sudan to Lake Tanganyika and reaching a length of 6 ft (1·8 m). Finally, *P. amphibius* is found in Lake Rudolf and the eastern part of Africa. The African lungfishes are found chiefly in marshy areas but *P. aethiopicus* is essentially a lake-dweller; nevertheless it regularly rises to the surface to breathe air. In spite of their appearance of sluggishness, these fishes are surprisingly aggressive carnivores and large specimens are treated with great respect by local fishermen.

The lungfishes are of considerable interest to students of evolution because of their retention of such primitive features as a spiral valve in the intestine and the persistence into the adult of the notochord or primitive cartilaginous rod that in other bony fishes is reduced out of recognition by the developing bony elements of the vertebral column. Thus the modern lungfishes provide a possible clue to the soft structures of those species known only from fossils. FAMILIES: Ceratodontidae, Lepidosirenidae, ORDER: Dipnoi, CLASS: Pisces.

African lungfish *Protopterus* distinguished by its long and slender pectoral fins.

M

MACKERELS, small members of the family that includes the bonitos and tuna fishes, beautifully streamlined fish with pointed jaws and a body tapering to the slender base of the forked tail. The best known and economically the most important are members of the genus *Scomber*. The Common mackerel *S. scombrus* has two dorsal fins well separated from each other and a series of small finlets behind both the dorsal and anal fins. The back is dark green-blue with dark wavy lines on the upper part of the flanks and the undersurface is pearly white shot with rosy tints. It occasionally reaches 6 lb (2·7 kg) and is found on both sides of the North Atlantic, ranging from the Mediterranean to Ireland on the European side. The mackerel is a pelagic fish forming enormous shoals at the surface near coasts in summer and feeding on small crustaceans and other planktonic animals (fish and fish larvae). In winter the shoals disband and move into deeper water where they remain in a state approaching that of hibernation. Off the Atlantic coasts of North America huge fisheries exist for the mackerel and shoals that are 20 miles long and ½ mile broad (32 km by 0·8 km) have been seen, representing a million barrels of fish. Spawning takes place in coastal waters, large females laying about half a million minute eggs each.

The Spanish mackerel *S. colias* is a more southerly species found on both sides of the Atlantic and in the Mediterranean. It differs from the Common mackerel in having rather faint bars on the body but a series of dark spots or blotches on the lower flanks. In addition, there is a series of enlarged scales in the region of the pectoral fins forming a corselet similar to that of the tunny. A swimbladder, absent in the Common mackerel, is present in this fish. It is a member of the so-called Club mackerels, related species of which are found off coasts of all temperate regions.

The name Spanish mackerel is also given to members of the genus *Scomberomorus*. An American Atlantic species, *S. maculatus*, grows to 12 lb (5·5 kg) and is very beautifully coloured in greens and blues with black spots on the flanks and golden hues underneath. It is valued both as a food fish and for its sporting qualities. The related Monterey Spanish mackerel *S. concolor* was first seen in the Bay of Monterey in the autumn of 1879 and 1880, where it was caught in very large numbers. The species then vanished and has not been found since. The largest of the American Atlantic species is the kingfish or cavalla *S. cavalla*, a dark-coloured fish without spots which grows to a length of 5 ft (1·5 m) and a weight of 100 lb (45 kg). The Indo-Pacific *S. commerson*, named after the naturalist Philibert Commerson who accompanied Bougainville round the world, is another large species of commercial importance.

Related to the mackerels and Spanish mackerels are the species of *Cybium*. The seer *C. commersonii* of India grows to 4 ft (1·2 m) and is a greatly esteemed food fish in that country. In Hawaii and Japan the guaha *Acanthocybium solandri*, named after the naturalist Daniel Solander who accompanied Captain Cook to the Pacific, is a large species that reaches 6 ft (1·8 m) in length and has large and knife-like teeth serrated at the edges. A related form is found in the Atlantic.

The name mackerel is applied to some of the smaller tuna fishes in various parts of the world. The Frigate mackerel *Auxis thazard*, often known as the Plain bonito, is an Atlantic species for which there are a few British records. The remaining members of the family Scombridae have the first dorsal fin long, extending back to meet the soft-rayed second dorsal fin. This group contains the bonitos and the tuna fishes. FAMILY: Scombridae, ORDER: Perciformes, CLASS: Pisces.

MADTOMS, North American catfishes of the Horned pout family but distinguished from other members by the long adipose fin and rounded tail, the two being joined in such species as the Tadpole madtom *Noturus gyrinus*. In all madtoms there is a poison gland at the base of the pectoral fin spines so that these rather small fishes are dangerous to handle (possibly the name madtom is in some way connected with their venomous properties). There are a number of species, including some that are blind cave-dwelling forms. The stonecat *N. flavus* reaches 8 in (20 cm) in length and occurs in a large part of North America in fast-flowing brooks and streams, where it lurks under stones. The Tadpole madtom, which only

Beautifully streamlined Common mackerel with pointed jaws and forked tails.

reaches 4 in (10 cm) in length prefers muddy waters. FAMILY: Ictaluridae, ORDER: Cypriniformes, CLASS: Pisces.

MAHSEERS, large carp-like fishes of the genus *Barbus* from Indian freshwaters. The mahseers are considered to be amongst the greatest of the freshwater sporting fishes, reaching at least 6 ft (1·8 m) in length (some authors give 9 ft or 2·7 m). They are found in the rivers of the foothills of the Himalayas and northern India. Some species have relatively few scales along the body but these are correspondingly larger and may be the size of the palm of a hand. A number of species has been described but the large size of the adults, and therefore the difficulty of preserving them, has meant that relatively few specimens have been available for detailed study. The larger species of *Barbus* in Africa are sometimes referred to as mahseers although they never reach the enormous size of their Indian relatives, rarely exceeding 40 lb (18 kg) in weight.

MALAYAN ANGEL *Monodactylus argenteus,* a brackish water Indo-Pacific fish with a strong resemblance to the true angelfishes (species of *Pterophyllum* of the family Cichlidae) but placed in a quite separate family. It is also known as the fingerfish and there are three or four other species placed in the same genus. The Malayan angel has a deep body covered with very small silvery scales and the fins are long. It grows to about 10 in (26 cm) and is a popular aquarium fish because of its elegant shape and subtle colours. It can survive in freshwater but does best in salty water. FAMILY: Monodactylidae, ORDER: Perciformes, CLASS: Pisces.

MARLINS, large tropical oceanic fishes related to the sailfish and the swordfish and included under the general heading of billfishes. The bony snout is often as long as, or longer than, that in the sailfish but does not reach the length of the 'sword' in the swordfish. Great strength is given to the vertebral column, especially in the tail region, by overlapping processes on the vertebrae.

The Black marlin *Istiompax marlina* is variously referred to as the Silver or White marlin. It is characterized by its pectoral fins which cannot be folded back against the body (true of the sharks also). It is widespread in the tropical Indo-Pacific area and grows to 11½ ft (3·5 m) and can weigh up to half a ton (500 kg). The Blue marlin *Makaira ampla* of the Pacific, also known sometimes as the Black marlin, grows to 1,400 lb (630 kg) and often has stripes on the body which causes some confusion with the Striped marlin *M. audax.* The Blue marlin is of great commercial importance and is caught on long-lines off Pacific islands. The Striped marlin of the Pacific is a

The Pacific Striped marlin leaping clear of the water off Tocopilla, Chile. The bony snout is long though it does not reach the length of the 'sword' in swordfishes.

solidly built fish with definite vertical stripes on the body. It grows to 500 lb (225 kg).

The usually impressive snout in the billfishes would appear to be an effective weapon for attack and defence but the evident streamlining elsewhere on the body and the high speeds that these fishes attain suggest that the evolution of this long snout may have been determined chiefly by the hydrodynamics of fast swimming. FAMILY: Scombridae, ORDER: Perciformes, CLASS: Pisces.

MENHADEN *Brevoortia tyrannus* (and related species), herring-like fishes related to the *shads and found in enormous shoals along the coasts of the western Atlantic. The menhaden has a fairly deep and compressed body that is armed with sharp serrations (scutes) along the belly, a single soft-rayed dorsal and anal fin, and a series of dark spots on the flanks beginning just behind the gill opening. As in the shads, there is a series of radiating bony striations on the gill cover, but the menhaden can be immediately distinguished by a characteristic double row of ridge-like scales along the back from the head to the base of the dorsal fin. The several species of menhaden are found from Nova Scotia to Bahia Blanca in Argentina, but are absent from the tropical shores of America and the West Indies. As in the herring, there appear to be distinct populations, at least in

B. tyrannus, along the North American coast. The northern fishes are larger, fatter, and yield more oil than those of the south, and they spawn in summer whereas their southern relatives spawn in late autumn or in winter.

The size of the menhaden shoals is enormous, to judge from the great catches made along North American coasts. In 1956 and 1959, the catches from the Gulf and Atlantic coasts of the United States totalled 2,000 million lb (900 million kg). This is the only North American fishery to yield such a catch and it is rivalled only by the even greater catches of anchovies off the coasts of Peru and Chile. Great fluctuations occur and periods of abundance are followed by several lean years, although this does not necessarily affect the entire fishery. Only a very small part of this huge catch is used as food for man, the bulk of it being devoted to the manufacture of oil and fish meal or sold as fish scraps. FAMILY: Clupeidae, ORDER: Clupeiformes, CLASS: Pisces.

MILKFISH *Chanos chanos,* a silvery fish somewhat resembling a herring, found in saltwater and estuaries throughout the tropical and subtropical Indo-Pacific region but not in the Atlantic. The milkfish has a compressed body with small, silvery scales and a large forked tail. FAMILY: Chanidae, ORDER: Gonorhynchiformes, CLASS: Pisces.

MILLER'S THUMB *Cottus gobio,* also known as bullhead, a rather grotesque freshwater fish found in clear, fast-running and shallow streams in Europe. The head is broad and flat, the body round and lacking scales except along the lateral line. The pectoral fins are large. The colour varies to accord with the bottom on which the fish rests. It spends most of its time under stones, only darting out to catch a passing fish or insect larva. The eggs are guarded by the male which will display by expanding its gill covers to an intruder. Its common name derives from the shape of a miller's thumb which, used in testing flour by rubbing it between the thumb and forefinger, often became rather spatulate.

The Alpine bullhead *C. poecilopsis* is found in northern and central Europe and can be distinguished from the Miller's thumb by its long and narrow pelvic fins which reach as far as the vent. FAMILY: Cottidae, ORDER: Scorpaeniformes, CLASS: Pisces.

MINNOW, AMERICAN, a general term used in the United States for small carp-like fishes belonging to over 40 genera. The term is not used with any precision and many of the species referred to as 'minnow' have such alternative names as dace, chub and shiner, none of which is used in the same sense as it is in Britain. Only a few of the very many species known as 'minnows' can be mentioned here.

The genus *Notropis* includes the Common shiner *Notropis cornutus,* a species which grows to about 9 in (23 cm) and was once abundant in the New York area. It is now very rare there but is still found in other places on the eastern side of the continent. The scales are high and narrow and rather large in proportion to the size of the fish. The ground colour is olive on the back with silvery sides and belly and a mottling of dark patches on some scales. Although too small to be of much interest to the adult angler, generations of young fishermen must have cut their teeth on this fish. Its range, however, is becoming more and more restricted.

The Golden shiner *Notemigonus crysoleucas,* to which many other common names have been applied, has a wide range, occurring from Nova Scotia to Manitoba and northern Ontario southwards to the Gulf. It lacks the small barbels present in the Common shiner and has a fleshy, scaleless keel between the pelvic fins and the long anal fin. At spawning time the dark brown to olive-green body becomes suffused with a gold. This species reaches about 9 in (23 cm) in length and lives in weedy areas in large rivers and ponds.

Most of the American minnows are small fishes but some can reach a weight of 3 lb (1·5 kg). The fallfish *Semotilus corporalis* normally grows to just over 12 in (30 cm) in

rivers but is very much larger in lakes and a fish of 3 lb (1·5 kg) is not rare. Its common name was bestowed on it because it is often found at the foot of waterfalls, although it seems to be equally at home in the still waters of deep lakes. Fallfish are nest-builders. In spring the male digs a nest in the bottom of the river and when the eggs have been deposited he covers them up with stones heaped in a mound (the stones are often surprisingly large). A close relative of the fallfish is the Creek chub or Horned dace *S. atromaculatus,* a nest-building species found only in streams, but in this case the male makes several smaller nests.

The squawfishes are the largest of the minnows. There are four species in the United States of which the largest, the Colorado squawfish *Ptychocheilus lucius,* is now threatened with extinction; poisonous chemicals killed off the largest population of these fishes in 1962. The Umpqua squawfish *P. umpquae* is found only in the Umpqua River in Oregon. The Northern squawfish *P. oregonensis* occurs from British Columbia across to the Washington, Idaho and Montana tributaries of the Columbia River. The maximum size of the squawfishes is debatable. In the early part of this century fishes of 4 ft (120 cm) were reported, but recently few have been caught more than 2 ft (60 cm) long.

More typical of the minnows are the species which reach only 2–3 in (5–8 cm), such as the various American species of dace. The Black-nose dace *Rhinichthys atratulus* lives in clear streams from Nova Scotia to North Dakota and has the typical 'minnow' colouring of a silvery body with olive mottlings. There are a great number of similar species the identification of which is baffling to all except the experts.

Although the minnows have no economic importance they fulfil an important role in the general ecology of streams, rivers and

lakes and are often the first wild fishes that we encounter in youth. It is sad, therefore, to note that with other American fishes the minnows are in many areas becoming depleted, in numbers of individuals, in numbers of species and in their range. In the last century many species ranged over hundreds of miles and all small streams had thriving populations. Streams are now polluted with chemicals or dried up under drainage schemes and certain species are reduced to areas remote from centres of population. An American ichthyologist, Dr R. R. Miller, has produced details of the distribution and numbers of some species showing that fishes such as the Moapa dace *Moapa coriacea* have been reduced to possibly as few as 500 individuals. FAMILY: Cyprinidae, ORDER: Cypriniformes, CLASS: Pisces.

MINNOW, EUROPEAN *Phoxinus phoxinus,* a small and slim carp-like fish from the freshwaters of Europe and Asia. The body is typical of the slender carp-like fishes (bleak, dace, etc.). The back is olive or grey with dark spots and the flanks silvery with dark vertical streaks in some fishes and a bright golden band running from behind the eye. The belly is yellow or white, sometimes scarlet. The scales are tiny, almost invisible to the naked eye. Minnows grow to 6 in (15 cm) and live in rivers and streams with sand or gravel bottoms. They are found in large shoals, especially at spawning time in April to June. In spite of their preference for clear and highly oxygenated water, minnows can adapt well to aquarium conditions. FAMILY: Cyprinidae, ORDER: Cypriniformes, CLASS: Pisces.

MOLLIES, small freshwater species of the genus *Mollienesia,* from the northwestern parts of South America, members of the live-bearing group of toothcarps. Mollies are amongst the commonest fishes kept by

European Common minnow, in catching it small boys get their first lesson in angling.

aquarists and their colours have been altered by selective breeding. In the wild, *M. sphenops* has a ground colour of olive, but by careful breeding a black variety has been produced. In some European countries this has been referred to as the Black molly, but in other countries the name Black molly has been given to the black variety of *M. latipinna*. The latter should, in a good strain, have a large dorsal fin but this character has often been eliminated by careless breeding.

Amongst the mollies are species in which only females are found. Professor Carl Hubbs and his wife made this surprising discovery while examining specimens of the Amazon molly *M. formosa*. It appeared that the development of the eggs could be triggered off by males of other species without their sperm making any direct contribution to the genetic make-up of the offspring. FAMILY: Poeciliidae, ORDER: Atheriniformes, CLASS: Pisces.

MOSQUITOFISH *Gambusia affinis*, a small freshwater fish from North America belonging to the live-bearing group of toothcarps. Its common name derives from its food of mosquito larvae. The mosquitofish occurs in Trinidad and other Caribbean islands and is widespread in the southern parts of the United States. The female closely resembles the female guppy but can be distinguished by the presence of small black spots on the tail. The male resembles the male guppy in shape but lacks the bright colours of that fish, the body being olive-brown with occasional spots. The mouth is directed upwards and the fishes swim just below the surface, feeding on mosquito larvae or other small animals. Since the mosquitofish is able to destroy its own weight of mosquitoes in one day, it became the most important fish to be introduced into countries where malaria-carrying mosquitoes were prevalent. Unfortunately, its virtues blinded public health authorities to the fact that it also preyed on the eggs and young of other fishes to such an extent that local species often became rare or were destroyed altogether. In Bangkok (Thailand) the native panchax *Aplocheilus panchax* has now become rare and the unique little *Phenacostethus*, which was known only from there, has disappeared. In the streams near Laguna de Bay in the Philippines, the mosquitofish flourishes but *Gulaphallus* has gone. *Micropanchax schoelleri* of the lower Nile cannot now be found, while the mosquitofish flourishes. Dr G. S. Myers, who has done much to point out the dangers of the mosquitofish, first encountered the problem when the staff at a hatchery for Black bass reported that the mosquitofish, introduced as a 'forage fish' for the bass, were in fact destroying a large proportion of them. In his own goldfish pond, Dr Myers discovered that the total weight of goldfish increased threefold over a period of seven years compared with the weight that had existed when the pond was stocked with both goldfish and mosquitofish. FAMILY: Poeciliidae, ORDER: Atheriniformes, CLASS: Pisces.

Molly, the black variety.

Sailfin molly *Mollienesia velifera*, selectively bred for the aquarium, is more colourful than the wild form.

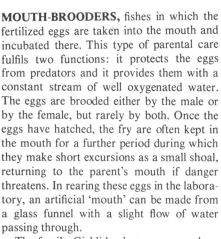

MOUTH-BROODERS, fishes in which the fertilized eggs are taken into the mouth and incubated there. This type of parental care fulfils two functions: it protects the eggs from predators and it provides them with a constant stream of well oxygenated water. The eggs are brooded either by the male or by the female, but rarely by both. Once the eggs have hatched, the fry are often kept in the mouth for a further period during which they make short excursions as a small shoal, returning to the parent's mouth if danger threatens. In rearing these eggs in the laboratory, an artificial 'mouth' can be made from a glass funnel with a slight flow of water passing through.

The family Cichlidae has many members that practise mouth-brooding. It is found, for example in the African genera *Tilapia* and *Haplochromis* and the South American genus *Geophagus*. The eggs are usually laid in a shallow depression excavated by the male after a nuptial display by him. In most species the female then scoops up the eggs into her mouth together with sperm from the male. In *Tilapia heudelotii* the male incubates the eggs, while in *Pelmatochromis guentheri* the male and female take it in turns. The eggs are held in the mouth and throat, which may be somewhat expanded so that a brooding fish is noticeable on that account. Care of the eggs and young may last up to five weeks, during which time the parent cannot feed. In some species, however, methods of collecting microscopic organisms (diatoms, algae, etc.) involving a mucous stream or minute rakers on the gill arches may serve to provide a little sustenance.

The cichlid fishes produce fairly small eggs but in the Sea catfishes of the genus *Arius,* which are also mouth-brooders, the eggs are few and very large (up to 20 mm in diameter). They are brooded by the male and feeding is out of the question during the incubation period.

Blind cave fishes of the family Amblyopsidae are also believed to be mouth-brooders, eggs having been found under the gill covers.

MUDMINNOW, a name given to several species of fish of the genera *Umbra* and *Novumbra* found in the fresh waters of North America and parts of Europe. The European

The mouth-brooder *Haplochromis multicolor.*

Mouth-brooding cichlid fish with its young swarming towards its mouth for shelter.

mudminnow *Umbra krameri* is a small fish found in moorland pools in western Austria and eastern Hungary. Despite their name they are not related to the minnows but are relatives of the pikes. The Alaska blackfish is the best known member of this group. FAMILY: Umbridae, ORDER: Salmoniformes, CLASS: Pisces.

MUDSKIPPERS, a family of small goby-like fishes living in brackish waters and mangrove swamps of the Indo-Pacific region. Their common name refers to their habit of leaving the water and skipping across the exposed sand or mudflats at low tide. Their overall shape is similar to that of the gobies, with a steep forehead and tapering body, but the eyes bulge from the top of the head and the pectoral fins have become modified with a fleshy base so that they can support the body. In some species the pelvic fins are also modified in this way, although in others they are joined to form a sucker.

One of the most widespread species is *Periophthalmus koelreuteri* of the Indian Ocean. It spends a great deal of its time, when the tide has receded, perched on the edge of small pools in mangrove swamps with the tip of its tail just in the water. When disturbed it will skip to the next pool, often with jumps of 2 ft (60 cm), rarely missing its target. These leaps are made by curling the body and then straightening it suddenly. It can also leap along the surface of the water. This species grows to about 5 in (12 cm) in length but certain of the Indo-Malayan species grow to about 12 in (30 cm) and are dug

Mudskippers *Periophthalmus chrysospilos*, small goby-like fishes of Malaya, living in brackish water, on a muddy beach at low tide.

up from holes in the mud by local fishermen.

The limb-like pectoral fins are provided with extra strong muscles and can be used for 'walking'. They are thrust forward, the rest of the body being dragged after. The mudskippers are able to absorb oxygen in two ways. The gill cavities can be filled with water before the fish emerges but exchange of gases can also occur in the mouth and throat, which are well supplied with fine blood vessels. Thus, gill-breathing probably

takes place for the first part of their stay out of water, but after this the gills and throat must still be kept moist for air-breathing.

Because of their need for a moist atmosphere and their tendency to leap, these fishes are difficult to keep in aquaria, but apparently once these difficulties have been overcome the fishes become quite tame and will often feed from their owners. FAMILY: Gobiidae, ORDER: Perciformes, CLASS: Pisces.

NO

NILE PERCH *Lates niloticus*, the largest of the freshwater fishes in Africa. It is found in the Nile, in some of the African lakes and in the larger West African rivers such as the Congo and the Niger. Its distribution reflects an ancient drainage system that linked some of the present rivers of West and Central Africa with the Nile system. Most specimens of the Nile perch are 4–5 ft (1·2–1·5 m) in length, but giants of 6 ft (1·8 m) and weighing more than 250 lb (113 kg) are by no means rare. These powerful fish make a splendid adversary for the angler and have been introduced into other parts of Africa both as a food fish and for sport. Nile perch have now been introduced into Lake Victoria, where they have some effect on the important fisheries for *Tilapia*.

The Nile perch was well known to the ancient Egyptians, who drew accurate pictures of it on the walls of their tombs. These fishes were not infrequently embalmed and placed in tombs. At Esneh on the Nile in Upper Egypt, the Nile perch seems to have been worshipped as an important god and this town was later renamed Latopolis, the City of Lates. Some of the fishes were so well preserved that even the fin membranes are intact.

Investigation into their biology has shown that they spawn in relatively sheltered conditions in water of about 10 ft (3 m). The eggs are pelagic and contain a large oil globule which gives them buoyancy. The adults are fish-eaters and are sometimes cannibalistic. In certain parts of Africa the Nile perch is an important element in local fisheries. FAMILY: Centropomidae, ORDER: Perciformes, CLASS: Pisces.

NORWAY HADDOCK *Sebastes marinus* or redfish, a marine fish from the North Atlantic and a member of the order of Mailcheeked fishes. This is a fairly deep-bodied fish with a perch-like appearance. The head is spiny and scaled as far forward as the eyes, there is a single dorsal fin which is notched between the spiny and soft portions, and the general body colour is a bright red. The Norway haddock is found in the northern parts of the North Atlantic, both along American and European coasts, and it lives at depths of 300–700 ft (90–200 m). It is of some commercial importance, particularly to the Norwegians but also along American coasts, where it is known as the rosefish. The Norway haddock is a viviparous species and a female of about 13 in (32 cm) has been known to bear as many as 20,000 young, the eggs being extremely small. When released from the female, the young are only 6 mm long. This fish reaches 3 ft (90 cm) and specimens weighing up to 20 lb (9 kg) have been recorded, although commercial catches are usually half this size.

A closely related species, *S. viviparus*, is also found in the North Atlantic. It is a smaller fish, only growing to 2 ft (60 cm) in length and is of no commercial value. A third and rather similar fish is *Helicolenus dactylopterus*, another deep-water fish which differs from the other two in having a slate-blue mouth and throat. It is a well-flavoured fish but attains only 18 in (45 cm). FAMILY: Scorpaenidae, ORDER: Scorpaeniformes, CLASS: Pisces.

OCEAN SUNFISHES, large disc-shaped oceanic fishes apparently lacking a tail which has earned them the alternative name of headfishes. The body is greatly compressed, the head large and the dorsal and anal fins prolonged into paddle-like structures. The most striking feature of these fishes, however, is the abrupt termination of the body behind the dorsal and anal fins so that they seem to be all head. During development the rear end of the vertebral column atrophies and there is a rearrangement of the small bones of the tail, somewhat as in a normal fish when the tail has been amputated at an early stage. The result is that the muscles of the body that should attach to the base of the tail no longer do so and instead they are attached to the bases of the dorsal and anal fins. This increases the power of these fins and they are the principal means of locomotion, the fish gently flapping them as it propels itself slowly along. Pelvic fins, as well as the swimbladder, have been lost. The skin is leathery and up to 3 in (7·5 cm) thick. The mouth is unexpectedly small and the teeth are fused together into a beak.

The Ocean sunfish *Mola mola* is the largest in this family. It can reach 11 ft (3·6 m) in length and weigh up to a ton. It is found in all oceans and even comes as far north as the British Isles. It derives its name from its alleged habit of basking on its side at the surface of the water on hot days, feeding on small crustaceans, jellyfishes and fish as they float by. It probably descends to lower levels in bad weather. Sunfishes swim slowly but are reputed to be able to squirt jets of water from the gills to give themselves an extra spurt. With their thick skins, they have few predators and they make little effort to escape when caught; the skin has been known to ward off rifle bullets.

Five species of sunfishes are known, placed in three genera. The Truncated sunfish *Ranzania truncata* rarely grows to more than 3 ft (90 cm) in length. The mouth in this species is apparently unique amongst fishes in that it closes as a vertical slit and not horizontally. In the earliest picture of a sunfish, published in 1613, this curious mouth is clearly shown. The Tailed sunfish *Masturus lanceolatus* is a rare species in which there is a small pointed tail.

Young sunfishes are nothing like the adults. They hatch at about $\frac{1}{10}$ in (2·5 mm) and at first resemble the larvae of any other fish with a normal tail. These juveniles are the smallest free-swimming larvae of any large fish and in order to attain the full adult weight of one ton they must increase their body weight 60 million times. During development the larva's tail soon disappears and its body develops an impressive array of bony spines. When it is about $\frac{1}{2}$ in (1·2 cm) long the spines vanish and a new fringe-like tail appears, the body gradually changing in shape to resemble that of the adult. For many years the larvae were thought to represent a separate species of fish, which was named *Ostracion boops* (bo-ops meaning OX eye). It was only when intermediate stages were found that the true identity of the larvae was recognized. FAMILY: Molidae, ORDER: Tetraodontiformes, CLASS: Pisces.

P

PADDLEFISHES, primitive fishes related to the sturgeons and sharing with them a skeleton of cartilage and a spiral valve in the intestine. There are only two species of paddlefishes, one from the Yangtse in China (*Polyodon gladius*) and one from the Mississippi basin (*P. spathula*). The body, although naked, resembles that of the sturgeons except for the prolonged snout which is extended into a flat sword. This 'paddle' is sensitive and easily damaged and is not used, as might be expected, as a probe or digger in feeding, since these fishes tend to swim with their mouths open and gather their food in that way (small planktonic organisms). The barbels that are characteristic of the mouth of sturgeons are reduced to small protuberances under the paddle. The Mississippi paddlefish rarely grows to more than 150 lb (68 kg). The Chinese paddlefish is reported to reach 20 ft (6 m) in length. Paddlefishes spawn in turbulent waters and it is only in recent years that their larvae have been identified and studied. Like the sturgeons, the paddlefishes have become rarer owing to pollution of rivers. FAMILY: Polyodontidae, ORDER: Acipenseriformes, CLASS: Pisces.

PANCHAX, small egg-laying freshwater fishes belonging to the family of toothcarps and found in Africa and Southeast Asia. Many of the panchaxes are now included in the genus *Aplocheilus,* but their former

The use to which the grotesque 'spoonbill' of the paddlefish is put is still speculative.

placement in *Panchax* earned them their common name. In Africa, members of the genus *Micropanchax* are also referred to as panchaxes. The Asian species grow to about 3 in (8 cm) and the African species to about 2 in (5 cm). The Dwarf panchax *A. blocki* from Ceylon has a shining blue-green underside which has given it the alternative name of Green panchax. The Blue panchax *A. panchax,* found from India across to Malaysia, is rarely imported into Europe although it is extensively kept and reared in the Far East. The African panchaxes, and especially *M. macrophthalmus,* are often on sale in Europe and are attractive additions to an aquarium. FAMILY: Cyprinodontidae, ORDER: Atheriniformes, CLASS: Pisces.

PARROTFISHES, a family of colourful tropical marine fishes related to the wrasses. The name parrotfish has sometimes been applied to superficially similar but unrelated fishes but is best restricted to the Scaridae. Parrotfishes are moderately deep-bodied and have a fairly long dorsal fin but shorter anal fin. The fin spines are rather weak. The teeth in the jaws are fused to form a 'beak' and this, together with their very bright colours, earns them their common name. Parrotfishes feed on coral, biting off pieces and grinding them very thoroughly with the pharyngeal teeth in

Pachypanchax playfairi, one of the panchaxes, living in the freshwaters from East Africa to Madagascar and the Seychelles.

Parrotfish.

the throat. This is then swallowed, the food extracted and the calcareous matter excreted, often in regular places where small piles of coral debris accumulate. Parrotfishes are, in fact, responsible for most of the erosion that occurs on reefs. Many species show strong homing instincts, returning to the same spot after foraging for food, and schools of parrotfishes have been seen regularly following the same route through the coral landscape. At night, some species, such as the Rainbow parrotfish *Pseudoscarus guacamaia,* secrete a tent of mucus around themselves. This may take up to half an hour to produce and as long to break out of in the morning. This mucous envelope would seem to be a protective device which perhaps prevents the odour of the fish from reaching predators.

Parrotfishes usually reach 2–3 ft (60–90 cm) in length, but a Tahitian species has been reported to attain 12 ft (3·6 m). In some species, such as *Scarus coeruleus* of the Atlantic, the larger individuals develop a curious bump on the forehead. The extraordinarily bright colours of the parrotfishes (often vivid patches of varying green and red) have made identification of species difficult. The young fishes are often quite different from the adults and the latter may show striking sexual differences, sometimes greatly complicated by sex reversal with or without the appropriate change in colour. In the Surf parrotfish *Scarus fasciatus* of the Atlantic this sexual dichromatism is so pronounced that the male and female can hardly be recognized as the same species. The species known as *S. taeniopterus* and *S. croicensis* were long thought to be distinct species until it was realized that only males of the first had ever been found and only females of the second.

The parrotfishes make excellent eating and in some areas are of commercial importance. FAMILY: Scaridae, ORDER: Perciformes, CLASS: Pisces.

PENCILFISHES, a family of slim, pencil-like fishes from the Amazon basin, belonging to the suborder of characin-like fishes, the Characoidei. A small fleshy adipose fin is sometimes present behind the rayed dorsal fin, but some authorities would prefer to place all the pencilfishes in the single genus *Nannostomus*. These fishes live in slow-flowing and weedy waters and many feed from the surface. In aquaria they tend to swim in an oblique position with the head directed upwards. Almost all the species not only have a characteristic colour-pattern but also develop a differing pattern at night, the nocturnal colouration being darker than that of the day.

The Dwarf pencilfish *N. marginatus* is less slender than most of this genus. The back is olive, the flanks silvery with three longitudinal dark bands (the middle one edged with red) and the dorsal fin has a crimson blotch. At night the blotch darkens and a small dot appears on the gill cover. This species grows to 1½ in (4 cm) and is easy to keep in an aquarium. The Two-banded pencilfish *N. bifasciatus* is similar but has only two longitudinal stripes; at night there is only one faint band and three blotches.

If kept in an aquarium, these fishes should be provided with a heavily planted area and the water should be kept at 77–82°F (25–28°C). FAMILY: Lebiasinidae, ORDER: Cypriniformes, CLASS: Pisces.

PERCHES, a family of spiny-finned fishes that have been considered central to the great radiation of perch-like fishes that comprise the order Perciformes. This order contains nearly 150 different families, ranging from the diminutive blennies to the large tunas, from the ragfishes to the surgeonfishes, and the icefishes to the archerfishes. The many thousand species of perch-like fish vary widely in their general form but all share with the common perch the development of spiny rays in the fins, a protrusile upper jaw and, at least originally, sharp-edged scales.

The family Percidae contains the darters, the Pike perches and the true perches (the name perch is often used, however, for fishes of other perch-like families, e.g. the Nile perch, family Centropomidae).

The European perch *Perca fluviatilis* is widespread in England and Ireland but rare in Scotland and Norway. It is common throughout the rest of Europe as far as the Soviet Union. It is a deep-bodied fish with two barely separated dorsal fins, the first spiny with a prominent black spot near the rear. The back is olive brown, the flanks yellowish (often brassy) with about six, dark vertical bars, and the belly white. The tail and the lower fins are often tinged with red. The perch prefers slow and sluggish waters but can live almost everywhere. When in fairly fast streams, these fishes form small shoals in the eddies. Perches are predators, feeding throughout life on small fishes and invertebrates. Beloved of anglers, because of the ease with which they take the bait, perches have been caught up to 6 lb (2·7 kg) in England and up to 10 lb (4·5 kg) on the continent of Europe. They spawn amongst weeds in shallow waters in late spring. The males first congregate at the spawning grounds and when the females arrive several males will accompany one female as she lays long strings of eggs entwined in weeds. Perches make excellent eating.

The American perch *P. flavescens* is

The European perch has given its name to a large order of spiny-finned fishes.

closely allied to the European species and is found over large parts of central and southern United States, in some regions reaching as far north as 60°N. The body is greenish-yellow and it is slightly smaller than its European counterpart, attaining a weight of 4 lb (1·8 kg).

Related to the perch is the ruffe or pope of Europe, which has been described elsewhere.

In the Danube basin there are other related but rather rare species. They include the schratzer *Gymnocephalus schraetser,* a species allied to the ruffe, the streber *Aspro streber* and its relative the zingel.

The multitude of perch-like fishes show that the basic body plan has been highly adaptable and has enabled fishes of this type to conquer an enormous range of habitats. FAMILY: Percidae, ORDER: Perciformes, CLASS: Pisces.

PIKE, freshwater fishes of the northern hemisphere. The European pike *Esox lucius,* is a mottled yellow-green fish with an elongate body, the short and soft-rayed dorsal and anal fins being set far back towards the tail. The position of the dorsal and anal fins is characteristic of predatory species that lie in wait for their prey and then make a sudden dash. The head is long and the large jaws are armed with sharp teeth which are replaced at intervals during the life of the

A pike catches its prey.

fish. Pike tend to lurk amongst weeds, blending well with their background, until the prey is sighted. The pike will then cruise very slowly forward, only the slightest movements of the fins indicating motion, until with an incredibly swift final lunge the victim is seized sideways in the jaws, juggled into position and swallowed. The pike swallows fishes such as the perch head first since the spiny fins and gill covers would otherwise stick in its throat.

The pike is the largest of the permanently freshwater British fishes, the record being a monster weighing 53 lb (24·5 kg) caught in Ireland. There are many legends of larger pike, some of which may well be true. The famous Kenmure pike, caught towards the end of the 18th century in Loch Ken, was said by one authority to have weighed 72 lb (32·6 kg), but by another to have weighed only 61 lb (27·6 kg). Most of the head of this noble fish is kept in Kenmure Castle and, although not complete, it was thought by Dr

A pike when swallowing its prey lifts its gill covers, exposing its blood-red gills.

Tate Regan of the British Museum (Natural History) to be from a fish that might well, if in good condition, have weighed 72 lb.

Another legend associated with the pike is that, although voracious and even cannibalistic, it will not eat the *tench. The latter is called the Doctor fish by country people. The story goes that the pike, as well as other fishes, rub their wounds against the tench's slimy body, which heals the wounds and guarantees immunity to the tench. The legend is, however, unfounded since the pike, while not particularly fond of tench, is in some areas fished for with tench as the bait.

The pike is widely distributed all over Europe except on the Iberian Penninsula and across the northern parts of the Soviet Union. It is also found in North America, from the Great Lakes to Alaska. In North America it is referred to as the Northern pike to distinguish it from its American relatives. As in Europe, the pike has generated many legends in North America. The Canadian Eskimos relate stories of a Giant pike capable of swallowing canoes. The largest rod caught Northern pike, however, weighed only 46 lb (20·8 kg) and measured 52 in (132 cm).

The muskellunge or muskie, *Esox masquinongy,* from the north-east of North America is a rather different proposition. Muskies weighing 60 lb (27 kg) or more are by no means uncommon and the rod caught record is about 70 lb (about 32 kg). These large fishes have so far all proved to be females, with ages ranging from 20 to 25 years. The muskie, whose predatory habits are similar to those of the Northern pike, can be distinguished by its rather smaller scales.

In addition to these giants, there are three smaller species of pike in North America which are usually referred to as pickerels. The Chain pickerel *Esox niger,* comes from the south and east of the United States. In

color it resembles the European pike but the mottlings often have a brick-like appearance. The largest specimen caught weighed 9½ lb (4·3 kg) but a fish of 3 lb (1·4 kg) is usually considered a good size for an adult. The Red-fin pickerel and the Grass pickerel are very closely related and some authorities prefer to call them subspecies, respectively *Esox americanus americanus* and *E. `a. vermiculatus.* Neither fish reaches more than 14 in (36 cm) in length. Both have shorter snouts than other pikes and the scales on the body are relatively large.

Pike make extremely good eating and in the past, both in England and on the Continent, these fishes were kept in ponds for culinary purposes.

Zoologically, the pikes occupy a rather isolated position, their nearest relatives being the Alaskan *blackfish and the European *mudminnows. FAMILY: Esocidae, ORDER: Salmoniformes, CLASS: Pisces. K.B.

PIKE PERCHES, fishes of the genus *Stizostedion* that are true members of the perch family but show a similarity in general form to the pike. The European Pike perch *S. lucioperca* is an elongated, pike-like fish widely distributed across Central Europe

The European pike-perch, also known as the Zander, is a true perch that is pike-like.

and introduced into southern England and southern Scandinavia. A population exists in the Baltic which migrates into the lagoons from the sea in winter. This species is also known as the zander. There are two dorsal fins, the first with stout spines. The mouth is armed with large canine-like teeth interspersed with many smaller ones. The back and flanks are greenish-grey with vertical dark bars in the young and there are longitudinal rows of dark spots on the two dorsal fins. The young feed on small aquatic animals but the adults are greedy predators feeding chiefly on fishes. The Pike perch grows to 4 ft (120 cm) and a weight of 22 lb (10 kg). The flesh is good to eat.

Closely related to the Pike perch of Europe is the walleye *S. vitreum* of the United States and Canada. Its name derives from the blind appearance of the eyes. In the last century some walleyes were introduced into a river in Cambridgeshire, England, in mistake for Black bass, but this population is now extinct and only a stuffed rod-caught specimen survives. All Pike perch in England are the European species. Commercial fisheries exist for the walleye in North America and this industry has noted the great fluctuations in the size of populations from year to year. This appears to be due to the remarkable fecundity of the females, one female being able to lay up to half a million eggs, combined with the yearly variations in the conditions suitable for the survival of the eggs and fry. The average life-span is seven years but an 18-year-old female fish has been recorded. FAMILY: Percidae, ORDER: Perciformes, CLASS: Pisces.

PILCHARD *Sardina pilchardus,* a marine fish of the eastern North Atlantic and Mediterranean belonging to the herring family and widely known in its marketed form as both pilchard and sardine. The pilchard somewhat resembles the herring in its cylindrical body and fairly smooth belly, the series of small serrations along the belly (scutes) being poorly developed. It differs from the herring in having the last two anal rays longer than the rest, the colouring of the back rather greenish as opposed to bluish, and the presence of a dark spot behind the gill cover, followed by a series of small spots along the flanks (sometimes absent). The pilchard grows to 8 in (20 cm) in length and is found from North Africa to the southern coasts of Norway and also in the Mediterranean and adjoining seas. The fishes of the North African coasts and the Mediterranean have slightly more gillrakers and are considered to belong to a distinct subspecies *S. pilchardus sardina.* The species spawns in autumn and winter in the southern part of its range, but in late summer in the north.

The pilchard is of considerable economic importance to several European countries. Adult fishes are caught off the coasts of Cornwall, England, and although the fishery is rather small, the canned products are of excellent quality. Larger fisheries exist along the French coasts of Brittany and the Bay of Biscay. Off the coasts of Spain, southern France and in the Mediterranean, the juvenile fishes, of about a year and a half, are caught in enormous numbers and are referred to as sardines. In Basque country the sardines are caught by ring-nets, the fishes being enticed into compact shoals either by casting *rogue* (salted Norwegian cod's roe) onto the water or by the use of powerful incandescent lamps at night.

The name sardine, and derivatives of it, is used almost throughout the world for small and silvery herring-like fishes, often only distantly related to the pilchard. In England, only the young of the pilchard are recognized for trade purposes as sardines, the tinned young of other species being marketed under other names.

Elsewhere along temperate coasts (except the western Atlantic coasts) the pilchard is replaced by members of the genus *Sardinops.* The species of *Sardinops* are outwardly very similar to the pilchard. In Japan, *S. melanosticta* forms the overwhelming bulk of the great Iwashi fisheries (the anchovy *Engraulis japonicus* and the Round herring *Etrumeus teres* make up the rest). Large pilchard fisheries also exist along the Pacific coast of North America, and off the coasts of South Africa, Australia and New Zealand. FAMILY: Clupeidae, ORDER: Clupeiformes, CLASS: Pisces.

PILOTFISH *Naucrates ductor,* a small fish habitually associated with sharks and larger fishes and related to the mackerels and tunas. This pelagic fish is found all over the world in tropical and temperate oceans. The name comes from its alleged habit of not only accompanying sharks and sometimes other large fishes but of actually leading them to their prey. The pilotfish feeds on the scraps of food left by its host and thus deserves the name commensal (literally 'feeding from the same table'). Pilotfishes swim round sharks, making brief sorties and returning, but it is doubtful if they act as pilots. V. V. Shuleikin calculated that sharks swim three times as fast as a pilotfish. He suggested the pilotfishes are carried along by the shark's boundary layer, that is, the layer of water over its surface which travels at the same speed as the shark.

Young pilotfishes are often found sheltering amongst the tentacles of jellyfishes, a habit shared with the young of the Horse mackerel and the Portuguese man-o'-war fish.

The pilotfish has a mackerel-like body with the first dorsal fin reduced to a few low spines. The second dorsal fin and the anal fin are moderately long and are opposite each other. The body is dark blue on the back and silver on the sides with about six vertical dark bars on the flanks which fade with age. The fish grows to about 2 ft (60 cm) in length.

Fishes of the genus *Seriola,* and especially *S. zonata,* also have an association with sharks. This fish can be distinguished from the rather similar pilotfish by the presence of seven small spines joined by a membrane in front of the soft-rayed dorsal fin (four to five separated spines in *Naucrates*). Two other fishes have been reported as associating with sharks, the Rainbow runner *Elagatis bipinnulatus* and the Starry jack *Caranx stellatus,* both of which have been seen escorting Grey sharks (*Carcharinus*) off the Galapagos Islands. FAMILY: Carangidae, ORDER: Perciformes, CLASS: Pisces.

PIPEFISHES, a family of highly elongated and rather specialized fishes related to the trumpetfishes, shrimpfishes and Sea horses. They have a world-wide distribution and although mainly marine include some freshwater species. The long, thin body is completely encased in bony rings but it is surprisingly flexible and prehensile. The fish is well camouflaged for a rather secretive life amongst weeds. The pelvic fins and the tail are often lacking. The prehensile body is developed to its greatest extent in the Sea horses, the head being bent at an angle to the body. There are pipefishes that approach this arrangement but still retain the head in the normal position.

The pipefishes show a most interesting method of caring for their young. In the most primitive forms (e.g. *Nerophis*) the fertilized eggs are stuck together on the underside of the male. In the next and more advanced group the eggs are embedded singly in a spongy layer that develops along the belly of the male. Finally, in forms like *Doryrhamphus* the bony plates encasing the body are enlarged to form a groove in which the eggs are placed. This is carried to the extreme in the Sea horses where the male has a distinct brood pouch.

There are six species of pipefishes found along British shores. One of the largest of these is the Great pipefish *Syngnathus acus,* a species which reaches 18 in (45 cm) in length. It has a small anal fin and a small tail. As in all pipefishes the rays of the dorsal fin are soft and flexible and each ray can be moved independently. This is important because like the Sea horses, the pipefishes swim by undulations of the dorsal fin. The small Worm pipefish *Nerophis lumbriciformis* rarely grows to more than 6 in (15 cm). The body is dark brown and the body plates are not easily seen. It is often found on the shore under stones and weeds. In July the males can be found with eggs stuck to the underside of their body.

Most pipefishes, a family of highly elongated and specialized fishes, live in the sea. A few, like this *Syngnathus pulchellus*, of the Congo, have become adapted to a freshwater life.

Most pipefishes are rather drab in colour, but the male of the Straight-nosed pipefish *Nerophis ophidion* has a greenish body with blue lines along the abdomen. Some of the pipefishes are quite small. *Doryrhamphus melanopleura* from coral reefs of the Pacific region reaches only 2½ in (6·5 cm) in length. It is bright orange-red with a longitudinal bright blue band from the snout to the tail, the latter being orange at its base, followed by blue with a white margin.

Most pipefishes live among corals or weeds in shallow water, but a few live in burrows and *Corythoichthys fasciatus*, of the Indo-Pacific, inhabits the intestinal cavity of bêche-de-mer. *Syngnathus pelagicus*, on the other hand, is pelagic and lives amongst the sargassum weed floating at the surface in the Atlantic.

Some pipefishes can live contentedly in tropical aquaria provided that an adequate supply of live food is available. *Syngnathus spicifer* and *S. pulchellus* from the Congo are frequently imported but have rarely been bred in captivity. Even *Nerophis ophidion* from British coasts has populations in the fresh parts of the Baltic and has been kept in aquaria with only very slightly salted water.

The hobbyhorses or pipehorses are rather rare little pipefishes found largely in the Pacific. In many ways they bridge the gap between the pipefishes and the Sea horses. The genus *Acentroneura* contains small species which rarely exceed 3 in (7·5 cm) in length. The head is very slightly tilted from the main axis of the body and the tail is prehensile. To break the outline of the fish there are little sprig-like fringes irregularly scattered about the body, a type of camou-

flage also found in the young of some pipefishes (e.g. *Larvicampus runa*) but one that attains its greatest development in the Sea dragons. See Sea horses. FAMILY: Syngnathidae, ORDER: Gasterosteiformes, CLASS: Pisces.

PIRANHAS or caribes, small but very ferocious freshwater fishes from South America belonging to the family Characidae. They are renowned for their carnivorous habits and are amongst the most infamous of all fishes. Travellers' tales relate cases where large animals and even men have been attacked and the flesh picked off their bones in a very short space of time. At river crossings in South America a look-out is kept for the shoals of piranhas so that people fording the river can be warned. There are several species involved, the largest growing to about 15 in (38 cm). The jaws are short and powerful and are armed with sharp cutting teeth. Their main diet is fish or mammals but they are reputed to be strongly attracted to the smell of blood so that a single bite will draw hundreds of other members of the shoal to the same spot.

The White piranha *Serrasalmus rhombeus* of the Amazon is one of the largest species. The body is olive to silver with irregular dark blotches. The Red piranha *Rooseveltiella nattereri,* also from the Amazon, grows to 12 in (30 cm) and has an olive-brown back, light brown flanks and numerous bright silver spots on the body. The belly and the fin bases are, appropriately enough, blood red; the dorsal and anal fins are black.

Provided that one is not squeamish, the piranhas make interesting aquarium pets. They are not unattractive but must be provided with live food to keep them in the best condition. If 20 or more are kept together they will attack anything that moves in the water. If only one or two are kept, however,

Piranhas, South American river fishes, are credited with unusual ferocity, yet some species, including the Red piranha, are kept as aquarium fishes.

they will cower in the corners of the tank until they have 'egged' each other on to attack. As in the phenomenon known as 'feeding frenzy' in sharks, it appears that intensive feeding is stimulated by the sight of others also attacking. FAMILY: Characidae, ORDER: Cypriniformes, CLASS: Pisces.

PLAICE *Pleuronectes platessa,* perhaps the most popular of all the edible European flatfishes. The common name derives from an Old French word for flat. The plaice is one of the most easily identified species because of the irregular orange spots on the upper surface which persist after the fish is dead (similar spots in the flounder soon disappear when the fish is out of water). The blind side is a translucent white. Unlike the flounder, there are no rough scales on the head or at the start of the lateral line, but there are small tubercles between the eyes. In contrast to most of the flatfishes, the plaice is a sedentary species, found mainly over sand or gravel. It is, therefore, very susceptible to overfishing and the maintenance of a fishery depends on strict control of catches to balance the natural replacement each year. Experiments have been conducted in the rearing of young plaice for restocking depleted areas and also in the transferring of plaice from British North Sea coasts, where they are numerous, to the eastern shores of the North Sea where growth conditions are better. Plaice grow to 33 in (83 cm) and may reach 15 lb (6·7 kg) in weight. FAMILY: Pleuronectidae, ORDER: Pleuronectiformes, CLASS: Pisces.

PLATYS, live-bearing cyprinodont fishes from freshwaters of the New World placed in the genus *Xiphophorus* (formerly *Platypoecilus,* from which the common name was derived). The genus *Xiphophorus* also contains the swordtails. These fishes are at-

tractive and easy to keep in an aquarium. The platy *X. maculatus,* which grows to 2½ in (6 cm), is found in the rivers of the Atlantic drainage of Central America. In the wild, the normal colour is an olive green with a pair of black spots near the tail, but it is a very variable species and red and black varieties are also found. These characters have been developed by breeders to produce stable red, orange and yellow varieties with assorted black markings. The Wagtail platy was the result of a cross between a wild platy and the golden variety. Wagtails have orange and red bodies with a black dorsal fin and tail. The Variegated platy *X. variatus* comes from southern Mexico. It too is very variable in its colours but usually has bands or zig-zagging rows of spots along the flanks. Many colour varieties have now been bred by aquarists. The Green swordtail *X. helleri,* which is greenish in the wild, has been crossed with the red variety of the platy to produce the common Red swordtail.

Platys are not only of interest to the aquarist. Their ability to cross with other species and the range in colour forms that can be produced have been of considerable interest in studies on genetics and a great deal can be learned from them of the mechanism of inheritance. FAMILY: Poeciliidae, ORDER: Atheriniformes, CLASS: Pisces.

POISONOUS FISHES, species which have flesh or organs that cause poisoning when eaten or those capable of injecting venom. Man has been aware from earliest times that certain fishes are dangerous, either to handle or to eat, and amongst local peoples such species have usually been well known and avoided. It is only in fairly recent years, however, that the causes of fish poisoning and the way in which fish venoms act have been properly investigated.

1 **Poisonous fishes.** It is well known that

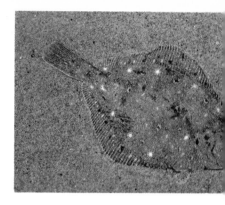

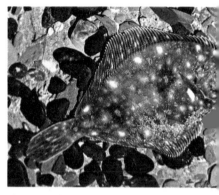

A plaice can be recognized by its red spots which persist when the fish is dead. Plaice can change colour to match the colours of the sea-bed on which they are lying, as is shown in these pictures of the same specimen.

mild or severe poisoning can result from eating poorly preserved fishes. This is especially true of mackeral, tuna and related scombroid fishes in which decomposition results, through bacterial action, in the release of a histamine-like substance which can cause allergy reactions.

Until quite recently it was widely held that fish poisoning resulted from eating spoiled fish, although Moray eels and pufferfishes were recognized as often harbouring some special toxin. In 1958 Dr J. Randall pieced together recorded cases of fish poisoning and showed that the most prevalent form of poisoning was that known as ciguatera, a term that had been coined a century before to describe the illness resulting from eating the marine snail *Livona pica*, a staple seafood throughout the Caribbean. Randall was puzzled that from time to time previously edible species of fishes would suddenly become poisonous or whole areas of a reef would have to be abandoned by local fishermen and could later be fished again apparently without harm. He was able to show that ciguatera poisoning was generally found amongst the large fish-eating species such as barracudas, Horse mackerels and groupers that fed on smaller fishes browsing around the reefs. He also found that ciguatera poisoning affected fishes in just a small area of the reef and was not universal. He de-

Many colour varieties of platys have been bred by aquarists and some with abnormally shaped fins.

duced that ciguatera poisoning is caused by a small but poisonous bottom-living organism, probably a blue-green alga and that the poison becomes concentrated as one animal feeds on another through the food chain. By the time that man eats a large fish-eating species of grouper or barracuda, the toxin is sufficiently concentrated to produce very severe symptoms. Typically, the symptoms are weakness, diarrhoea, tingling and numbness of the lips, hands and feet, nausea, joint and muscular pain, poor co-ordination, difficulty in breathing, burning urination, itching and confusion of the senses of heat and cold. The stomach disorders pass fairly quickly but the upset to the nervous system may last for weeks. Most victims recover but some deaths have been recorded.

The poisoning caused by Moray eels and pufferfishes may be a form of ciguatera poisoning or may result from toxic substances normally in the flesh of these animals. In Japan pufferfishes are prepared by highly trained cooks and served as a dish called *fugu*. In spite of the elaborate preparation of *fugu*, pufferfishes are still the major source of fish poisoning.

2 **Venomous fishes.** In many fishes the spines of the fins or those associated with the bones of the head are capable of inflicting a wound into which poison is injected. At least 40 species of bony fishes have venomous organs, including certain catfishes, the weevers, scorpionfishes and the toadfishes. In the catfishes the spines of the dorsal and pectoral fins are not only sharp and serrated but contain poison cells in the skin covering the spine. In European waters the two species of weeverfish and the stingray are the most venomous fishes. The first four or five rays of the dorsal fin in the weevers, as well as the spine on the gill cover, are sheathed in skin covering a groove in which the poisonous tissue lies, rupture of the skin releasing the poison which then flows down the spine and into the wound. In the stingray *Dasyatis pastinaca* there are one or two long spines near the base of the tail with a channel in which lies the poison-secreting tissue. These fishes will lash out with the tail when disturbed and should be handled with great care to avoid an extremely painful wound. Death may occur if the spine stabs in the chest or stomach since the poison quickly affects the muscles of the heart. One of the most lethal of all fishes is the stonefish *Synanceja verrucosa*, a grotesque-looking fish but one which is able to blend all too successfully with its surroundings of rock or coral. The poison spines which bear a deep groove on either side into which the poison glands discharge, are located in the dorsal fin. These fishes lie motionless on the bottom and many cases are recorded of swimmers stepping on them. Death can occur in two hours. In the toadfishes the spines of the gill cover and the

The Spotted triggerfish *Balistoides conspicillum*, of the Indo-Pacific, is one of a number of species responsible occasionally for ciguatera poisoning.

first two dorsal spines are hollow with the poison gland lying at the base so that pressure on the spine forces the poison into the wound in much the same manner as a hypodermic needle.

No specific antidotes have been developed for fish venoms. One method of treatment is to tie a ligature above the wound (if it is on the hand or foot) and immediately to immerse the limb in iced water for at least five, but not more than ten, minutes. The ligature must then be removed and the limb replaced in the iced water for another two hours.

POLLACK *Pollachius pollachius,* a cod-like fish found in the eastern Atlantic as far north as Norway, but absent from the Mediterranean. It resembles the cod but lacks a barbel on the chin, has smaller pelvic fins and has elongated, light-coloured smudges on the flanks. The pollack feeds on small fishes, especially sand-eels, as well as worms and crustaceans. It reaches 24 lb (11 kg) in weight and is of some commercial value. FAMILY: Gadidae, ORDER: Gadiformes, CLASS: Pisces.

PORCUPINEFISHES, a family of tropical marine fishes in which the teeth in each jaw are fused completely together to form a beak

In spite of porcupinefishes blowing themselves up and erecting their spines they are sometimes swallowed by sharks. Nobody knows what effect this has on the sharks.

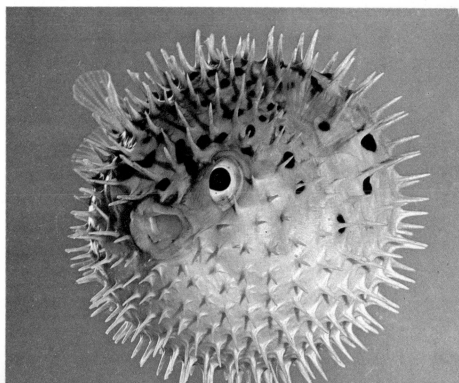

(Diodontidae meaning two teeth). They are related to the *pufferfishes and are best described as pufferfishes with well-developed spines on the body. The spines, which are modified scales, normally lie against the body. As in the pufferfishes, the porcupinefishes are capable of inflating the body with air or water as a means of defence, the fish presumably being too large, in that condition, to be swallowed by predators. With inflation, the spines on the body become erected and provide an additional means of defence.

The most frequently illustrated species is *Diodon histrix,* one of the several forms commonly sold to tourists dried and inflated as a curio or even as a lampshade. FAMILY: Diodontidae, ORDER: Tetraodontiformes, CLASS: Pisces.

PUFFERFISHES, fishes principally of tropical waters, related to the porcupinefishes and capable, like them, of inflating their bodies with air or water as a means of defence. These are clumsy looking fishes with scales often modified into spines. The head and chest are bulky but the body narrows thereafter. The soft-rayed dorsal and anal fins lie far back near the tail. If a puffer is removed from the water it gulps in air until it becomes blown up like a balloon. It will also do this when threatened by a predator in water, presumably becoming too big to be swallowed. When full of air it floats helplessly at the surface and cannot swim until the air has been released. Unlike most fishes, the puffers use the pectoral and dorsal fins as the main propulsive units, the small anal fin and the tail acting as rudders. In both upper and lower jaws the teeth have become fused on each side leaving a gap in the middle. The fish thus appears to have four teeth, giving rise to the family name of Tetraodontidae or 'four-teeth.' They are carnivorous fishes and since they are clumsy

swimmers they rely on subtle camouflage in approaching their prey.

Some species of puffers are poisonous to eat and they advertise this fact by their much brighter colours. The poison in pufferfishes is known as tetrodoxin and it is frequently fatal (see poisonous fishes). Nevertheless, a dish called *fugu* is prepared from puffers and is considered to be a great delicacy in Japan.

Puffers rarely exceed 3 ft (91 cm) in length and many species are much smaller than this. Several freshwater species are kept by aquarists. The Parrot pufferfish *Colomesus psittacus,* from South America and the West Indies, grows to 6 in (15 cm) and will live peacefully with other fishes in a tank

but will tend to attack its own species. The Common pufferfish from India and Malaysia *Tetraodon cuticuta* is the species most often imported. It is a hardy fish, easy to keep and growing to 6 in (15 cm). Like all puffers, it does well on live food. The back is olive green, the flanks yellowish and the belly pale brown-grey and there is a dark blotch edged with gold on the flanks in front of the dorsal fin. Unlike most puffers, it lacks the prickles (modified scales) found in the skin of other species. Although easy to keep and obliging in its readiness to inflate, this species is rather irascible and will attack other fishes. FAMILY: Tetraodontidae, ORDER: Tetraodontiformes, CLASS: Pisces.

Pufferfishes, apart from other peculiarities, look almost as if they are artificially painted.

RAINBOWFISHES, a group of fishes of the family Atherinidae related to the silversides and found in the fresh and brackish waters of Australia.

The Dwarf rainbowfish *Melanotaenia maccullochi* and the Red-tailed rainbowfish *M. nigrans* are commonly imported as aquarium fishes. They rarely grow to more than 4 in (10 cm) in length. Like all atherinids, two dorsal fins are present. Their colours are subtle, their charm lying in the iridescent flank patterns. FAMILY: Atherinidae, ORDER: Atheriniformes, CLASS: Pisces. (Ill. p. 149.)

RAYS, or batoid fishes, a group of cartilaginous fishes which share a number of features with sharks but are placed in a separate order on the basis of two main structural differences. First, the gill slits lie on the underside of the head and not along the sides of the head as in sharks; second, the pectoral fins are almost always greatly expanded and wing-like and the leading edge joins smoothly onto the head. The highly flattened body and large pectoral fins enable these bottom-living fishes to lie unnoticed on the bottom or cruise close to the bottom by undulatory movements of the pectoral fins. Since the mouth is also underneath the head, sand and mud would normally be taken in with the respiratory current, but in rays this problem has been solved by drawing water in through the two large spiracles behind the eyes. Certain rays, however, are pelagic (e.g. the huge Manta rays) and these breathe normally, the water being drawn in through the mouth. The rays resemble the sharks in having a skeleton composed of cartilage with no trace of bone although the vertebral column, and sometimes the elongated snout, may be strengthened by calcification, as in the blade-like saw of the sawfishes. They also resemble the sharks in having denticles that cover the body (modified into the bucklers or thorns of the Thornback rays, or into the stinging spines of the stingrays); in the development of rows of teeth in the jaws, although in the rays these are not the typical sharp-pointed teeth of sharks but are usually flattened to form a crushing or grinding mosaic or pavement; and in various anatomical features connected with their very similar method of reproduction, the most obvious being the presence of claspers or mixopterygia, the modified appendages of the pelvic fins used by the male to transfer sperm to the female during copulation. Like many sharks, the rays give birth to live young which hatch and develop in the uterus of the female, the only exception being members of the family Rajidae or skates in which the young are born in horny egg-cases (mermaid's purses). The claspers are rather far apart in the rays and probably only one can be inserted into the cloaca of the female during mating, a fact that may be coupled with the development of only one uterus in many rays.

About 340 species of rays are known and these can be placed in six main groups. The Electric rays have a round, disc-like body and rather short tail, but their most striking feature is the pair of electrical organs on either side of the disc (muscle modified into a honeycomb of tiny plates to form 'batteries' capable of delivering up to 220 volts—see Electric fishes). The skates have a body that is more pointed in front, often diamond-shaped or almost triangular and the tail is rather longer and more slender without a well-developed tail fin. The group, often referred to merely as rays, includes the stingrays of both marine and freshwaters, the Eagle rays and the Cow-nosed rays, in which the tail is slender, often whip-like, and armed with one or more sharp spines on top and near the base capable of injecting venom into a wound. The Devil rays or mantas are often huge fishes, over 20 ft (6 m) in width, that have abandoned life on the bottom for a pelagic existence, the mouth and gills being adapted for taking in large quantities of water and straining out the small animals of the plankton. The sawfishes have a large blade-like snout edged with teeth and the body more closely resembles that of a shark than a ray. Finally, the guitarfishes are a group with an even greater similarity to sharks in the general form of the body but are placed with the rays because the gill slits are underneath the body and the pectoral fins are joined to the head.

Although the rays appear early in the fossil record, ray-like fishes being found in Upper Jurassic rocks, they are clearly an offshoot of the sharks that have become adapted to life on the sea bed. Burying is thought to be the major factor that both stimulated and directed the course of the evolution of the rays. The shift of the gill slits to the underside of the body would not only allow 'jet-propelled' take off but would also enable the pectoral fins to expand round the head and thus produce the wing-like pectorals of the modern rays. It seems likely that the free-swimming pelagic rays represent a later colonization of the middle and surface layers of the sea. The invasion of freshwaters by certain families of stingrays was also probably a later development. ORDER: Hypotremata, CLASS: Chondrichthyes. (Ill. p. 150.)

REMORAS or Shark suckers, curiously specialized fishes in which the first dorsal fin has become modified into a sucking disc by which the fish attaches itself to sharks, other large marine creatures or even to ships. The body is elongated and flattened on top and the sucker lies over the head. The sucker is one of the most remarkable examples of the adaptation of a body part for quite a different function from its original one since this disc is in fact a highly modified fin. The finrays have become flattened and deflected alternately to the left and to the right to form a series of ridges, sometimes with serrated edges. The rim of the sucker is raised and the plate-like finrays can be adjusted to form a strong vacuum. The grip of a remora is remarkably strong, especially on a slightly rough surface, and it is possible to tear the disc from the fish before the latter will relinquish its hold. The various species are distinguished chiefly by the number of plates or lamellae in the disc, which range from ten in *Phterrichthys* to 20–28 in *Echeneis*. Some species are more elongated than others but in all the belly and the back are the same general colour. This, coupled with the fact that the lower jaw is longer than the upper, has earned these fishes the Spanish name of *reverso*.

It is not certain what advantage is derived by the remora from attachment to another animal. The arrangement may simply be one of phoresy or the transport of one organism on the body of another. It is also possible that the remora feeds on the scraps left by a shark. There have been many records of remoras entering the mouths of Manta rays and several species of large sharks, as well as some of the larger billfishes. In this, they seem to resemble the Cleaner fishes but there is no evidence that they undertake the cleaning duties (the removal of parasites) of the former. In at least one instance fairly large remoras (*Echeneis naucrates* in this case) have been recorded from the stomach of a Sand shark. Remoras are good swimmers and often leave their host to forage and then return.

Aristotle mentioned the remora but probably never saw one. Pliny recorded that the remora attached itself to the hulls of ships and was able to bring them to a sudden halt, a legend that persisted right through the Middle Ages and was only finally explained when Sven Ekman, the great oceanographer, demonstrated how sailing ships could indeed be brought to a sudden stop by the phenomenon of dödvand or 'dead water' (the retarding action of underwater waves at the interface between fresh and salt water off river mouths). The remora was also held to possess magic powers and a potion made from it was believed to delay legal proceedings, arrest age in greying matrons and slow down the course of love.

In several parts of the world fishermen have evolved an ingenious method of fishing with the remora. A line is attached at the base of the tail and the fish is then released into the water. When the remora has fixed itself to some large fish or turtle, the line is then hauled back to the boat. It is remarkable that this fishing method should have been evolved independently by fishermen in the western Atlantic and in the Indo-Pacific region. The first record of this technique comes from Pierre Martyr who accompanied Columbus on his second voyage to the Antilles (1494). Konrad Gesner used Martyr's description and produced an illustration of an extraordinary creature with a huge cowl on its head in the act of catching a manatee, before the startled eyes of a turtle. With various modifications, this illustration was reproduced for another two centuries before remora fishing was rediscovered by Europeans. FAMILY: Echeneidae, ORDER: Perciformes, CLASS: Pisces. (Ill. p. 145.)

ROACH *Rutilus rutilus,* one of the commonest of the carp-like fishes of Europe but also found right across Asia to the Amur basin. The roach is a fairly high-backed but slender fish, the upperparts being grey or blue-green fading to silvery on the flanks and belly and the fins red. It is found in both rivers and lakes, the young fishes shoaling and readily taking any bait offered but the larger adults becoming more solitary and difficult to catch. Roach grow to 16 in (40 cm) and weigh over 3 lb (1·4 kg). The young feed on algae and plankton but later turn to worms, insects, crustaceans, small fishes and fish eggs, as well as aquatic plants and molluscs. The roach is very variable in form depending on the type of water mass that it inhabits. Lake forms are usually deeper-bodied than those from flowing water and this was once considered a good basis for recognizing several species, one of which was from brackish water. All are now placed in the same species.

Roach have the unfortunate habit of readily hybridizing with the bream (a larger fish) and several specimens of 'roach' that were believed to be of record size later proved to be hybrids. It also breeds with the rudd. The species are not easy to separate but the most useful, though not completely reliable, character is the position of the dorsal fin. In the roach the dorsal fin begins over, or in front of, a vertical line from the base of the pelvic fins, whereas in the rudd the dorsal fin begins behind this line. Roach × bream hybrids also closely resemble the roach but can be distinguished by their longer anal fin which has 11–16 branched rays. FAMILY: Cyprinidae, ORDER: Cypriniformes, CLASS: Pisces. (Ill. p. 149.)

ROCKLINGS, small and elongated cod-like fishes of shallow waters and especially rock pools, from which they derive their common name. They are found off the shores of Britain and the European continent. The general body form is similar to that found in the other cod-like species but in many rocklings there is more than one barbel round the mouth. The Three-bearded rockling *Gaidropsarus vulgaris* has two barbels near the nostrils and one under the chin; it is the largest of the eastern Atlantic species, growing to 20 in (51 cm). The Four-bearded rockling *Rhinonemus cimbrius* has an additional barbel near the upper lip and the Five-bearded rockling *Ciliata mustelus* has a total of five barbels. The young of all these species are silvery and pelagic and look quite unlike their brownish and spotted parents. The difference between young and adults is so striking that the young were at one time placed in a separate genus *Couchia.* FAMILY: Gadidae, ORDER: Gadiformes, CLASS: Pisces. (Ill. p. 151.)

RUFFE *Gymnocephalus cernua,* a perch-like fish from lakes and rivers of Europe. It is also known as the pope, a name used in a derogatory sense but for obscure reasons. The ruffe is a small relative of the Common perch *Perca fluviatilis,* reaching 9 in (23 cm) in length. It is widely distributed throughout northern and central Europe as well as in southeast and central England. It resembles the perch but the division between the spinous and soft parts of the dorsal fin is not so distinct. The body, which is more slender than that of the perch, is olive to brown-green with irregular dark patches. The flesh makes excellent eating, especially when fried and in Germany it is used for soup. Baltic fishermen are said to slap the sides of their boats to attract these fishes. It is also recorded that in the last century country people in some parts of England would enjoy themselves by impaling a cork on the spiny rays of the dorsal fin of the ruffe, then releasing the fish so that it would be an easy prey for other fishes. FAMILY: Percidae, ORDER: Perciformes, CLASS: Pisces.

A well-known freshwater fish of Europe with a curiously checkered history.

SAILFISH *Istiophorus platypterus*, a large oceanic scombroid fish with a sail-like dorsal fin. This fish was formerly referred to as *I. gladius* and several other species were recognized, but recent studies have shown that all belong to a single, world-wide species occurring in all tropical and subtropical seas. The sailfish has the powerful torpedo-shaped body of fast oceanic swimmers. The dorsal finrays are enormously extended to form a 'sail' along the back. Pelvic fins are present (as in the related swordfish but not in the marlins). The tail is crescent-shaped and there are small finlets behind both the dorsal and the anal fins. The upper jaw is extended into a 'bill' or 'sword' which is longer than the head and is rounded in cross-section (flattened in the swordfish). In the juveniles the upper and lower jaws are the same length and are provided with pointed teeth, but by the time that the fish is 2 in (5 cm) long the upper jaw has outgrown the lower and the teeth have disappeared. Just in front of the tail there are two keels on the side of the body (a single keel in the swordfish). The body and the dorsal fin are blue or blue-black, often ornamented with small dark spots.

The sailfish is an exceedingly fast swimmer, the huge dorsal fin being folded down at high speeds. It has been said that they can reach 60 mph (100 kph) and although this is by no means impossible, no accurate measurements have been made. On calm days the sailfish basks at the surface with the dorsal fin fully erect, giving rise to the, perhaps correct, assumption that this fin is actually used as a sail. They feed on fish and squids. They are highly esteemed by anglers because of their fighting qualities, the fishes making tremendous leaps when hooked. A fish of 12 ft (3·6 m) long and weighing over 200 lb (90 kg) is an unforgettable sight as it leaps and twists to free itself from the line. FAMILY: Istiophoridae, ORDER: Perciformes, CLASS: Pisces.

SALMON, highly palatable anadromous fishes of the northern hemisphere belonging to the genera *Salmo* and *Onchorhynchus*. Of all the fishes in the world, the Atlantic salmon *Salmo salar* is perhaps the most famous. It has been eaten for at least 2,000 years, has had books and poems devoted to its virtues and habits, has made the owners of stretches of good salmon rivers wealthy, and artists and photographers have spent a lifetime trying to capture the salmon's triumphant leaps as it makes for its spawning grounds. Cave men eagerly sought the salmon and the drawings and models of this fish found in caves in the Pyrenees suggest that they well appreciated the nobility of the salmon. The thrill of spearing a salmon with a sharpened length of wood is now gone and regretfully the salmon is to many people a fish that is bought by the tin or caught only by the wealthy.

The Atlantic salmon lives in the North Atlantic and breeds in the freshwaters of Europe and North America. It is the only salmon in this whole region. In the North Pacific, however, there are several species belonging to the related genus *Onchorhynchus*, namely the Chinook salmon *O. tschawytscha*, the coho *O. kisutch*, the sockeye *O. nerka*, the Pink or Humpback salmon *O. gorbuscha* and the Chum or Dog salmon *O. keta*. These are all confined to the western side of Canada and the United States. A further species, *O. masu*, is found on the eastern seaboard of northern Asia. The largest of these is the Chinook, which can weigh over 100 lb (45 kg) and the smallest is the Pink salmon, which rarely exceeds 10 lb (4·5 kg). In their general biology, these species of *Onchorhynchus* resemble the Atlantic salmon in ascending rivers to spawn, the young descending to the sea either shortly after hatching (Pink salmon) or months or years later. One principal difference between these species and the Atlantic salmon is that the former do not return to the rivers to spawn a second time but die on completion of their first spawning.

In England, the various names given to different stages in the life history of the Atlantic salmon is an indication of the interest shown in these fishes. The newly hatched young with their yolk sac are known as 'alevins'. Juveniles of about 5 in (13 cm) with their bodies marked by dark bands are called 'parr'. After 18 months to two years the parr change to a silvery colour and are ready to migrate; these are the 'smolts'. Salmon of about 2 ft (60 cm) long that have been to sea for a year or so and are coming up the rivers for the first time to spawn are known as 'grilse'. Lastly, salmon that have spawned and are limply drifting back to the sea are called 'kelts' (or blackfish or redfish).

The adult salmon is an elongated, powerfully built yet graceful fish. The fins are soft-rayed, the tail is slightly emarginated and a small adipose fin is present. In colour the fishes are silvery with small black 'freckles' and a darker back, but when the breeding season approaches the male becomes suffused with a reddish tinge and its jaws become curiously hooked. The adult fishes feed in the sea for one or two years before they return to the rivers and are in good condition for the climb ahead of them. Quite often they will approach the mouth of a river but lie off it for another year before making the ascent. The salmon run up the rivers in August to September and the major spawning period is in the early winter. In some areas a second run of salmon occurs in spring. During the actual spawning run they need all the energy reserves they have built up since they do not feed in freshwater. It is not known why salmon, although fasting, will take the flies and spinners of the fisherman.

The journey upstream and the act of spawning are exhausting. The fish which two months before had firm red flesh and a well-rounded body with clear skin is now pale, soft and flaccid and liable to infection. Slowly the kelts drift back to the sea, where they feed and recover, the salt water killing off any parasites that they have picked up in freshwater. Those that have survived will return to spawn again and in a very few cases the same fish has been found to have spawned four times. Breeding has a profound effect on the scales of salmon. Calcium is reabsorbed from the scales and at the same time a certain amount of erosion of the scales takes place. The result is that when the growth of the scales is resumed on the feeding grounds a very characteristic ring is formed, much like the distinctive annual ring of a tree.

It has often been said that salmon return to their natal stream to spawn and the individual marking of fishes with numbered tags has shown that, at least for the recaptured fishes, this is perfectly correct. Over 400,000 young salmon were marked from one Canadian stream before they migrated to the sea, and of these 11,000 were recaptured in their natal stream and none in any other stream. Salmon disperse widely once in the sea, those in the Fraser River opening onto the Pacific coast of North America reaching as far as the Aleutian Islands, and the question arises how do the salmon find their way back to the river mouth once more? Recent work has suggested that the salmon may well orient by the sun, the so-called solar compass method or celestial navigation already demonstrated in certain birds, as well as in ants, bees and crustaceans. Experiments on the White bass *Roccus chrysops* in Lake Mendota showed that the fishes were able to compensate for the apparent height of the sun through the day and thus to maintain a straight course. In the case of salmon, however, there is the further problem of selecting exactly the right tributary that will lead to the stream where the fish was spawned. Some very ingenious experiments by Dr Arthur Hasler have shown that the salmon has a very highly developed sense of smell and is able to recognize the odour of its natal stream. Taking fishes that had chosen a particular fork in the river during their ascent, it was found that they invariably chose the same fork again except when the nostrils were plugged with cotton wool, when they apparently chose at random. A final problem yet to be solved is how or why salmon ever colonize new streams.

Most rivers are fairly easy to ascend but if weirs have been built the salmon display extraordinary tenacity in trying to leap over them, trying again and again until they either succeed or fall back exhausted. A large salmon can make a leap of 10 ft (3 m) which is normally quite sufficient. But if an entire spawning run has been blocked by a hydro-electric dam, it is now the practice to provide a series of pools or fish-ladder involving a number of small leaps to bypass any large dam.

The journey upstream continues into the smallest brooks and streams, often where there is only just enough water to cover the back of the fish. Here the nest or 'redd' is built, the male making a large trough in the pebbles by lashing with its tail. Several males will often make their redds within a few feet of each other. The female then lays the eggs in the redd (about 800 eggs per lb weight of fish) and the male fertilizes them and covers them over with gravel. Juvenile salmon were often noticed haunting the spawning sites and it was eventually realized that these smolts were in fact precociously mature and were scuttling in under the adult male to deposit sperm. Possibly this has some survival advantage in ensuring that all the eggs are fertilized.

The eggs and alevins are eagerly sought by trout and perch and to protect them from such predators they are often pushed down 7 in (18 cm) amongst the pebbles. Probably under half the eggs are actually fertilized and not all of these will hatch. The time taken to hatch is directly related to the temperature of the water, and ranges from five weeks in warm waters to as long as five months in very cold water. This has been of service in the transporting of salmon eggs to streams in other countries since it is merely necessary to keep them cool and moist.

The newly hatched alevins are about $\frac{1}{2}$ in (1·3 cm) long and they remain among the pebbles living on the food in their yolk sac. When about 1 in (2·5 cm) long they leave the nest and those that survive lead a secluded life in shallow waters feeding on small insect larvae. They reach about 4 in (10 cm) in the first year and 6 in (15 cm) in the second year. During this time they bear the parr markings of 8–10 dark oval blotches on the flanks with a red spot between each oval. Usually in the second year (occasionally in the first or the third) a silvery pigment develops over the parr marks and the fishes are then termed smolts (if the silvery pigment is scraped away the parr markings are visible below). The smolt then migrates to the sea, spends a year or more feeding, returning as an adult to struggle back upstream to its birthplace.

There is reason to fear that the days of the Atlantic salmon are now numbered. So many European rivers are now polluted or no longer have salmon runs. In the 18th century, for example, the Thames was one of the finest salmon rivers and the fishes could be seen leaping at London Bridge. With the growth of London, the discharge of sewage into the river began to affect the numbers of fishes caught, and with the Industrial Revolution this was aggravated by the discharge of industrial wastes. Finally the upstream migration of salmon became impossible and the last salmon to be seen in the River Thames was recorded in June, 1833. The salmon has disappeared from Portugal, Switzerland, Denmark, the Low Countries and is very rare in France and Spain. A similar situation exists along the eastern coast of Canada and the United States, while the spraying of insecticides for the control of Spruce bud worm has had disastrous effects on the salmon fisheries of the western seaboard of North America. Not only are salmon being prevented from spawning, however, but the size of the stock available to spawn is being diminished by the development of an extensive seafishery off Greenland following the discovery of large concentrations of Atlantic salmon there.

The salmon that were introduced in the last century and the early part of this century into the Argentine, New Zealand and other countries in the southern hemisphere are thriving and the situation might one day arise in which the salmon of the North Atlantic may be confined to the colder waters of the South Atlantic. FAMILY: Salmonidae, ORDER: Salmoniformes, CLASS: Pisces. (Ill. p. 149, 151.)

SANDEELS, small, silvery eel-like fishes, in no way related to true eels, found around the coasts of the Atlantic Ocean. They spend a lot of their time buried in sand. They have pointed jaws well adapted for burrowing, a long dorsal fin and no pelvic fins. Their main importance lies in their being an important item of diet for many commercially valuable fish like cod and halibut. FAMILY: Ammodytidae, ORDER: Perciformes, CLASS: Pisces.

SARDINE *Sardina pilchardus,* a small herring-like fish commonly marketed in tins, in fact the young of the *pilchard.

SARGASSUMFISH *Histrio histrio,* a small fish 6–8 in (15–20 cm) long, belonging to the family of frogfishes, which lives amongst the floating weeds of the Sargasso Sea. Like the anglerfishes, it has a 'fishing rod' or illicium modified from the first dorsal fin ray. It is very beautifully camouflaged in blotches of yellows and browns to match the Sargassum weed and is found also in other tropical areas where this weed occurs. It moves slowly amongst the fronds using its pectoral fins rather in the manner of arms and can modify its colours to match its surroundings. The body is stocky and appears clumsy, but if dislodged from the weed it can move surprisingly quickly in its efforts to regain the safety of the sargassum. To complete its camouflage, the outline of the fish is broken up by small, irregular flaps of skin. FAMILY: Antennariidae, ORDER: Lophiiformes, CLASS: Pisces.

SAURY PIKE *Scombresox saurus,* an elongated surface-living fish, up to 18 in (45 cm) long, resembling the garfishes (family Belonidae) found in the eastern Atlantic and Mediterranean. It is also known as the skipper from its habit of leaping out of the water. The jaws are somewhat elongated, but less so than in the garfishes, and the teeth are minute. There is a row of small finlets behind both the dorsal and anal fins. The Saury pike migrates northward in summer and may reach Norway. FAMILY: Scombresocidae, ORDER: Atheriniformes, CLASS: Pisces.

SAWFISHES, members of a family of flattened cartilaginous fishes somewhat resembling the guitarfishes but with the snout greatly elongated and bearing a series of 16–32 teeth on either side. Like the guitarfishes, the sawfishes have a rather shark-like body, with small pectoral fins which are not used for propelling the body forward, the motive power for swimming being derived from sinuous movements of the body, as in sharks. The sawfishes, however, have the gill slits on the underside of the head and are thus clearly allied to the rays and not to the sharks. They are found in tropical marine and brackish waters but also occur in some tropical fresh waters.

The curious 'saw' is a flattened blade of cartilage, calcified to give it rigidity, and the teeth along its two edges are implanted in sockets. The saw has always been assumed to be a weapon for defence and for attacking prey (other fishes) but observations have shown this to be only partially true. A specimen at the Lerner Marine Laboratory in Bimini (Bahamas) was seen to strike sideways at a fish, impale it on one of its saw teeth, and then retreat to the bottom where the impaled fish was rubbed off and eaten. The proverbial use of the saw to cut up larger fishes, and attack whales and even boats is, however, unfounded.

The Common sawfish *Pristis pectinatus* is found in the Atlantic and Mediterranean and is known to reach a length of 18 ft (5·4 m). The related *P. perotteti* has been caught some 450 miles (724 km) up the Amazon and is also found in Lake Nicaragua. Other species are known from fresh waters throughout the tropical world and in Thailand a specimen of 26 ft (7·8 m) has been caught and a monster of no less than 46 ft (14 m) has been reported. Although sawfishes have been reported as 'docile' considerable respect is shown for them by local fishermen, both in the water and when landed.

The sawfishes can be distinguished from the rather similar Saw sharks by the ventral position of the gill slits. The Saw sharks are true sharks, the gill slits being on the side of the head slightly above the pectoral fins. FAMILY: Pristidae, ORDER: Hypotremata, CLASS: Chondrichthyes.

SCATS, a family of marine or estuarine perch-like fishes from the Indo-Pacific region. In Australia they are referred to as butterfishes since the flesh is 'soft as butter'. They are also known as argusfishes because the eye-like spots on the body suggest the hundred-eyed Argus of legend. The scientific name of *Scatophagus* means 'dung-eaters' and refers to their habit of feeding on refuse and excrement, although plants and animals (usually dead) are also eaten. Scats are small compressed fishes with deep bodies and they are found in coastal and estuarine waters from Africa and India to the northern coasts of Australia; they are particularly common in the Malaysian area. There are strong spines on the dorsal fin and on the gill covers and the presence of four spines in the anal fin is an unusual feature amongst the perch-like fishes and helps in identification. Little is known of their breeding habits and they have rarely been bred in captivity. They appear to deposit their eggs in crevices in rocks. The larvae pass through a stage that is unlike that of the adult, the *tholichthys* stage, in which a strong spiny armour develops on the head and nape but is later lost. The young feed on algae before adopting their parent's feeding habits.

These little fishes are popular with aquarists because they can be kept in freshwater, although they do better in brackish water. *Scatophagus argus* is one of the commonest species imported. In the wild it grows to 12 in (30 cm) in length but stays very much smaller in aquaria. In this, as in other species, the colours can vary considerably and the background colour can range from greenish silver to the colour of coffee. The lower half of the body has irregular rows of black spots about the size of the eyes, but above the lateral line the spots may coalesce to form vertical bars. A reddish tinge may develop forming vertical bands in older fishes, and more red is found in the Australian species. The spines are said to cause inflamed wounds.

Members of the genus *Solenocta* are also imported for aquarists. These fishes have a much lower dorsal fin in contrast to the rather triangular fin of *Scatophagus*. FAMILY: Scatophagidae, ORDER: Perciformes, CLASS: Pisces. (Ill. p. 150.)

SCORPIONFISHES, a family of heavily built and often poisonous fishes belonging to the order of Mail-cheeked fishes. Many are from temperate waters, usually living in rocky areas, but some, like the bizarre lionfish, are found in tropical seas. They are chiefly bottom-living forms with large mouths and in some species an ornamentation of bony and fleshy spines and appendages on the head camouflage them against a background of rocks, corals and marine plants. Many have pungent or even poisonous spines in their fins which has given them their common name. The most poisonous of all scorpionfishes, and perhaps the most poisonous of all venomous fish, is the stonefish the camouflage of which is so perfect that the fish is almost indistinguishable from its background. Many scorpionfishes bear live young. Closely related to the scorpionfishes are the gurnards which, however, do not have poisonous spines. FAMILY: Scorpaenidae, ORDER: Scorpaeniformes, CLASS: Pisces. (Ill. p. 145, 149.)

SEA BREAMS, marine perch-like fishes not closely related either to Ray's bream or to the freshwater breams, found mainly in warm and tropical waters. The body is usually deep with a single long dorsal fin, the first part of which has spines, and three spines in the anal fin. There are well-developed teeth in the jaws, sharp in front, often rounded and molar-like behind. Many species are known from the eastern Atlantic and the Mediterranean and a few penetrate north as far as British shores.

Sea breams are also known as porgies. FAMILY: Sparidae, ORDER: Perciformes, CLASS: Pisces. (Ill. p. 149.)

SEA HORSES, small highly specialized marine fishes related to the pipefishes. They are unique amongst fishes in having the head set at right angles to the body. In many ways the Sea horses represent an end-point in several trends already apparent in the pipefishes. The body is entirely encased in an armour of bony plates or rings but the tail fin is absent and the hind part of the body is prehensile and can be twined round seaweeds to anchor the fish. Swimming is accomplished by wave-like vibrations in the dorsal fin, the fish progressing in a characteristic upright position. Care of the young by the male has reached a point where an enclosed pouch is present, formed by the bony plates of the body. Camouflage reaches bizarre proportions in such members as the Australian Leafy sea horse *Phyllopteryx foliatus,* in which fleshy leaf-like appendages decorate the body simulating seaweed. This grows to 12 in (30 cm) which is large for a Sea Horse.

Because of its unfish-like appearance and the ease with which dried specimens could be brought back to Europe, the Sea horses have long excited interest. The head is surprisingly horse-like and in the *Hortus Sanitatis* of J. von Cube, published in the 15th century there is an illustration of a Sea horse complete with hoofed forelegs and hair on the body. Sea horses were used as talismans and in potions against a variety of illnesses. The ashes of the Sea horse, however, were deemed fatal if mixed in wine, and in cases where the victim survived he was said to be plagued with a permanent desire to bathe. Mixed with pitch, the ashes of these little fishes were believed to be efficacious for restoring hair, but taken alone they were also a wise remedy for the bite of a mad dog.

The behaviour of the living Sea horses is just as interesting as the ancient legends. These fishes can show remarkable colour changes to match their surroundings. Their eyes can move independently of each other and, using their heads, they can clamber about the weeds in which they live, 'chinning' themselves from one strand to another. Not infrequently, several adults come together and twine their prehensile tails, a charming 'dance' in the adults but possibly lethal in the juveniles who are sometimes unable to free themselves and thus die of starvation. When breeding the male and female of most species wrap their tails round each other the eggs then being passed from the female by a cloacal appendage into the brood pouch of the male along his belly. The brood pouch is lined with soft tissue into which the eggs sink in little compartments while blood vessels in this tissue enlarge transforming the pouch into a spongy 'womb'. A parallel can be drawn between the vascular tissue surrounding the eggs and the placenta found in mammals. The male may be visited by a number of females. Eggs that do not find a pocket in the pouch fail to develop but those that do succeed hatch within the pouch and remain in their pocket until the yolk is used up. The 'birth' or ejection of the young seems to be exhausting for the male. Firmly grasping some support with the tail, he rubs the pouch against shell or rock until the young and assorted pieces of tissue are ejected. There seems to be no truth in the contention that the young thereafter resort to the pouch for shelter when danger threatens. A large male may give birth to as many as 400 young, each a little replica of the adult.

Sea horses live in shallow warm temperate and tropical seas around the world but have a patchy distribution being absent from large stretches of the coast of West Africa and in the Indo-Pacific area may be present in one region but absent in another. There are about 100 species known. They feed on tiny pelagic organisms which they suck up with their long snouts.

At least one species is not infrequently found off the south coasts of England, the Long-snouted sea horse *Hippocampus ramulosus* (formerly known as *H. antiquorum)*, a species which is quite common in the Mediterranean. The Short-snouted sea horse *H. hippocampus* only rarely occurs north of the Brittany coast. These two species are found amongst weeds in shallow water and, for Sea horses, are not very spectacular. The common Atlantic sea horse *H. hudsonensis* of the Western Atlantic coast, however, can produce magnificently intense colours ranging from white, through the normal browns and greens, to bright red and deep purple. The Hedgehog sea horse *Hippohystrix spinosissimus* of Australia has small spines. FAMILY: Syngnathidae, ORDER: Gasterosteiformes, CLASS: Pisces. (Ill. p. 147.)

SHADS, marine herring-like fishes that migrate into fresh waters to breed. Their common name may stem from the same root that gave rise to scad, that is from an Anglo-Saxon word for shadow. The best known of the European shads are the Allis shad *Alosa alosa* and the Twaite shad *A. finta*. These fishes are deeper-bodied than the herring and can be recognized by the bony

striations on the gill cover. The Allis shad is the larger of the two and reaches 2 ft (60 cm) in length with a weight of 8 lb (3·6 kg). Both species have a black spot behind the gill cover and in the young a series of black spots continues down the flanks. These spots are lost, however, in the adults of the Allis shad. The Allis shad is found on both sides of the North Atlantic but the Twaite shad is limited to European coasts. It is also found in some lakes in Switzerland and Italy and there is a semi-landlocked form, the Killarney shad, found in Ireland.

Related species of shads are found in the Caspian Sea and along the North American coast and are of economic importance in both areas. In the Indo-Pacific region the shads also play a useful role in native fisheries. The best known species is the hilsa *Hilsa ilisha* of Indian waters, a species that grows to 2 ft (60 cm) and is caught in enormous quantities as it enters rivers. FAMILY: Clupeidae, ORDER: Clupeiformes, CLASS: Pisces.

SHARKS, an order, Pleurotremata, of cartilaginous fishes that includes about 250 species found both in the oceans and in fresh waters and ranging in size from less than 1 ft (30 cm) in length, the Midwater shark *Squaliolus laticaudus,* to at least 45 ft (13·5 m) in the Whale shark. The sharks belong to a class of fishes that includes the rays (order Hypotremata) and the chimaeras (subclass Bradyodonti), the three orders sharing such common features as an entirely cartilaginous skeleton (no bone present but the cartilage is sometimes strengthened by calcification), the development of tooth-like placoid scales (denticles) on the body, the gills opening externally by a series of gill-slits (covered over in the chimaeras, however), and reproduction by internal fertilization, the young in many cases being born alive after hatching in the uterus of the female. Sharks are usually elongated, with a fusiform or cigar-shaped body, the snout being more or less pointed and the upper lobe of the tail often being much better developed than the lower lobe. The gill-slits, which lie on the side of the head (under the head in rays), are usually five in number but there are six in the Frilled shark and six or seven in the Cow sharks. Water is drawn in through the mouth and pumped out through the gill-slits, although in the Whale shark a continuous flow of water may be achieved by the fish merely swimming with its mouth open. As in the rays and chimaeras, there is no swimbladder and since the fish is heavier than water it must constantly swim to avoid sinking. The body is therefore highly streamlined and the large pectoral fins provide considerable 'lift' by acting as hydrofoils. Some species, such as the Carpet sharks, spend a certain amount of time resting on the bottom but species, such as the

Mackerel sharks, spend their entire lives cruising in mid-water or at the surface and such species are characterized by almost symmetrical tails on a narrow base, small second dorsal and anal fins and rather sickle-shaped pectoral fins. The large and oily liver of a shark is probably of use as a buoyancy organ in species such as the Basking shark that often lie motionless at the surface. Sand sharks are said to gulp air and to retain it in the stomach to provide buoyancy. In swimming, the motive power is derived from sinuous movements of the body, the fins being fairly inflexible and used to control rolling, yawing and pitching as well as controlling the direction of movement. Species such as the Mackerel sharks are not only extremely fast swimmers but can also leap clear out of the water.

One immediately obvious feature of sharks is their rough covering of placoid scales or denticles. These are tooth-like having a pulp cavity surrounded by dentine and covered by a thin layer of enamel. The tooth-like denticles arise from a flat basal plate. The tooth is often capped by another flat plate which may bear low keels on its upper surface. The denticles may be fairly small and close together to produce the sandpaper surface of the Grey sharks or they may be rather sparse and thorn-like as in the Bramble shark. The jaw teeth in sharks have essentially the same structure and lie in rows in the jaws, the outer series functional and the inner series ready to fold outwards and replace those that are lost. The three principal types of teeth are the triangular cutting or shearing teeth found in such fishes as the Great white shark, the slender awl-like teeth of the Mackerel sharks, and the rather flat pavement of teeth for crushing and grinding found in the Smooth hounds. In addition to the main cusp of the tooth, one or more secondary cusps may be developed and in the Cow sharks there are a large number of cusps that have suggested the alternative name of Comb-toothed sharks for these fishes. In the Horn sharks there are cutting teeth in the front of the jaw but crushing teeth at the rear. Sharks are mostly carnivores, feeding on fishes and a wide range of invertebrates but known also to scavenge refuse from ships or harbours and in the process to swallow an extraordinary range of inedible objects amongst which can be listed bottles, tins, boxes, a native drum, the head of a buffalo and articles of clothing. The Whale shark and the Basking shark, however, have taken to filtering small crustaceans and other animals from the plankton by means of a mesh of fine gill-rakers.

Sharks have the reputation for being amongst the most dangerous of all marine animals, but out of the 250 species known only 27 have definitely been implicated in attacks on men. The most dangerous of all is the Great white shark, both because of its aggressiveness and its large size, and more attacks have been accredited to this species than to any other. The Mako shark is the most frequently involved in attacks on boats, mostly unprovoked. Other large species that are dangerous are the Hammerhead sharks, the Tiger shark and some of the Grey sharks. Often a series of attacks will occur along a previously 'safe' beach and these appear to be due to a rogue shark newly arrived in the locality. The movements of the swimmer in the water are probably more important in attracting sharks than such things as the colour of a bathing suit. Although sharks occur in all seas, shark attacks are limited to waters over 70°F (21°C) so that the zone between 21° N and 21° S is one in which attacks can occur throughout the year while to the north and south of this zone attacks are mainly limited to the summer months. In both hemispheres attacks are rare or unknown north of about 42° N, the most northerly being Greece, Port Said and Genoa (44° N) and the coast of New Jersey northwards to South Amboy. No effective shark repellant has yet been developed and experiments on copper acetate and black nigrosine dye have shown that these are not always reliable. Bubble curtains from perforated pipes of compressed air have also been ineffective and by far the best protection has been provided by shark nets surrounding bathing beaches. It should be borne in mind, however, that the number of shark attacks is infinitesimal compared with road accidents and that actual fatalities are no more numerous than those caused by lightning.

Reproduction in sharks involves an act of copulation, fertilization being internal. In males parts of the pelvic fins are modified into claspers, or myxopterygia, bearing a groove down which the sperm is passed and there are one or more hooks which are used to engage the cloaca of the female during mating. One or both claspers may be inserted, the male wrapping its body round that of the female (some dogfishes) or bringing its body into close contact (larger sharks); a gentle rhythmic motion of the tail region has sometimes been observed. Fertilization takes place in the anterior part of the oviduct or in the nidamentary or shell gland. Here the eggs are coated with an envelope which in the egg-laying species is horny and in some species (dogfishes) has a long tendril from each corner. The embryo then completes its development on the sea floor, nourished all the while by its yolk. In the ovoviviparous species the eggs are coated with only a very thin shell by the shell gland and then pass to the uterus where they hatch, continue their development and are later born. In some species, however, the young are retained in the uterus for longer than their yolk supply would last and various methods have evolved for nourishing the young. In some species the

embryo is fed by secretions from the uterus (uterine milk), but in others an 'umbilical cord' develops from the embryo to its yolk sac and the latter becomes attached to the wall of the uterus to form a placenta similar to that found in mammals. Another method of nourishing the embryos is by means of yolk from unfertilized eggs. Typical of the oviparous or egg-laying sharks are the Horn sharks, Whale shark, most Cat sharks and some of the Carpet sharks. Most other sharks are ovoviviparous but some of the Grey sharks and Hammerhead sharks are truly viviparous, the embryos being directly nourished by the mother.

Sharks are of some commercial importance as food although in world catches they now represent only about 1% of the total fish caught. The flesh is very lean since the oils are concentrated in the liver. Shark livers once provided a valuable source for vitamin A and during the Second World War $\frac{3}{4}$ of the vitamin A produced in the United States was derived from shark livers (mainly the Soupfin shark *Galeorhinus zygopterus*). With the artificial synthesis of this vitamin, however, shark liver oils have become of less importance. Sharkskin or shagreen can be made from sharks but the finest product comes from a stingray *Dasyatis sephen* in which the denticles are closely packed together. By abrasion, polishing and dyeing a very beautiful and ornamental surface can be produced. Shark fins from the Soupfin shark are also a valuable product much appreciated in the East.

There are 20 families of sharks, representing a primitive group that reached its zenith in Carboniferous times but then declined in face of competition from the bony fishes. Except for the Grey sharks, all the other families contain genera that are known from fossils in rocks dating back to the Cretaceous period or even the Jurassic. The modern sharks show considerable diversity in shape and habits and in spite of their eclipse by the more advanced bony fishes they must still be reckoned as a successful group of fishes. ORDER: Pleurotremata, CLASS: Chondrichthyes. (Ill. p. 145.)

SHRIMPFISHES or razorfishes, a family of curious flattened fishes the bodies of which more closely resemble the blade of a knife than in the so-called knifefishes. The shrimpfishes are related to the snipefishes and the Sea horses. The snout is elongated, with a tiny mouth at its tip, and the hind end of the body is even more curious in that it is bent downwards in such a way that the first dorsal fin is in the position usually occupied by the tail, while the latter is in the position normally taken by the anal fin. The first dorsal is represented by a massive spine followed by a few small rays. In the genus *Centriscus* the tip of the spine is jointed and

movable. The reason for this very unusual joint is not known, but *Centriscus strigatus* has been observed resting head downwards with the tip of the spine at right angles to the body, possibly gaining some stability through contact with the surface of the water. Equally unusual and puzzling is the fact that this part of the spine is supplied with nerves and sensory cells.

Shrimpfishes are mainly found in the Indo-Pacific region, where they swim in small groups in shallow water. For a long time it was debated whether they swim head up or head down, for they rarely swim horizontally. Dr Robert Rofen finally solved this problem by keeping some of these fishes in an aquarium. He found that they usually feed head downwards but if they encounter an overhanging surface they will follow it round until they end up with the head upwards, that is to say, upside down. With the dorsal and anal fins and the tail bunched together, they are best adapted for swimming with the head down and the back of the fish pointing forwards. This might appear clumsy but shrimpfishes are in fact surprisingly agile, darting about with great rapidity. They are so thin that when they turn sideways amongst weeds the little shoal seems to disappear. A favourite haunt appears to be amongst the long spines of tropical Sea urchins, where they take up a position parallel to the spines and are both difficult to see and safe from predators.

Shrimpfishes feed on the tiniest particles of food, which are sucked up by the pipette-like mouth. There are only a few species of which the largest is the Australian *Centriscus cristatus,* a species which occasionally reaches 12 in (30 cm) in length. The body is silvery with a deep red band from the mouth to the eye, continuing to the spine of the 'tail' as an orange line. The belly is pale yellow with about ten oblique red bars on it.

Little is known of the breeding habits of the shrimpfishes. They are of no economic value but are used as ornaments on some of the Pacific islands. FAMILY: Centriscidae, ORDER: Gasterosteiformes, CLASS: Pisces.

SILVERSIDES, small marine or freshwater fishes with a bright silvery band down the flanks, related to the flyingfishes. They are almost worldwide in distribution being found in the freshwaters of Australia, where they are known as rainbowfish. They have two dorsal fins, the first with rather weak spines and the second soft-rayed. The eggs have long filaments sprouting from them which help anchor them to weeds or seaweeds. The Common sandsmelt *Atherina presbyter* found off the coast of northwest Europe grows to about 6 in (15 cm) and is common in harbours, bays and estuaries. These fishes are gregarious and feed on small crustaceans and other invertebrates. With their bright silver band on the flank they make excellent bait for trolling and spinning. The second European species is Boyer's sandsmelt *A. mochon* (formerly *A. boyeri*), a less common species which can be distinguished by its slightly larger eye and fewer rays in the anal fin (13–15 as against 15–19 in the Common sandsmelt).

There are several freshwater species on the western side of the Atlantic. The Brook silverside *Labidesthes sicculus,* from a wide range of waters in the eastern parts of the United States, grows to only a few inches in length and is semi-transparent and pale green with a violet iridescence. It lives in enormous shoals and when alarmed by predators these scatter rapidly, the fishes skittering over the water, which has earned them the name of skipjack.

Along the shores of Lower California is found the grunion *Leuresthes tenuis* that grows to 6 in (15 cm) and normally lives in shallow water. It has remarkable breeding habits. It spawns at night high up on the beach at the time of high spring tides, the fish allowing themselves to be washed as far up the beach as possible by the surf and then wriggling forward over the wet sand. The female digs herself into the sand and the male wraps himself around her. The eggs are shed and fertilized about 2 in (5 cm) below the surface. The fishes then wriggle back into the surf. The eggs remain in the sand until the next high spring tide when they hatch within a very short time of first being wetted, the larvae making their escape to the sea. Since the spawning of the grunion is so closely correlated with the tides, it is thought that these fishes are able to appreciate the phases of the moon. FAMILY: Atherinidae, ORDER: Atheriniformes, CLASS: Pisces. (Ill. p. 146.)

SKATES, a family of flattened cartilaginous fishes belonging to the order of rays but differing from all other ray-like fishes in producing eggs and not giving birth to live young. In the United States, a variety of species are known as skates, but in England two principal species are known as skates and the remainder as rays, the distinction depending to some extent on the degree to which the snout is pointed. Similar distinctions are made in other European languages but these do not always correspond with English usage. Typically, the skates are highly flattened fishes with large wing-like pectoral fins that spread evenly from the snout and then taper more or less abruptly. The tail is slender, equal to, or shorter than, the body and there are two dorsal fins set far back towards the end of the tail. The eyes are on top of the head, followed by a pair of conspicuous spiracles through which water is drawn to aerate the gills. The body, and sometimes the pectoral 'wings', are often lined with spines or bucklers (modified den-

ticles). The gill slits are on the underside as is also the mouth, which bears a series of flat pavement-like teeth in each jaw. In some species the snout is produced into a point or rostrum. The skates lay large eggs enclosed in a horny rectangular capsule with short pointed tendrils at each corner; these are commonly found on beaches and are known as mermaids' purses. The young remain within the egg capsule for at least four months and sometimes as long as 14 months. Skates are world-wide in their distribution, mostly in shallow waters but a few in depths down to over 7,000 ft (2,000 m). Some species have weak electrical organs developed along the side of the tail and these are possibly used for echolocation of prey, mates, obstacles and predators. Colour is very variable between species and between individuals and can to some extent be controlled to match the background. The majority of skates are fairly small, reaching 1 or 2 ft (30–60 cm) in length but a few may reach 8 ft (2·4 m). The skates are more important commercially off European coasts than in the western North Atlantic but are of local importance to fisheries elsewhere.

The Common skate *Raja naevus* of European waters is a member of a large genus with over 100 species the identification of which is often extremely difficult. It is the most abundant of the long-snouted species found off the coasts of Britain and is caught from shallow water down to depths of about 200 ft (60 m). The back is a dark brown or grey, sometimes with eye-spots and the belly is grey (never white). These fishes may reach 7 ft (2·1 m) in length and weigh up to 200 lb (90 kg). Anglers find that once hooked, skates are extremely difficult to raise, the fish making every effort to remain on the bottom. The Long-nosed skate *R. oxyrhynchus* is also often caught by anglers. It is more triangular than the Common skate and grows to a length of 5 ft (1·5 m).

The most common of the British species is the Thornback ray *R. clavata*. It has very well-developed spines not only down the back and tail but also on the pectoral fins. Like other species, the Thornback is mainly a bottom-feeder, browsing on crabs, Sand eels *Ammodytes* spp and other fishes.

Other European species include the Cuckoo ray *R. neavus*, the homelyn *R. montagui*, the Shagreen ray *R. fullonica* and the Bottle-nosed ray *R. marginata*. The identification of these and other species depends largely on good illustrations showing the characteristic shape and colours of the fish. One of the most common of the western North Atlantic skates is the Little skate *R. erinacea* which occurs from Nova Scotia to Carolina. It grows to about 20 in (51 cm) and is frequently used by schools and colleges for teaching purposes.

For centuries fishermen and sailors have

trimmed the pectoral fins and modified the heads of dead skates to produce a curious dragon-like creature to be sold as a basilisk, Sea eagle or monkeyfish to the credulous. These curios are known as Jenny hannivers. FAMILY: Rajidae, ORDER: Hypotremata, CLASS: Chondrichthyes.

SLEEPER SHARK *Somniosus microcephalus,* also known as the Greenland shark, a large fish of the temperate and Arctic waters of the North Atlantic with closely related species in the Mediterranean, the Pacific and Antarctic waters. The body is large and bulky. There are two dorsal fins without spines in front and the upper lobe of the tail is slightly larger than the lower lobe. This species is said to be very lethargic and easy to catch, offering little or no resistance when hauled to the surface in spite of its often great size. It can reach 24 ft (7·2 m). It is caught by the Eskimos of Greenland, sometimes on a thin line hauled by a fisherman in a small kayak. Sleeper sharks are the only species of shark found in Arctic waters but members of these northern populations have in the past been recorded as far south as Massachusetts and the English Channel. The Sleeper shark produces large numbers of eggs, which range in size but may be as large as those of a goose. For many years it was thought that it was an oviparous species, the eggs being laid in mud and later hatching. Recent work has shown, however, that the Sleeper shark is ovoviviparous, the eggs hatching within the uterus of the female and the embryos continuing their development there.

The family of Sleeper sharks also contains the Luminous shark *Isistius brasiliensis,* a small shark that grows to about 18 in (46 cm) and has numerous small light organs scattered on the body that give off a vivid greenish glow. Similar light organs are found in the Pigmy shark *Euprotomicrus bispinatus,* also a member of this family. The Pigmy shark is one of the smallest of all sharks, the largest recorded specimen being only 10½ in (27 cm). FAMILY: Dalatiidae, ORDER: Pleurotremata, CLASS: Chondrichthyes.

SMELT, small estuarine fishes related to the salmons. The European smelt *Osmerus eperlanus* is an elongated, compressed fish somewhat resembling a small trout but with a silvery body and slight blue-green tinges on the fins. A small adipose fin is present and the lateral line is short, not extending beyond the pectoral fins. The mouth is large, with fine teeth in the jaws, and there are conical teeth on the roof of the mouth and several large fang-like teeth at the front of the tongue. Smelt live in large shoals in the estuaries and coastal waters of Europe and are commonly used by fishermen for bait.

They are anadromous fishes, migrating up into fresher water to spawn. A peculiar feature of the smelt (from whence it may have derived its common name) is the odour of the flesh, which resembles that of cucumbers. In the days before many of the large European estuaries became so polluted that fish were rarely found in them, fishermen were said to be able to detect the presence of smelt by the smell of cucumbers. By the middle of the last century, the Thames estuary was so polluted that the smelt disappeared but in recent years stringent measures against pollution have resulted in a recolonization of this area and smelt have been recorded once more. The smelt rarely grows to more than about 8 in (20 cm) but is considered to be a great delicacy. Connoisseurs claim that smelt should be eaten within an hour of capture, should not be washed at all but lightly fried or grilled.

Other species of smelt are found in the coastal waters of the temperate regions of the northern hemisphere. *Thaleichthys pacificus* from the northeast Pacific grows to about 12 in (30 cm). It has earned the common name of candlefish since the flesh is very oily and the American Indians made use of this by drying the fishes and then setting light to them in the manner of candles. This is the largest of the species of smelt. One of the smallest species is the Sacramento smelt *Spirinchus thaleichthys* from the San Francisco area. It grows to only 3 in (7·5 cm) in length and is found in vast shoals along the coast. FAMILY: Osmeridae, ORDER: Salmoniformes, CLASS: Pisces.

SNAKEHEADS, a group of elongated freshwater fishes from Africa and Asia. The affinities of this group are somewhat uncertain and for the present they are placed near the vast assemblage of perch-like fishes, the Perciformes. They have long, cylindrical bodies, a very reptilian-looking head and long soft-rayed dorsal and anal fins. The body is usually mottled with shades of brown, sometimes with hints of red, the colour pattern being distinctive for each species, but the markings blend well with the background. They are aggressive, predatory fishes, usually 2½ ft (75 cm) long with large and pugnacious jaws.

Snakeheads often live in foul, stagnant waters and like many other fishes in this type of environment they have developed accessory breathing organs. The gill chambers have little pouches that are folded and well supplied with blood vessels for the absorption of oxygen. When the water dries up they bury themselves in the mud but are also capable of moving overland with peculiar rowing movements of their pectoral fins.

In Southeast Asia they are important food fishes, largely because of their ability to stay alive for a long time out of water and thus remain in good condition until sold. There are two genera, *Ophicephalus* (literally 'snakehead') and *Channa,* which has a single species that lacks pelvic fins. They have been successfully introduced into parts of the United States. FAMILY: Ophicephalidae, ORDER: Channiformes, CLASS: Pisces.

SNAKE MACKERELS, oceanic fishes of moderately deep waters, related to the true mackerels, the frostfish and the swordfish. The common name refers to their general resemblance to elongated mackerels. The first dorsal fin consists of spines joined together by a membrane, which begins behind the head and gradually becomes lower until a second dorsal fin arises about ⅔ of the way along the body followed by a few isolated spines with individual membranes (finlets). There are two lateral lines along the flank, one just below the dorsal fin and the other along the midline of the body. The eyes are large and the mouth is armed with dagger-like teeth.

Gempylus serpens is found in all tropical seas but will occasionally wander into cooler waters. It is a species that grows to at least 5 ft (1·5 m) in length. It is sometimes found at the surface at night, while in the daytime Snake mackerels are caught from time to time with long lines set at some depth for tunas. Like many oceanic fishes, the Snake mackerel seems to make a daily vertical migration. It was during the night that a specimen was washed on board the Kon-tiki during its voyage across the Pacific. Although this is not a unique occurrence, the publicity focused on this specimen made the Snake mackerel better known than many other uncommon oceanic fishes. FAMILY: Gempylidae, ORDER: Perciformes, CLASS: Pisces.

SNAPPERS, marine perch-like shore fishes of warm waters. The snout is fairly pointed, the mouth prominent and the jaws armed with sharp teeth, thus giving the fishes their name of snappers. There are over 200 species, some rather deep-bodied, some very colourful, but most presenting considerable difficulties in identification. A few species enter freshwater. The larger species grow to over 3 ft (90 cm) and in certain tropical countries the snappers are important food fishes. A few species have been implicated in ciguatera poisoning but the latter is to be expected in any large and predatory reef-inhabiting fish (see poisonous fishes). The Red mumea *Lutjanus bohar* is apparently always poisonous in the Samoa region. As a general rule, snappers from close inshore are greenish and banded, marbled or spotted, whereas those from deeper waters are usually reddish. The colour-pattern, as in several other groups of marine fishes, may change radically during the growth of the individual, as for example in the cinnamon-fish *L. nematophorus.* FAMILY: Lutjanidae, ORDER: Perciformes, CLASS: Pisces.

SNIPEFISHES, a family of marine fishes of moderately deep water, related to the pipe-fishes and shrimpfishes. They have compressed, oval bodies and a long snout. The first dorsal fin is pointed, with a massive spine, and is quite separate from the second dorsal fin. The body is covered with tough and rather rough scales but on the chest and shoulders there is a lattice-work of bony bars. The mouth is small and weak and placed at the tip of the snout. *Macrorhamphosus scolopax* lives at depths of about 300 ft (100 m) in the North Atlantic and Mediterranean but comes to the surface at night. It is pinkish in colour and reaches 6 in (15 cm) in length. The related *M. gracilis* has a much more elegant shape and is found farther south in the Atlantic.

In the southern hemisphere the genera *Notopogon* and *Centriscops* are found and are popularly known as the bellowsfish from their resemblance to an old-fashioned pair of bellows. The Banded bellowsfish *Centriscops obliquus* is widespread, growing to about 10 in (25 cm) and having six oblique black bars on a pinkish background. These fishes come into shallow water and have been kept in captivity in New Zealand, where it was noted that they can swim as easily backwards as forwards. Normally, when swimming, the snout points downwards. They are easily alarmed and then perform surprisingly agile leaps for such seemingly ungainly fishes. They feed on small crustaceans, eggs and plankton, which they suck up with their long snouts. FAMILY: Macrorhamphosidae, ORDER: Gasterosteiformes, CLASS: Pisces.

SNOEK *Thyrsites atun,* an important food fish in the southern hemisphere, silvery with a bluish-black back and dark bands along the sides, up to 4ft (1·2 m) long and 20 lb (9 kg), ranging from South Africa to Argentina, Chile, New Zealand, and Australia, where it is known as barracouta, or sea-pike. Snoek swim in large shoals preying on other fishes, especially a sardine *Clupea sagax,* which they wear down by their greater stamina.

Until a few years ago nothing was known of the life-history. Then a South African biologist on a research ship took roes from ripe male and female snoek, released their contents in an aquarium of seawater and studied the development of the fertilized egg to the larva. FAMILY: Gempylidae, ORDER: Perciformes, CLASS: Pisces.

SNOOK, a name associated with certain marine fishes but most usually applied to the perch-like fishes of the family Centropomidae, living in tropical seas, estuaries and freshwaters. The centropomids include the tiny glassfish *Chanda ranga* of India (formerly known as *Ambassis lala*), the giant Nile perch *Lates nilotica* of African lakes and the palmer *L. calcarifer* from the coasts of the Indo-Pacific region. The centropomids have fairly elongated bodies and in some species the spinous and soft parts of the dorsal fin are joined. They are mostly predators with bands of fine teeth in the jaws.

The Common snook *Centropomus undecimalis* has separate spiny and soft dorsal fins and the series of lateral line scales down each flank is marked as a dark stripe. This species is found in the tropical Atlantic, particularly in coastal regions. Mangrove swamps harbour large numbers of snook and frequently they are found far up rivers in freshwater. They grow to over 4 ft (1·2 m) and can weigh up to 44 lb (20 kg).

In Australia, the name snook is used for the Narrow-barred mackerel *Scomberomorus commeroon*. In South Africa, snook or *snoek is a fish resembling the barracuda. FAMILY: Centropomidae, ORDER: Perciformes, CLASS: Pisces.

SOAPFISHES or soapies, fishes of the marine family Leiognathidae, which, when handled, secrete a slippery mucus that makes them difficult to hold. Presumably this is used by the fish as a defence mechanism against predators. In America these fishes are also called slipmouths and in Australia they are referred to as ponyfishes. The soapfishes have deep and very compressed silvery bodies with the dorsal and anal fins beginning at the deepest point of the body so that the profile of the fish is almost disc-like. A characteristic feature is the protrusile mouth which is usually extruded when the fish is taken from the water, giving it a horse-like appearance and earning it the name of ponyfish. A protrusile mouth enables a fish to seize or suck in small food particles from the bottom, although in the genus *Secutor* the mouth is in fact protruded upwards. The soapfishes are small shoaling fishes which often enter brackish lagoons, especially as juveniles. In spite of their small size and relatively little muscle, they are so numerous in some areas that they make an important contribution to protein resources and are caught and sun-dried in large numbers.

Some of the Sea perches (family Serranidae) have also been given the name of soapfishes because of their mucus covering which bubbles up like soap-suds when the fish is active and especially when handled. The Three-spined soapfish *Rypticus saponaceus,* a 12 in (30 cm) fish found off the tropical Atlantic coasts of America and Africa, is an example of a serranid soapfish. FAMILY: Leiognathidae, ORDER: Perciformes, CLASS: Pisces.

SOLES, a family of rather elongated flatfishes of considerable economic importance. The eyes are on the left side, the mouth is small and the snout projects well beyond the mouth to give the fish its characteristic appearance. It can be noted that the Lemon sole *Microstomus kitt* is not a true sole but belongs to the plaice family. The Dover sole *Solea solea* has a long oval body and the dorsal fin begins over the head and reaches almost to the tail. The eyed side is dark brown with darker blotches. It lives in shallow water in the Mediterranean and along European shores as far north as the coasts of Britain, but becomes rarer in the north. Occasionally it enters estuaries and in winter it migrates into slightly deeper and warmer waters. It is caught by trawl, especially in the southern North Sea and the Bay of Biscay. The sole reaches 2 ft (60 cm) in length and can weigh as much as 9 lb (4 kg). The name Dover sole was coined in the last century before refrigeration when an enterprising gentleman organized a series of coach stages between Dover and London so that the fishes could be brought to the London markets with the greatest possible speed.

The Thickback sole *Microchirus variegatus* is very much smaller and thicker. It has a more southerly range and is of no economic importance. Of all the European soles it is the most easily identified, having transverse black bands on the body. A fairly rare Atlantic sole is *Bathysolea profundicola*, a deep-water species found down to nearly 4,000 ft (1,290 m) in the North Atlantic and Mediterranean. The Naked sole *Gymnachirus williamsoni* from Florida coasts is less elongated than the European species and has a pretty pattern of dark chocolate bands on a reddish background.

The flatfish most commonly kept by aquarists is *Achirus fasciatus,* which is known as the Dwarf flounder but is a true sole. It is found in fresh and brackish waters in the southeast of the United States and in the wild grows to 6 in (15 cm). The eyed side is a mottled grey-brown. It is unfortunate that this particular species should be nocturnal, buried in the sand for most of the day but coming out at night to feed. It thrives on worms but will also eat small pieces of plants. FAMILY: Soleidae, ORDER: Pleuronectiformes, CLASS: Pisces.

SPINY DOGFISHES, a family of small sharks characterized by the presence of a sharp spine in front of the first and second dorsal fins and by the absence of an anal fin. The most common species of both sides of the Atlantic is the Spiny dogfish, Spur dog or Piked dogfish *Squalus acanthias*. It has an elongated, slender body with a pointed snout and is dark grey-brown sometimes spotted with white. The two spines of the dorsal fin

bear grooves containing venom-secreting tissue so that a jab from one of these spines can be extremely painful. The Spiny dogfish is a voracious eater of crabs, mussels and fishes and is considered a scourge by fishermen, especially along the American Atlantic coast. This fish is a shoaling species that sometimes occurs in enormous numbers; off the coast of Massachusetts some 27 million Spiny dogfish are said to have been caught in one season and 20,000 were once caught in a single haul off the coast of Cornwall in England. At one time they were dried and used as fuel on fishing boats. In parts of Europe, the Spiny dogfish is used as a food fish. It reaches about 4 ft (1·2 m) in length (males rather smaller) and is ovoviviparous, the young hatching within the uterus of the female after completing what must be one of the longest gestation periods of any vertebrate, birth taking place after 18–22 months. The Spiny dogfish is essentially a coastal, shallow-water species.

This family contains a number of curious species. The Portuguese *Centroscymnus coelolepis* is apparently the deepest-living of all sharks, having been recorded from a depth of 8,917 ft (2,718 m). Some of the species of *Etmopterus* are amongst the smallest of all sharks, reaching a maximum of just over 12 in (30 cm). In *Etmopterus lucifer* the lower surfaces of the fish are densely but irregularly scattered with tiny light organs. These photophores are cup-shaped and backed by a dark pigment. They have a lens in front and are equipped with an iris-like structure of pigment cells which presumably regulates the amount of light emitted. Members of the genus *Oxynotus* have bodies that are triangular in cross section, the back being strongly compressed and rising up to a high dorsal fin. FAMILY: Squalidae, ORDER: Pleurotremata, CLASS: Chondrichthyes.

SPINY EELS, eel-like fishes of the fresh waters of Africa and Asia but quite unrelated to the true eels. Characteristic of the family is the elongated body and the pointed snout with its tubular nostrils at the end. Along the back and before the dorsal fin there is a row of sharp spines (40 or more) which the fish erects when it is handled and by wriggling backwards, it can lacerate the hands. Some species are found in waters that are poor in oxygen, some occasionally enter estuaries and others are found in mountain streams that are rich in oxygen. Most are nocturnal and during the day bury themselves in the sand or amongst plant debris with only the snout protruding.

Normally the colouring is attractive but not brilliant, with various patterns of brown and grey predominating. In the Fire eel *Mastacembelus erythrinus,* however, there are vivid red markings on the body and although this is a rather large species it is currently finding favour with aquarists. Reputedly these fishes will come to recognize their owners when kept in tanks by themselves. Most Spiny eels kept by aquarists rarely grow to more than 12 in (30 cm) in length but in the wild they can reach 3 ft (100 cm). FAMILY: Mastacembelidae, ORDER: Perciformes, CLASS: Pisces. (Ill. p. 148.)

SPRAT *Sprattus sprattus,* a small herring-like fish found off the Atlantic coasts of Europe and in the Mediterranean. It closely resembles the herring, but is much smaller and rarely exceeds 6 in (15 cm) in length. Since sprats commonly shoal with juvenile herrings the two are often confused and at one time the sprat was thought to be the young of the herring. The sprat, however, is inclined to be greenish rather than bluish along the back and it can be fairly easily distinguished by the much stronger serrations of the scutes along the belly (this is obvious if the 'keel' of the fish is stroked from tail to head). The sprat is a pelagic species that feeds on plankton in the surface waters and the eggs are also pelagic, floating near the surface and not lying at the bottom as in the herring. The sprats of the Baltic and the Mediterranean differ slightly from the rest and are considered distinct subspecies.

Unlike the young of the herring, the sprats have a very high fat content and are of great commercial value, the herring at this size being rather lean. Whitebait is usually a mixture of sprats and young herrings and at one time it was even thought that whitebait represented a distinct species. Commercially marketed sprats are also sometimes mixtures of the two species and their quality is thereby reduced, a fact that has been said to account for the decline in the popularity of the sprat in northern England. Large numbers are caught in Norwegian waters, especially in sheltered fjords near Stavanger and Haugesund, and after capture by ringnets the fishes are confined to pens in order to give time for the gut to empty and thus to produce a perfect fish for canning. These Norwegian 'sardines' are marketed as brisling.

There are no other members of this genus in the northern hemisphere, but four species of *Sprattus* occur off the coasts of New Zealand, southern Australia and south-eastern South America, where they are of some commercial importance. Members of the related genus *Ramnogaster* occur off the coast of Argentina and also enter estuaries. FAMILY: Clupeidae, ORDER: Clupeiformes, CLASS: Pisces.

SQUIRRELFISHES, a common name usually applied to certain fishes of the sub-order of berycoid fishes and especially to those of the family Holocentridae. The pro-file of the head and the large eyes faintly resemble a squirrel but hardly enough to justify the common name. To students of evolution, the berycoid fishes are of great interest because this group appears to have been ancestral to the great group of perch-like forms (order Perciformes) and thus to be an intermediate group between the primitive soft-rayed fishes and the more specialized of the spiny-finned Acanthopterygii.

The holocentrid squirrelfishes are usually bright red with silvery spots or bands on the flanks. The scales are large and bear serrations or sharp points on the hind edge so that the fish is rough to handle. There are also sharp spines on the head and on the bones of the gill cover (the opercular series). Most squirrelfishes are nocturnal and have large eyes. They live in shallow water, particularly around coral reefs, and during the day hide in cracks, coming out at night to feed. They have a world-wide tropical distribution.

In Australia they are known as soldier-fishes. The Red soldierfish *Holocentrum rubrum* is perhaps the most widespread in the Indo-Pacific region. It tends to live in slightly deeper water than most of its relatives being found down to 90 ft (27 m). The body is bright red and each longitudinal row of scales bears a silvery stripe; the fins are rosy red with black markings. It grows to about 12 in (30 cm) in length. Like other members of the genus *Holocentrum,* this fish shows a strong territorial behaviour and the fishes are therefore solitary. In the related genus *Myripristis,* however, individuals commonly shoal together. Most squirrelfishes make noises when courting and under certain conditions these can be heard out of water. FAMILY: Holocentridae, ORDER: Beryciformes, CLASS: Pisces.

STARGAZERS, two families containing bottom-living perch-like fishes, the eyes of which are set on top of the head, the fish appearing to stare upwards, hence the common name. The principal difference between these two families is that the uranoscopids have electric organs. They are marine fishes found in all tropical and temperate waters, from the shallows to the depths. They have stocky, depressed bodies, large heads and a mouth that is directed upwards. The European stargazer *Uranoscopus scaber* is common in the Mediterranean. It grows to 1 ft (30 cm) long and has little flaps of tissue inside the mouth that resemble small worms. These appear to act as lures, enticing fishes inside the mouth.

The electric organs are formed from muscles and are lodged in pits behind the eyes. Although small, the discharge from these organs reaches 50 volts. It is thought to be partly a means of defence and partly a means of stunning small fishes. Stargazers also defend themselves by means of poison-ous spines above the pectoral fins. The spines are grooved and there is a poison gland at their base, the poison running along the groove and into the wound. It has been known to be fatal to humans. These fishes are extremely difficult to see, even when in shallow water, because they bury themselves in the sand with only the eyes and tip of snout showing. In some species the nostrils open into the mouth so that a stream of sediment-free water can be drawn in.

One of the best known of the dactylosco-pids is *Dactyloscopus tridigitatus.* It is found in the warmer parts of the Atlantic. FAMILIES: Uranoscopidae, Dactyloscopidae, ORDER: Perciformes, CLASS: Pisces.

STICKLEBACKS, a family of very common freshwater and marine fishes of the northern hemisphere, characterized by the series of sharp spines in front of the soft-rayed dorsal fin. The Three-spined stickleback *Gasterosteus aculeatus* is found in almost every brook and pond in England and is common throughout Europe, across Asia to Japan and in North America. There are, as the name suggests, three spines before the soft dorsal fin and the pelvic fins are each reduced to a single spine. It was formerly thought that there were several species of sticklebacks with three spines, but Professor Léon Bertin finally showed that there is a single but variable species. Thus populations from northern waters and in the sea produce larger individuals which have a series of bony plates or scutes along the flanks. Those from the south are smaller and the scutes are reduced to about two at the front of the body. The species reaches a maximum of about 4 in (10 cm) in length.

In spring, the male Three-spined stickleback changes to a bright blue with red on the chest. He then constructs a nest from plant strands which are stuck together with a sticky secretion from the kidneys. The nest is ball-like and the male enters it and makes a large central chamber. The nest may be placed in a hollow on the bottom but nests have also been found in old tins lying in the water. The male defends the nest from other males or from intruders but entices gravid females to enter and deposit their eggs. After the eggs are fertilized, the male guards the nest and aerates the eggs by fanning movements with the pectoral fins, carefully removing any dead or infertile eggs.

Sticklebacks are extremely voracious and probably rival the bluefish, although on a much smaller scale. A naturalist of the 18th century once observed that one of his sticklebacks consumed 74 young dace of $\frac{1}{4}$ in (6 mm) long and two days later ate a further 62 dace and was presumed to have been capable of taking more. These fishes are easy to keep in captivity provided that live food is given. The life span appears to be three or four years. Although essentially a freshwater species, some live in rock pools and a few have been caught several miles out to sea.

Two other species are found in Europe and Asia. The Ten-spined stickleback *Pungitius pungitius* is less common in England than the previous species and is often found in brackish water. It is, however, widespread across Europe and occurs in North America. Other species of *Pungitius* are found in Asia. The marine Fifteen-spined stickleback *Spinachia spinachia* grows to about 9 in (23 cm) in length and is commonly found around European coasts. It is more elongated than the freshwater species and leads a solitary life amongst weeds. It has a brown, well camouflaged body and also constructs a nest.

In North America there are two species of sticklebacks, the Four-spined stickleback *Apeltes quadracus* and the American brook stickleback *Culea inconstans*, which usually has five spines and is the more northerly of the two. The latter species may have four or six spines but more usually five. Some variation also occurs in the other species, the Three-spined occasionally having two or four spines and the Fifteen-spined sometimes having fourteen or sixteen.

Although the sticklebacks are common fishes that have been studied since the beginnings of modern ichthyology in the 16th century, they still present rather a puzzle. They have long been linked with the Sea horses and pipefishes, but this relationship seems questionable. The only fossils found have been very similar to the modern forms so that their nearest relatives, apart from the tubemouths, are still in doubt. FAMILY: Gasterosteidae, ORDER: Gasterosteiformes, CLASS: Pisces.

STINGRAYS, a family of ray-like fishes with a venomous spine at the base of the tail capable of inflicting a painful or even fatal wound. The greatly flattened body and wing-like pectoral fins vary in outline from round to triangular or diamond-shaped followed by a thin and whip-like tail that may be longer than the body. The eyes are on top of the head and close behind are the spiracles through which water is drawn to aerate the gills, the latter being on the underside behind the mouth. On the upper side and near to the base of the tail (not at its tip, as is commonly thought) is the sting, a sharp spine with a pair of grooves down the hind edges in which lie the glandular cells that secrete the venom. The spine, which is usually 3–4 in (7·5–10 cm) long but may be up to 15 in (38 cm) in a large fish, is sometimes followed by one to four additional spines. The sting is used solely in defence, the fish lashing the tail from side to side or up and down, sometimes with sufficient force to drive the

spine deep into a plank or through a limb. There are about 90 species of stingray, ranging in size from less than 1 ft (30 cm) across the disc of the body to 6–7 ft (1·8–2·1 m) in the case of Captain Cook's stingaree *Dasyatis brevicaudata* of Australasian waters and *D. centroura* of the western North Atlantic. A common species off the Atlantic shores of Europe and in the Mediterranean is the stingray *D. pastinaca*, a species that was well known to Pliny, who repeated the fable that the sting would wither a tree if driven into the trunk. Stingrays lie on the bottom and are often extremely well camouflaged, so that great care should be taken when wading on sandy or muddy beaches where these fishes are known to occur. Some 1,500 accidents with stingrays are reported in the United States every year, mostly of a minor, but nonetheless very painful nature, although some fatalities have been recorded when the sting has penetrated the abdomen causing paralysis of the muscles of the heart. In many parts of the world the spines are used as tips for native spears. The stingrays are bottom-living fishes that feed on shellfish, crustaceans and fishes, the food being crushed or ground up by a pavement of teeth in the jaws. All species are ovoviviparous, the young hatching within the uterus of the female and only later being born.

Members of the genus *Potamotrygon* are found in freshwaters in South America, where they are greatly feared by the local fishermen. The Butterfly rays, often placed in a separate family Gymnuridae, have very short tails, in some species without a sting. The Lesser butterfly ray *Gymnura micrura* is fairly abundant along part of the American Atlantic coast and grows to a width of about 3 or 4 ft (about 1 m), but the rather rare Atlantic coast Giant butterfly ray *G. altavela* reaches 12 ft (3·6 m) from the tip of one pectoral 'wing' to the other. The Butterfly rays are highly coloured, with lace-like markings of browns, greens and purples.

The Round stingrays (family Urolophidae) are circular in outline and have short and stubby tails, again armed with a sting. The Round stingray *Urolophus jamaicensis* of the western North Atlantic is very common in Jamaican waters and is particularly dreaded by the fishermen. FAMILY: Dasyatidae, ORDER: Hypotremata, CLASS: Chondrichthyes. (Ill. p. 150.)

STOCKFISH *Merluccius capensis*, the South African cod and member of the same genus as the North Atlantic cod. The stockfish is the most important element in South African trawl fisheries, far exceeding other fishes in both numbers and weight. In 1959–60 the catch amounted to 150 million lb (68 million kg). In Europe and America the name stockfish is generally used to denote cod that have been split and hung up to dry.

FAMILY: Gadidae, ORDER: Gadiformes, CLASS: Pisces.

STONEFISH *Synanceja verrucosa*, the most venomous of all the scorpionfishes. It is a bottom-living species of the Indo-Pacific region most often found off the coasts of Australia and South Africa. The heavy and ugly body, up to 14 in (35 cm) long, is covered by warts and small flaps of skin that render it almost invisible against a background of rock or coral or if the fish is partly buried in sand. The poisonous dorsal spines are quite capable of killing a man. FAMILY: Synancejidae, ORDER: Scorpaeniformes, CLASS: Pisces.

STURGEONS, primitive, often large fishes from temperate waters of the northern hemisphere, descended from the ancient palaeoniscids (see fishes, fossil). The dense bony skeleton of the palaeoniscids has, however, been replaced by cartilage, the scales have been lost and the dermal armour is represented by a series of bony plates or bucklers. The biting mouth is now an underslung, protrusile sucking mouth. The sturgeons are, however, larger than their ancestors, some reaching well over 20 ft (6 m) in length. Although not related, the sturgeons have a rather shark-like appearance which is heightened by the steeply rising tail.

Sturgeons are found throughout most of the cold and temperate waters of the northern hemisphere, some species living in the sea and migrating up rivers to spawn, while others live permanently in rivers or are landlocked in lakes. There are about 25 species, all rather slow-moving that browse on the bottom. Fleshy barbels surround the mouth and are used to detect prey (usually bottom-living invertebrates). There is a spiral valve in the intestine, a primitive feature also found in the sharks.

The largest of the sturgeons is the beluga *Huso huso* of the Volga and the Black and Caspian Seas for which a length of 28 ft (8·4 m) and a weight of 2,860 lb (1,300 kg) have been recorded. A related species, *H. dauricus* from the Amur basin and the Far East, is smaller. The Atlantic sturgeons all belong to the genus *Acipenser*. The largest from the New World is the White sturgeon *A. transmontanus* of the Pacific coasts of North America which now grows to about 300 lb (135 kg) but in the past has been known to reach over 1,200 lb (540 kg). These fishes rarely go to sea until they are almost mature, the younger individuals living in rivers and migrating up and down stream each winter and spring.

The common Atlantic sturgeon *A. sturio* reaches a weight of 700 lb (315 kg), although the males are smaller. They live in the sea and migrate into rivers to spawn. Formerly widespread and occurring in most European rivers, Atlantic populations now survive only in the Guadalquivir in Spain, the rivers of the Gironde in France and Lake Ladoga in the Soviet Union. Stragglers may reach Great Britain but by ancient right they are royal fish and belong to the monarch. Some of the American sturgeons are confined to lakes, for example the Shovel-nose sturgeon *Scaphirhynchus platyrhynchus,* a species with a long and flattened snout.

Sturgeon are valuable commercial fishes, particularly prized for the eggs or caviar removed from fishes migrating up rivers to spawn. The eggs are separated and soaked in salt, the quality of the caviar being determined by the length of time the eggs are soaked and the strength of the brine. The swimbladders are an important source of isinglass, the skin is tanned and the bony plates are used for ornaments. The flesh is delicious and although caviar is extremely expensive it is possible to buy sturgeon cuts quite cheaply.

Beluga that are not caught as they migrate up rivers continue upstream to spawn in deep holes. Such migratory sturgeon have definite breeding seasons but the Lake sturgeon *A. fulvescens* of the United States has continuously ripening eggs. The age of large sturgeon is of great interest to the fisheries and it is recorded that a Russian fish weighing almost a ton (1,000 kg) was estimated to be 75 years old. FAMILY: Acipenseridae, ORDER: Acipenseriformes, CLASS: Pisces.

SUNFISHES or centrarchids, a family of common freshwater fishes from North America containing the crappies, bluegills and Black basses. The two dozen species are perch-like, with a spinous anterior portion to the dorsal fin and in some species the body is deep and compressed. These fishes are nest builders, the male scooping out a hollow and guarding the eggs once the female has deposited them. The *Black basses (species of *Micropterus*) have been dealt with elsewhere. The crappies (species of *Pomoxis*) from the northeast of the United States, which can grow to 21 inches (54 cm), are popular sport fishes that have now been introduced into fishing waters elsewhere in the country. The White crappie *P. annularis* prefers rather still and turbid waters, whereas the Black crappie *P. nigromaculatus* is generally found in clear waters. The Bluegill sunfishes or bluegills are fairly deep-bodied and are characterized by a bony projection from the upper corner of the gill cover, popularly referred to as an 'ear flap'. The Pumpkinseed bluegill *Lepomis gibbosus* is one of the most colourful and best known species. The back is dark green to olive, the undersides yellow to orange, and there are red, blue and orange spots arranged irregularly on the flanks. There is a brilliant scarlet spot on the 'ear flap', from which this species

derives its common name. It reaches 9 in (23 cm) and is found in the maritime provinces of the United States and Canada. The Green sunfish *L. cyanellus* grows to the same size but is less colourful. The bluegill *L. macrochirus* has been introduced into all the States (except Alaska). Reaching 4 lb (1·8 kg) in weight, the bluegill can be recognized by the bluish colour of the lower jaw, lower part of the cheek and gill cover. The Red-ear sunfish *L. microlophus*, a smaller species, is dull olive with a red band on the gill cover. It is also known as the shell-cracker since it has strong teeth in the throat (pharyngeal teeth) with which it crushes snails on which it feeds. The Spotted sunfish *L. punctatus* is reputed to linger beside tree stumps and half-submerged logs waiting for insects or frogs to settle above it, thereafter charging the log to knock its prey into the water.

The Sacramento perch *Archoplytes interruptus* is the only species of sunfish found naturally in the rivers and streams of the western part of the United States.

The sunfishes, and especially the Black basses and the bluegills, have been introduced into a number of countries outside the United States including the cooler parts of East Africa. FAMILY: Centrarchidae, ORDER: Perciformes, CLASS: Pisces.

SURGEONFISHES, a group of marine fishes characteristic of coral reefs. Their name derives from the little bony keels, often extremely sharp and blade-like, on either side at the base of the tail (i.e. on the caudal peduncle). In some species these little 'knives' are hinged at the rear and can thus be erected to point forwards so that care should be taken when handling live specimens. In the *unicornfish there are several bony keels on each side of the peduncle. The surgeonfishes are deep-bodied and compressed, with small terminal mouths bearing a single row of cropping teeth in each jaw. They feed by scraping algae and other organisms from rocks and coral.

Some variation in colour is found in the surgeonfishes. In the Yellow surgeon *Zebrasoma flavescens* there are yellow and greybrown colour phases and the Common surgeonfish of the Atlantic *Acanthurus bahianus* has been observed to change when chasing another member of the species, from its normal blue-grey colouring to white anteriorly and dark behind. The Five-banded surgeonfish *A. triostegus,* an Indo-Pacific species that reaches 10 in (25 cm), has a dark, apple-green body with dark brown vertical bars. Also known as the convictfish, it has been involved in cases of fish poisoning. During development, the young surgeonfishes pass through a curious larval or acronurus stage in which the body has vertical ridges and does not closely resemble that of the adult.

In the Indo-Pacific area some of the surgeonfishes are popular as food and are extremely tasty; in fish markets the offending keels on the caudal peduncle are often cut off prior to display. FAMILY: Acanthuridae, ORDER: Perciformes, CLASS: Pisces.

SWEETLIPS, perch-like marine fishes belonging to the genus *Plectorhynchus,* and deriving their common name from their thick and rather luscious lips. The sweetlips are found commonly in the Indo-Pacific region. They have fairly deep bodies, a small mouth with conical teeth, and the spiny and soft portions of the dorsal fin are joined by a membrane. They grow to about 25 in (64 cm) and many are very strikingly coloured. In *Plectorhynchus chaetodonticeps* the body is brown with large white spots and bars. *P. golmani* has diagonal blue stripes on a silvery body, while the fins are yellow with blue spots. In some species, however, the young are quite different from the adults in colour, a situation which is not uncommon in reef-dwelling species and which in the past has often led zoologists to describe the young and the adults as two different species. FAMILY: Pomadasyidae, ORDER: Perciformes, CLASS: Pisces.

SWIMBLADDER, also known as gas- or airbladder, a silvery gas-filled sac lying along the top of a fish's body cavity just below the vertebral column. A swimbladder is absent in sharks but is present in most bony fishes. It has been secondarily lost in some groups. In the more primitive bony fishes the swimbladder is connected by a narrow tube to the throat (e.g. in the herring) but in the advanced fishes (e.g. perch) this duct closes and disappears at an early stage in the lifehistory. Many fishes in which the swimbladder is closed swallow air when young to fill the swimbladder before the duct degenerates. Perch fry, for example, if prevented from reaching the surface, are unable to fill the swimbladder. The primary function of the swimbladder in modern fishes is to give buoyancy so that they can use their fins for purposes other than merely preventing themselves sinking to the bottom (see fins).

The possession of a swimbladder presents some difficulties to fishes that migrate to and from deeper water. Since the pressure of water decreases as the fish rises to the surface, the volume of the swimbladder increases correspondingly. In a fish rising from considerable depths the swimbladder would soon displace all the other internal organs if there were no means of preventing this. In fishes in which the swimbladder still connects to the throat through a ductus pneumaticus the excess gas can be allowed to escape quite simply. In fishes without a duct the volume of gas is varied by absorption or secretion of gas, through the blood vessels of the oval gland and the gas gland respectively. Neither organ is found in fishes with a duct.

The centre of buoyancy is usually below the centre of gravity so that if the fish leans to one side it will tend to turn upside down. In addition, any upward movement of the fish will tend to expand the swimbladder, making the fish even more buoyant. For these reasons, the fins are rarely still but are constantly engaged in slight correcting movements.

The swimbladder has been lost secondarily in a number of bony fishes, including some deep-sea forms. It is absent in the large ocean-living tuna-like fishes, but the large quantities of oil in the flesh help to provide buoyancy.

The swimbladder evolved from the lungs found in primitive fishes (see air-breathing fishes) and in modern lungfishes is now only secondarily adapted for breathing air. It is also used as a resonator in some fishes in sound production.

SWORDFISH *Xiphias gladius*, a large oceanic fish with the snout produced into a powerful, flattened sword. Swordfishes are worldwide, mainly in tropical oceans but also entering temperate waters. They have been recorded off the coasts of northern Europe and occasionally stray as far as Iceland. Rather solitary fishes, they grow to a weight of 1,500 lb (675 kg) and are chiefly found in open waters often at the surface with the high but short dorsal fin cleaving the water like the dorsal fin of a shark. Where common they are exploited commercially, usually being caught by harpoon, and are also much sought after by anglers. Swordfish feed on fishes and squids and examination of their stomach contents shows they also penetrate to depths and feed on deep-sea fishes.

The 'sword' is reputed to be used to thrash amongst shoals of fishes, the swordfish feeding at leisure on the injured fishes. The fish has been known since ancient times both because of its size and because of instances when it has rammed wooden vessels. In the British Museum (Natural History) is preserved a piece of timber from a ship that has been penetrated to a depth of 22 in (56 cm) by the sword of a swordfish. It was also reported that HMS *Dreadnought* was punctured by a swordfish on its return voyage from Ceylon to London, the sword passing right through the copper sheathing of the hull. Swords are occasionally found broken off and embedded in the blubber of whales and it has been suggested that swordfishes mistake ships for whales. It is possible, however, that the swordfish, a fast and powerful swimmer of the open seas, credited with speeds up to 60 mph (96 kmph) has on occasions been unable to divert its course in time to prevent a collision. FAMILY: Xephiidae, ORDER: Perciformes, CLASS: Pisces.

SWORDTAIL *Xiphophorus helleri,* a livebearing cyprinodont fish from Mexico and Guatemala. The lower caudal fin rays in the male are prolonged into a 'sword', which is quite soft and used in sexual display. The swordtail has many remarkable features which make it a most instructive aquarium fish. In some instances the female, having given birth to up to 100 young, changes into a male, losing her dark 'pregnancy mark' as the anal fin changes shape and the male sword develops. Such males, once the transformation has been completed, are fully capable of fathering another 100 or so young. In some strains up to 30% of the females change sex. The change from male to female has never been recorded.

In the wild the swordtail is the 'green sword', but the species is variable. A cross with a reddish individual of the closely related species *X. montezumae* (the Montezuma sword) has produced the Red swordtail. A cross with a Wagtail platy has produced the Wagtail sword. FAMILY: Poeciliidae, ORDER: Atheriniformes, CLASS: Pisces. (Ill. p. 151.)

TARPONS, powerful, silvery fishes related to the tenpounders. They are strong swimmers and are renowned for their fighting powers when hooked. There are two species, the Atlantic tarpon *Tarpon atlanticus* and the Indo-Pacific tarpon *Megalops cyprinoides.* The two are outwardly so similar that many authors place them in the same genus. Recent studies have shown, however, that there are fundamental differences in the skull which suggest that the two tarpons are very different fishes. The body is fairly compressed with large silvery scales and there is a single dorsal fin with the last ray prolonged into a filament. Although primarily marine, the tarpons are not infrequently found in freshwater and sometimes even in foul waters. The Indo-Pacific tarpon reaches 3 ft (90 cm) in length, but the Atlantic tarpon is a huge fish, growing to 8 ft (2·4 m) and weighing up to 300 lb (135 kg). Like the ladyfish and the tenpounder, the tarpons begin life as a ribbon-like leptocephalus larva resembling that of the eels. FAMILY: Megalopidae, ORDER: Elopiformes, CLASS: Pisces.

TELESCOPE-EYES, deep-sea fishes with tubular eyes of the family Giganturidae and distantly related to the whalefishes. They are also called giant-tails. These fishes have cylindrical bodies and reach 9 in (23 cm) in length. The body is naked, the pectoral fins are set behind the head and very high up on the flanks and the lower lobe of the tail is elongated into a long banner. They live in all oceans at depths down to 12,000 ft (3,600 m). The tubular eyes give these fishes excellent binocular vision, an attribute that is rare in fishes but one that enables them to make accurate estimates of distances when pouncing on prey. Like many deep-sea fishes, the telescope-eyes have elastic stomachs and are capable of swallowing fishes larger than themselves.

Gigantura is a relatively solid looking fish and is unusual amongst deep-sea forms in having a silvery body. Its relative, the Pacific Telescope-eye fish *Bathyleptus lisae,* is much more fragile in appearance but both fishes have long, fang-like teeth. Almost nothing is known of the biology of these fishes and only

about 12 specimens of *Bathyleptus* have ever been caught. FAMILY: Giganturidae, ORDER: Cetomimiformes, CLASS: Pisces.

TENCH *Tinca tinca,* perhaps the most easily identified of all the carp-like fishes of European freshwaters. It is a stocky fish with very small scales, heavy and rounded fins and a body that is dark olive-green shot with gold. The belly is light grey or reddish grey with a violet sheen. One variety is green shot with gold with the mouth red. The tench, usually a rather sluggish fish, spends most of its time on the bottom rooting around the mud in ponds or slow-flowing waters. It hides away in winter, sometimes in the company of other tenches, almost in a state of hibernation but it will stir on very warm days. A really large tench can weigh up to 10 lb (4·5 kg) and any angler who has caught these large fishes will vouch for the fact that they can be anything but sluggish. When hooked their lethargy disappears as if by magic.

Old legends refer to the tench as the doctorfish because of its alleged habit of allowing injured fishes to rub their wounds on its healing slime. These healing properties were supposed to confer some kind of immunity from attack on the tench, but this is certainly not true since both perch and pike will readily eat this fish. The tench is also reputed to remove leeches from carp in much the same way as the Cleaner fishes remove parasites from other and larger species. FAMILY: Cyprinidae, ORDER: Cypriniformes, CLASS: Pisces. (Ill. p. 146.)

TENPOUNDER, the name given to the various species of *Elops,* silvery marine fishes somewhat resembling the herring. The tenpounder is now recognized as being related, not to the herring-like fishes, but surprisingly to the eels, these two outwardly dissimilar groups being united by the possession of ribbon-like leptocephalus larvae which later metamorphose into small replicas of the adult. The tenpounder is a slender fish with many small and silvery scales and a single soft-rayed dorsal fin. It shows several very primitive characters, such as the very high number of bony plates (branchiostegal rays)

which support the gill membranes, the presence of teeth along the parasphenoid on the roof of the mouth, and the presence of gular plates or paired plate-like bones under the lower jaw (see fishes).

The tenpounders are found in all tropical seas. They live in coastal waters and grow to over 3 ft (90 cm) in length. In the United States the fish is called the tenpounder or bonefish; in South Africa it is the springer (because it leaps when hooked) or Cape salmon; and in Australia it is the Giant herring or bananafish. This well demonstrates the confusion that can arise when an animal is referred to solely by its common name. FAMILY: Elopidae, ORDER: Elopiformes, CLASS: Pisces.

THREAD-FINS, perch-like fishes distantly related to the barracudas and the Grey mullets. They are marine and estuarine fishes found in all tropical waters. Their name derives from the form of the pectoral fin, which is in two distinct parts. The upper part bears the normal complement of branching rays but the lower part is made up of about six long filamentous rays unconnected by a membrane. The elongated rays can be moved independently of each other and it is thought that they may have some sensory function, possibly serving as organs of touch since these fishes inhabit murky waters.

Thread-fins have compressed bodies with the spiny first dorsal fin and the soft-rayed second dorsal fin well separated, as found in the barracudas and Grey mullets. The snout is pointed and overhangs the mouth, as in many fishes that grub on the bottom.

Thread-fins are valuable fishes since they are not only good to eat but provide a type of isinglass from their swimbladders. The largest species is *Eleutheronema tetradactylum* (i.e. four-fingers) from the Indian Ocean. It is sometimes called the Burnett salmon and off the coasts of India it has been known to reach 6 ft (1·8 m) and to weigh up to 320 lb (145 kg). Because of its rather pinkish flesh it has been given the name 'salmon'. The fish is a pale blue-grey with a yellow eye and yellow on the upper part of the pectoral fin. Blue and yellow are common colours in the thread-fins. *Polynemus sheridani,* a smaller species which reaches 18 in (45 cm) in length, has yellow on the lower half of the body, while the Striped thread-fin *P. plebejus* has a bluish body with fine yellow horizontal stripes. FAMILY: Polynemidae, ORDER: Perciformes, CLASS: Pisces.

TIGERFISHES, African freshwater fishes of the genus *Hydrocynus,* deriving their common name from their striped colouring and voracious appetite. The body is elongated and powerful and the mouth is armed with curved, dagger-like teeth. These fishes prey chiefly on other fishes and the largest species, *H. goliath,* which reaches 125 lb (56 kg) in weight, has been suspected of attacking cattle and even human beings. Fish eaten by the tigerfishes are either swallowed whole or have the soft parts cleanly bitten off.

Young tigerfishes shoal in shallow waters but larger fishes are mostly solitary, living in deeper water. Because of the importance of freshwater fishes as a source of protein in Africa, the tigerfishes have been the subject of various investigations, both as a source of food and because of their effect as predators on other useful species. It has been found that *H. vittatus* reaches its peak of efficiency as a predator on other fishes when it is 12–18 in (30–45 cm) long. Fishes smaller than this catch less relative to their body weight, while larger fishes also catch less because their bodies are fatter and their fins relatively smaller and they are thus less efficient swimmers. It is factors such as this that may set the limit on the maximum size to which such fishes can grow.

The tigerfishes are found in the Nile and in those rivers and lakes which once had a connection with the Nile. They are absent from Lake Victoria and the eastward-flowing rivers of East Africa, presumably because these were never in contact with the Nile system (the Murchison Falls presenting an absolute barrier to the passage of them into Lake Victoria). FAMILY: Characidae, ORDER: Cypriniformes, CLASS: Pisces. (Ill. p. 148.)

TILAPIA, perch-like fishes of the genus *Tilapia,* found principally in Africa but occurring also in Lake Tiberias and other water masses connected with the northern extension of the African Rift Valley. Species of *Tilapia* are found in lakes, streams and rivers, but some will penetrate into brackish waters. Typically, the body is fairly deep and compressed, with a long dorsal fin (the anterior rays being spiny) and a moderate anal fin. In some species a black spot occurs on the hind part of the dorsal fin, occasionally edged in yellow.

Because of their hardiness and palatability, species of *Tilapia* have been widely used in fish culture in ponds.

The two species most often imported for aquarists are *T. zillii* and *T. tholloni.* Both are plant-eaters and should not be put into tanks containing expensive water plants. FAMILY: Cichlidae, ORDER: Perciformes, CLASS: Pisces.

TILEFISH *Lopholatilus chamaeleonticeps,* one of the largest members of the family Pseudochromidae, reaching 3 ft (90 cm) in length. It is related to the Sea perches. There is a sharp crest at the back of the head. The body is fairly slender and the anal fin and single dorsal fin are fairly long. The discovery and the subsequent sudden disappearance of the tilefish present a rather curious story. The fish was first discovered in 1879. It was found at the bottom of the Gulf Stream slope of the shores of New England. The water mass in which the tilefishes were found was at that time warm since it was composed of Gulf Stream water that had travelled northwards from the Gulf of Mexico. The fishes were found in large numbers and a fishery subsequently developed. Three years later, after some extremely severe gales, the course of the Gulf Stream altered and the area in which the tilefishes lived was invaded by a much colder body of water from the Labrador Current. For some reason the tilefish is exceedingly sensitive to changes in water temperatures and this sudden cooling was enough to kill off the fishes in millions. In March 1882 an area of some 15,000 sq miles (40,000 sq km) was strewn with dead tilefishes. For the next 20 years no tilefishes were caught and it was presumed that the species was extinct. Then they slowly made a reappearance in the warmer waters of the Gulf Stream and their numbers gradually built up once more. The Pseudochromidae contains species which live in tropical waters and it would seem that the tilefish was able to take advantage of warm bodies of water that had for various reasons become pushed into temperate latitudes. FAMILY: Pseudochromidae, ORDER: Perciformes, CLASS: Pisces.

TOOTHCARPS, small, basically freshwater, fishes related to the Flying fishes, half-beaks and silversides. They are also known as topminnows or killifishes (although the latter term is one usually employed by aquarists to refer only to the egg-laying members of this suborder). The toothcarps are not related to the true carps. The group can be divided into the egg-layers (principal family Cyprinodontidae) and the live-bearers (principal family Poeciliidae).

The cyprinodonts or killifishes include the remarkable *Annual fishes whose whole lifespan is confined to the rainy season, the eggs only surviving through to the next season. Probably the most beautiful member of this group is the Argentine pearlfish. The panchaxes are typical cyprinodonts from Asia while the lyre-tails (genus *Aphyosemion*) are rather similar fishes from Africa. The cyprinodonts are, however, most common in the Americas. The genus *Fundulus* contains many species in North and Central America as well as some of the offshore islands. These are usually cylindrical fishes with flat heads, the mouth directed upwards and the dorsal and anal fins short-based. Some species, such as *Fundulus notatus* live and feed at the surface, while others like the golden-ear *F. chrysotus* may lie in the mud. The surface-living forms have a light golden mark on the top head. Certain of the species of *Fundulus* can tolerate salt water and *F. parvipinnis* of California is found in tide-pools while the Zebra killifish *F. heteroclitus* of eastern USA is found in brackish water. Some of the killifishes are very beautifully coloured, particularly those from Florida. The killifishes are so popular amongst aquarists that societies have been formed solely for the appreciation of this group of fishes.

One highly unusual cyprinodont is *Pantanodon podoxys,* a small species from Kenya and Tanzania which reaches $1-1\frac{1}{2}$ in (2·5–4 cm) in length. Unlike other toothcarps, it has no teeth in the jaws and has become adapted to filter-feeding on micro-organisms in the water. The tiny gillrakers are lined with very minute fans which can be opened or closed. This species has been successfully bred.

The live-bearing poeciliids include such species as the guppy, the mollies, the swordtails, the Four-eyed fishes and the mosquitofishes. These are all confined to the New World and are discussed generally under live-bearing fishes. FAMILIES: Cyprinodontidae, Poeciliidae etc, ORDER: Atheriniformes, CLASS: Pisces. (Ill. p. 146, 149.)

TRIGGERFISHES, marine fishes of warm seas related to the trunkfishes and pufferfishes. The common name derives from the trigger-like action of the enlarged first dorsal spine which can be locked in the upright position by the much smaller second dorsal spine. With the spine locked, the fish is both difficult to remove from rock crevices and difficult for a predator to swallow. The body is deep and compressed, and is covered by small bony plates. The mouth is terminal and small. The triggerfishes are often brightly coloured with grotesque or even absurd colour markings that contrast with their slow and rather dignified movement around the reefs. There are about 30 species, the largest rarely exceeding 2 ft (60 cm) in length. They have powerful teeth with which they crush molluscs and crustaceans. Their flesh is reported to be poisonous but it is not yet established that this is not simply a form of ciguatera poisoning (see poisonous fishes). In Hawaii the species of *Rhinecanthus* are called humahuma and have been immortalized in song. FAMILY: Balistidae, ORDER: Tetraodontiformes, CLASS: Pisces. (Ill. p. 150.)

The Lemon shark *Negaprion brevirostris*, 2.5 m long, is one of the commonest sharks in inshore waters of the American Atlantic coast.

Dorsal view of a remora, showing the large oval sucker on top of the head.

The scorpionfish *Pterois volitans*, of the Indo-Pacific, has venom glands in grooves along the sides of its beautiful spines.

Fry of silversides or Common sandsmelt.

Opposite: the European Sea horse *Hippocampus guttulatus* swimming in typical upright position.

Chriopeops goodei, the Blue-fin top minnow, one of the egg-laying toothcarps of North America.

Tench, or doctorfish, European carp credited with healing properties.

Two tigerfish leaping from the waters of the Niger River, above the Kainji Dam, Nigeria.

The Fire eel, one of the Spiny eels, popular with aquarists.

Atlantic salmon showing the dark bands on the flanks known as parr marks.

The roach is a freshwater fish which prefers still water with a profusion of water plants.

The male lyretail *Aphosemion ahli*, a small fresh water fish from tropical West Africa.

Scorpionfish showing its poisonous spines.

Two Red-tailed rainbowfishes of Australia.

This red sea bream shows the lateral line system very well.

Showing how a male stickleback greets a female, when she enters his territory.

The triggerfish *Rhinecanthus aculeatus* is known in Hawaii as the humuhumu-nukunuku-a-puaa.

A scat *Scatophagus argus*, named afther the legendary hundred-eyed Argus.

The stingray is fairly common in shallow waters, especially in summer, off the coasts of Europe.

The thornback ray moves gracefully through the water.

The five-bearded rockling is abundant on the coasts of Europe.

Male swordtail with young females. This male started life as a female and, after giving birth to several broods, underwent a change of sex and became a fully functional male.

Salmon leaping a waterfall in northern Brazil.

Female Sea trout migrating up a river to breed, leaping the rapids.

TROUT, members of the salmon family found in the freshwaters of the northern hemisphere. There is no scientific basis for the distinction between trouts and salmons and the names are merely applied by common usage. In England, the name trout refers to the Brown trout *Salmo trutta* (a member of the same genus as the Atlantic salmon, *S. salar*), while in the United States the word trout applies to Rainbow trout *S. gairdneri,* Cutthroat trout *S. clarki* and several other species, while Brook trout, Great Lake trout and so on refer to members of the genus *Salvelinus* (otherwise termed chars).

The question of trout species has long vexed ichthyologists. In addition to the Sea trout, Lake trout and River trout, several other species were thought to occur in Great Britain. They were distinguished by colour patterns and differences in shape. The gillaroo *S. stomachius,* for example, was characterized by a very thick stomach. Other 'species' included the sewen *S. cambricus,* the Black-finned trout *S. nigripinnis,* the Great lake trout *S. ferox* and the Brook trout *S.*

fario. The Sea trout was referred to as *S. eriox.* It has now been established, however, that all these forms belong to the single species *S. trutta* and that the differences are due to variations in feeding conditions and habits. The Sea trout with a partially marine habitat has developed a silvery colour; the thick stomach of the gillaroo results from its diet of shelled molluscs; the huge Lake trout enjoys the still and rich waters of lakes; dark and peaty water induces dark colour in fishes, and so on.

The Brown trout is closely related to the Atlantic salmon and the parr of the two species are very similar. The tail is less deeply forked in the Brown trout juveniles and there is always an orange or reddish tinge to the adipose fin. The natural range of the Brown trout is from England to the Pyrenees and eastwards across to the Urals, with a very small population in North Africa. Because of their sporting qualities, however, Brown trout have been introduced into the coastal regions of North America, Chile, Argentina, southern India, highland areas of East Africa,

South Africa, New Zealand and Australia. In warm countries trout have been limited to the upper reaches of rivers and have not interfered with the populations of local species further down. In the Drakensberg Mountains of South Africa, however, trout with its predatory habits introduced in the last century have thrived to such an extent that a small carp-like fish *Oreodameon quathlambae,* known only from that area, is now extinct. The danger of introducing a species to a new area cannot be too highly stressed.

The Brown trout is a solid, powerful fish, usually spotted but with great variability in the number, size and colour of the spots. The mouth is large and toothed and the tail is emarginate. These are swift, active fishes that favour highly oxygenated and cool waters. In Europe they can live at sea-level but in Africa the best conditions for their survival may well lie at 5,000–6,000 ft (1,500–1,800 m) above sea-level. In small mountain streams only a few inches deep, Brown trout will thrive, feed and breed but will never reach more than a few inches in length. The Great lake trout, on the other hand, will top the scales at 30 lb (14 kg), showing that trout, like many other fishes, are extremely sensitive to the amount of food and living space available.

The breeding habits and time of spawning of Brown trout are similar to those of the Atlantic salmon. Sea trout and forms living in estuaries migrate up rivers to breed, Lake trout move into the feeder streams and riverine forms merely run further upstream. Like the salmon, the trout female constructs a shallow nest, the redd, into which the eggs are deposited and there fertilized. The young trout pass through stages similar to those of the salmon (alevin, parr, smolt), the comparison being closer in the case of Sea trout. Throughout the whole of the northern hemisphere spawning occurs from September to April, although the actual time depends on water temperatures.

Although there is only one European species of trout, in North America there are several. One of these, the Rainbow trout, has been as widely distributed in other parts of the world as has been the Brown trout. In the Rainbow trout the flanks are pinkish and the back dark green to dark blue. Often there is a golden sheen on the flanks and the fins are always speckled (these are rarely speckled in the Brown trout). The Rainbow has a faster growth rate than the Brown trout under similar conditions and has been introduced into English trout rivers. The Rainbow has a migratory form, known as the steelhead, once thought to be a distinct species. In the United States Rainbow trouts can reach a weight of 30 lb (14 kg). The Cutthroat trout is native to the inland waters of the western part of the American continent. It derives its name from the red marking under the throat. As with all trout, the colours and markings of this species vary with the locality. The largest Cutthroat recorded was 39 in (1 m) in length and weighed 41 lb (18·5 kg). The Golden trout *S. uguabonita* is confined to parts of California with an altitude of over 8,000 ft (2,400 m). It rarely exceeds 20 in (51 cm) in length although a relative giant of 11 lb (5 kg) has been recorded.

For centuries, trout have been one of the most popular of sporting fishes and more books have been devoted to trout and the techniques for catching them than to any other fishes. They are well known for their cunning and the angler may have great difficulty in deceiving a large fish with an artificial fly. FAMILY: Salmonidae, ORDER: Salmoniformes, CLASS: Pisces.

TROUT-PERCHES, freshwater fishes of North America with a superficial resemblance to both the trouts and the perches. There are only three species, placed in a separate order. The common name stems from the presence of a trout-like adipose fin in two of the species, combined with a spiny

dorsal fin similar to that of a perch. It was long thought that the trout-perches represented an intermediate stage or missing link connecting the more primitive soft-rayed fishes with the more advanced spiny-rayed fishes. More recent studies have shown, however, that the trout-perches are in fact an evolutionary offshoot.

The sandroller *Percopsis orniscomaycus* has an adipose fin, rough spiny scales and spines on the fins. It grows to about 6 in (15 cm) and is found in Canada and the eastern part of the United States. *Columbia transmontana* is similar in appearance and occurs in the Columbia river basin.

The pirate-perch *Aphredoderus sayanus* is placed in a separate family, partly because the adipose fin is missing. There is, however, a more remarkable feature and one which students find difficult to forget once the species name has been turned into the humerous mnemonic 'say-anus'. In the young fishes the anus is in the normal position just in front of the origin of the anal fin, but as the fish grows the anus gradually moves forward until in the adult it lies in the throat. The pirate-perch, which is confined to the eastern side of the United States, reaches about 5 in

(13 cm) in length and lives on the bottom of lakes and slow moving waters where there is a thick layer of debris. FAMILIES: Percopsidae, Aphredoderidae, ORDER: Percopsiformes, CLASS: Pisces.

TRUMPETFISHES, rather specialized warm-water fishes related to the flutemouths, pipefishes and Sea horses and placed in the single genus *Aulostoma*. There are about four species known. They have elongated bodies with long flat snouts and a series of isolated spines bearing membranes in front of the dorsal fin. The dorsal and anal fins are set far back on the body. These fishes rarely grow to more than 2 ft (60 cm). They use their long snouts to ferret out small fishes and crustaceans around coral reefs and are adept at camouflage, frequently hiding head down amongst the coral. Dr Hans Hass noticed that, when passing into open water from one coral head to another, these fishes attempt to make the journey with another and larger fish. Dr Hass saw a trumpetfish shoot out of hiding to lay itself along the back of a parrotfish. The latter tried to dislodge its companion, but without success until they neared the next coral head, when the trumpet-

The Rainbow trout, a popular sport fish of western North America, in its breeding dress, a red belly.

fish swam quickly to safety. Trumpetfishes usually exhibit territorial behaviour, vigorously guarding their piece of reef. FAMILY: Fistulariidae, ORDER: Gasterosteiformes, CLASS: Pisces.

TUBE-MOUTH FISHES, small marine fishes with tube-like mouths found on both sides of the North Pacific and related to the sticklebacks. The term was formerly used collectively for all fishes with tube-like mouths (pipefishes, Sea horses, trumpetfishes and flutemouths) but it is preferable to restrict it to the aulorhynchids. *Aulorhynchus flavidus* from Canadian Pacific shores somewhat resembles a very slender stickleback with many spines along its back. *Aulichthys japonicus* from Japan is very similar in appearance. Like the sticklebacks, the Tubemouth fishes build nests. The late Conrad Limbaugh, a pioneer in combining scientific observation with underwater pleasure,

noticed huge shoals many yards in extent off the coast of California. The fishes build their nests amongst the roots and small fronds of the larger sea-weeds below the low water mark, the male cementing the nest together with a sticky secretion. After the female has laid eggs in the nest, the male guards them until they hatch. Spawning takes place throughout the year. FAMILY: Aulorhynchidae, ORDER: Gasterosteiformes, CLASS: Pisces.

TUNA FISHES or tunnies, large oceanic members of the mackerel family. Almost every feature of the tunas seems to be adapted for their life of eternal swimming. The body is powerful and torpedo-shaped, the dorsal and pectoral fins fold into grooves and the eyes are flush with the surface of the head, all of which help to reduce the drag caused by turbulent eddies as the fish cleaves the water. In addition, the scales are small and smooth and are reduced merely to a corselet round the

pectoral fins. The tail is crescentic, the ideal shape for sustained fast swimming, and the finrays are closely bound to the end of the vertebral column so that the tail is no longer a flexible appendage of the body but an integral part of it. Behind the second dorsal and the anal fins are small finlets that may serve to control the formation of eddies, while the sides of the caudal peduncle, or base of the tail, bear little keels for further streamlining. A swimbladder is absent but a considerable amount of oil is present which aids in buoyancy. One remarkable feature of these large fishes is that the energy expended in fast swimming warms the blood to a few degrees above that of the surrounding water—an unusual feature for a 'cold-blooded' vertebrate. The tunas are carnivorous fishes that feed on pelagic organisms and especially on squid. They are mostly tropical in distribution but some of the larger species are found in the colder northern waters. There are

The long snout of a trumpetfish.

A turbot, large North Atlantic flatfish, swimming.

six species of great tuna in the world: the albacore *Thunnus alalunga,* the yellowfin *T. albacares,* the blackfin *T. atlanticus,* the bigeye *T. obesus,* the bluefin *T. thynnus* and the longtail *T. tonggol.* Because of the size of these fishes and the difficulty of preserving specimens for comparative studies in museums, it is only recently that the confusion of names, both scientific and popular, has to some extent been resolved. Some species are world-wide in their distribution and have received a variety of common names, some of which are used for quite different species elsewhere. The names used here are those which are now generally agreed by fishery workers.

The bluefin of the Mediterranean and the Atlantic, often known merely as the tunny, is a large species that reaches 14 ft (4·3 m) and may weigh up to 1,800 lb (816 kg). The body is dark blue on the back, lighter on the flanks and silvery white with opalescent tints on the belly. The pectoral fins are short and the flesh is whitish. These fishes form the basis for an old and important fishery. The routes taken by the bluefins to their spawning grounds in special areas in the Atlantic, Mediterranean and Black Sea often pass close to the coast and such areas have been well known to the fishermen for centuries. In the Mediterranean, a system of nets, known as *madragues,* is set up to enclose a boiling mass of these powerful fishes. After spawning, the Mediterranean fishes pass into the Atlantic and migrate northwards, reaching the English Channel by

about June. This was once their most northerly limit, but since the 1920's they have been pressing north as far as Norway. A similar northward migration occurs along the western Atlantic coasts. Marked specimens from the Bahamas have been caught off the French coast but it is not yet known how much interchange there is between the eastern and western populations of the Atlantic. There is, indeed, much to be learned of the migrations of this important species. A subspecies of the bluefin, *Thunnus thynnus orientalis,* occurs in the Pacific.

The albacore is a smaller fish, reaching about 70 lb (32 kg) in weight. It can be immediately distinguished from the bluefin by its long sickle-shaped pectoral fins which reach as far as, or beyond, the second dorsal fin. It is world-wide in distribution, living near the surface in temperate seas but in deeper water in the tropics. Like other tunas, it is an important food fish and is especially valuable to the canning industry and, like the bluefin, it undertakes extensive migrations, specimens marked in California having been recaptured in Japan. These migrations are fairly strictly related to water temperatures and in the Atlantic the fishes migrate as far north as Iceland as water temperatures rise in the summer. The migrations of albacore in the North Pacific have been closely studied and there is reason to think that the same population inhabits the entire area.

The yellowfin is a large species that reaches a length of 8 ft (2·4 m) and can weigh up to

450 lb (204 kg). The longtail, however, is relatively small, reaching 30 lb (13·6 kg), but is important in many Indo-Pacific fisheries. The bigeye is a deep-water species. All the tunas are sporting fishes, the huge bluefin presenting a tremendous challenge to the skill of the angler. The world rod-caught record stands only a little short of 1,000 lb (454 kg). FAMILY: Scombridae, ORDER: Perciformes, CLASS: Pisces.

TURBOT *Scophthalmus maximus,* a large flatfish from the North Atlantic. The turbot is one of the flatfish species that rests on its right side, the left side being pigmented and bearing the eyes. It is a shallow-water species found in the Mediterranean and all along European coasts. The body is diamond-shaped, with large symmetrical jaws lined with sharp teeth. There are no scales on the body but the 'eyed' side is covered by warty tubercles. The turbot is mostly found on sandy bottoms in water of 10–200 ft (3–60 m). Turbot are avid fish-eaters and tend to concentrate in areas where food is plentiful such as shallow banks near the mouths of rivers. They lie in wait for their prey and like most flatfishes are well camouflaged.

The turbot is one of the best flavoured of British fishes. It grows to over 40 lb (18 kg) in weight and is extremely prolific, a female of 17 lb (7·5 kg) having been recorded with 9,000,000 eggs in the ovaries. FAMILY: Bothidae, ORDER: Pleuronectiformes, CLASS: Pisces.

UV

UNICORNFISH, members of the genus *Naso,* related to the surgeonfishes and given the name unicorn by early ichthyologists because of the curious conical horn which develops on the forehead in some members of the genus. In some species the horn may grow longer than the snout, giving the fish a most grotesque appearance. In juveniles the horn is merely a small bump but it increases in length with age. In other respects, the unicornfishes resemble the surgeonfishes in having rather compressed and oval bodies and long dorsal and anal fins armed anteriorly with spines. At the base of the tail, on the caudal peduncle, there are two razor-sharp keels which project like little knife blades and may be hooked forwards. These keels are not usually present in the young but develop as the fish grows. They are dangerous weapons, used in defence, and are found also in the surgeonfishes.

Unicornfishes have small mouths and are herbivorous. The genus is widely distributed in the Indo-Pacific region. The largest species, *Naso tuberosus,* is called the Humpheaded unicorn because the horn is developed as a large bulge on the forehead. The Brown unicornfish *N. unicornis* is one of the most common species. The body is brown, the dorsal and anal fins bear lines of blue and yellow and the base of the pectoral fins and areas round the keels on the caudal peduncle are blue. This species reaches 23 in (58 cm) in length. FAMILY: Acanthuridae, ORDER: Perciformes, CLASS: Pisces.

VIPERFISHES, slender-bodied deep-sea fishes belonging largely to the family Stomiatidae and related to the hatchetfishes. Under the same heading are placed certain members of other closely related families and the general name stomiatoid fishes is preferable for the whole group – a 'common' name is frequently meaningless in fishes that are not common.

Viperfishes of the family Stomiatidae are active pelagic fishes found in greatest numbers at about 6,000 ft (1,800 m); at night-time they rise to the surface waters. They have large heads and a mouth well equipped with vicious dagger-like teeth. To cope with swallowing large prey, the mouth can open to an extraordinary extent. To achieve this, the head is jerked upwards, a most unusual movement in fishes since the skull is normally very firmly attached to the anterior vertebrae. The skeleton is considerably modified to accommodate this unusual movement. In *Eustomias brevibarbatus,* for example, the first few vertebrae are widely spaced and are linked by a loop of cartilage which allows for the movement of the head.

The body in viperfishes tapers evenly from the head, the dorsal and anal fins being just in front of the tail. The pectoral and pelvic fins are reduced to a few long rays. Along the lower half of the flanks are rows of luminous organs giving the appearance of 'portholes'. There is usually a luminous gland under the eyes which is larger in the males than in the females and can be shut off by rotating it. Most of the stomiatoids have a barbel under the chin. In species such as *Melanostomias spilorhynchus* the barbel is fairly short, but in *Ultimostomias mirabilis* the barbel is no less than ten times the length of the body. In some species the barbel ends in a slight swelling, while in others it has been described picturesquely as resembling 'a bunch of grapes', 'strings of beads' or 'branches of a tree'. The swellings usually bear luminous organs which presumably serve to lure the prey nearer the mouth. Sir Alistair Hardy has noted that the tip of the barbel in *Stomias boa* resembles very strikingly a small red copepod. Possibly the barbels serve also as means of species recognition, while the more elaborately branched barbels may have a sensory function. From the bathysphere, William Beebe noted that at the slightest disturbance of the water near the barbel the fish immediately threshed around snapping with its jaws.

The stomiatoids living nearer to the surface are a shining silver, while the abyssal forms tend to be dark brown or black. These fishes are found in all oceans and none has been caught much over 12 in (30 cm) in length. There may, however, be larger species since William Beebe, during the first really deep-water dive, thought that he saw one of 6 ft (1·8 m).
FAMILIES: Stomiatidae, ORDER: Salmoniformes, CLASS: Pisces.

Juvenile unicornfish lacking the 'horn' on the forehead, which develops only with maturity.

WZ

WEEVERFISHES, marine bottom-living, poisonous fishes related to the Red mullets, stargazers and jawfishes. The name weever derives from an old French word, *wivere,* itself deriving from a Latin root meaning poisonous, a reference to the poisonous spines found in the weevers. There are two species found off the coasts of northern Europe, the Greater weever *Trachinus draco* and the Lesser weever *T. vipera*. The latter grows to about 6 in (15 cm) in length and is much more abundant than the former, which reaches 20 in (51 cm). The two species are fairly similar in appearance. The body is a deep yellow-brown with grey-blue streaks and the belly is a pale yellow. The most striking feature is the first dorsal fin, which contains 5–6 spiny rays and is black in colour. The poison glands are at the bases of these rays. In the Lesser weever there is another poison gland at the base of the spine projecting backwards from the gill cover. The spine is sheathed in skin but when this is ruptured the poison is released along the grooved spine and enters the wound. The venom, which resembles that of certain snakes, is not fatal but can be extremely painful.

The weevers frequent shallow water, burying themselves in the sand at the bottom with only the top of the head and the black dorsal fin visible. They are not infrequently caught in shrimping nets and there is a risk of treading on them while shrimping. FAMILY: Trachinidae, ORDER: Perciformes, CLASS: Pisces.

WELS *Silurus glanis,* a large catfish found in the bigger rivers of Europe; in the upper part of the Rhine and its tributaries and in rivers to the east of the Rhine which flow into the Black, Aral, Caspian and Baltic Seas. It also occurs actually in the Caspian and Baltic Seas. It is not native to Great Britain but has been introduced into some private lakes and has flourished.

The wels is a naked catfish with a small dorsal fin just behind the head and a long anal fin. There are two barbels on the upper jaw and four on the lower. The jaws have rows of fine teeth and there is a patch of fine

teeth in the roof of the mouth. The colour is variable, but is basically dark shades of blue-grey, brown or deep olive, lighter on the flanks, which are often mottled, and shading to pale grey on the belly. The fins often have reddish edges. Partial or complete albinos are fairly common.

The wels is a solitary fish, hiding in deep pools during the day and swimming into shallower water in the evening to feed on small fishes. It is a considerable predator and will eat not only fishes but frogs, birds and small mammals. There is a record from the last century of a child being eaten by a wels, a not altogether unlikely occurrence since

they can grow to about 9 ft (2·7 m) and reach a weight of 700 lb (318 kg). Records of even larger specimens may, however, be exaggerated. The wels spawns in shallow water and the eggs are laid on plant leaves. The parents guard the eggs until the young hatch out, looking very like tadpoles. Growth is very rapid, the fishes reaching 6 lb (2·7 kg) by the third year. A fish of 180 lb (82 kg) was found to be 24 years old, indicating that some of the largest specimens may well be 90 years old.

The wels is of some economic value. The flesh is eaten, the swimbladder and bones are used for glue, the skin is tanned into

Bottom-living Greater weeverfish of the coasts of northwest Europe.

leather and the eggs provide a sort of poor-man's caviar. The fish is eagerly sought after by anglers.

FAMILY: Siluridae, ORDER: Cypriniformes, CLASS: Pisces.

WHALE SHARK *Rhincodon typus,* the largest of all fishes but a harmless species found in the warm waters of the world. The Whale shark can be immediately recognized by the lines of pale spots on a greyish body and by the wide mouth at the end of the snout (the mouth being underneath in most other sharks). The body is heavily built, with ridges down the flanks, and the snout is blunt. Like the Basking shark, the Whale shark feeds on small planktonic animals, straining them from the water with a fine mesh of rakers in the throat region. There are, however, numerous small teeth in the jaws, of which 10 or 15 rows are functional at any one time. The fish cruises through the water with its mouth open when feeding, although Whale sharks have also been seen apparently feeding in a vertical position with their heads pointing upwards. As in the Basking shark, the enormous oily liver probably helps to maintain buoyancy and these fishes often lie at the surface where they are occasionally rammed by ships. The largest recorded Whale shark was 45 ft (13·5 m) in

White cloud mountain minnow.

length but there have been reports of specimens believed to be much larger than this and a length of 60 ft (18 m) may well be reached. A Florida specimen of 40 ft (12 m) was estimated to weigh 13½ tons (about 13,000 kg). In spite of this enormous size, the Whale shark shows none of the aggressive tendencies of its relatives and men have actually clambered onto them while they lay at the surface. Unlike many sharks, which give birth to live young, the Whale shark is an egg-layer and the egg cases are commensurate with the size of the fish, measuring over 2 ft (60 cm) in length.

Less than 100 specimens have been caught and described by scientists, although many more have been observed, and there is still much to be learned of the biology of these huge creatures. FAMILY: Rhincodontidae, ORDER: Pleurotremata, CLASS: Chondrichthyes.

WHITE CLOUD MOUNTAIN MINNOW *Tanichthys albonubes,* a small attractive fish 2 in (5 cm) long, from the streams of the White Cloud Mountains near Canton in China. *Tanichthys* means 'Tan's fish' named after Tan, a Chinese boy scout who first discovered the fish. It is one of the few Chinese species kept by aquarists and it has proved so easy to breed in captivity that it is

no longer necessary for supplies to come from China. The body is brownish with a brilliant golden-green band along the mid-line. The band is blue-green in the young. The dorsal and anal fins are yellow at the base and red beyond this.

Apparently some stocks of the White cloud mountain minnow are not pure *T. albonubes* but are the result of a cross between that species and a related cyprinid fish, *Aphyocypris pooni,* from Canton and Hong Kong. The latter species is sometimes called the venusfish and it has a yellow-green anal fin instead of the red and yellow of *T. albonubes.* In the hybrids the colours of the anal fin are mixed. FAMILY: Cyprinidae, ORDER: Cypriniformes, CLASS: Pisces.

WHITEFISH, silvery salmon-like fishes of the genus *Coregonus* confined to the colder parts of the northern hemisphere. It should be noted that the term 'whitefish' is also the correct name in Great Britain for the commercially important edible marine fishes such as plaice, cod, etc. In the southern part of their range they live in deep and cold lakes but farther north they inhabit rivers and some are found in brackish waters. In this respect they resemble the char. There is still great uncertainty as to how many species can be recognized. Some authorities consider that the population of each lake is specifically distinct, while others regard these as races or at most subspecies. The whitefishes have salmon-like bodies with silvery scales. There is a small adipose fin present and there are small fine teeth in the jaws. About six species are recognized in Europe and about 20 in North America.

In the British Isles the whitefish are confined to deep lakes fringing the Irish Sea and it is thought that they may once have been marine fishes which became land-locked at the end of the Ice Age. The Lochamben vendace is found in the lakes at Lochamben in Dumfriesshire, Scotland and the very similar Cumberland vendace lives in Derwentwater and Bassenthwaite in the English Lake District. The pollan is found in the four Irish lakes: Neagh, Erne, Derg and Ree. In spite of the various local names, these forms probably belong to the one species *Coregonus albula.* The gwyniad from Lake Bala, Wales, the Schelly from Haweswater, Red Tarn and Ullswater in the English Lake District and the powan from Loch Lomond, Scotland, are probably all races of *Coregonus lavaretus.* The only other British whitefish is the houghting *Coregonus oxyrhynchus,* a marine form now only rarely found in the North Sea but still fairly common in the Baltic. The houghting has a pointed snout that overhangs the mouth and is the largest of the British whitefishes, growing to 20 in (50 cm) in length.

Land-locked whitefish eat small insect

larvae, young fishes, shellfish and crustaceans. During the day the shoals are in deep water, but they come closer to the surface at night. Anglers rarely catch them by design but they are occasionally hooked on a fly or a worm.

One of the best known of the American whitefishes is the cisco or Lake herring, a widespread species. About 60 common names have been bestowed on the American whitefishes, representing perhaps only about 20 species.

Most of the deep lakes in northern Europe have their form of whitefish. One of the best known is the Blaufelchen *Coregonus wartmanni*. FAMILY: Salmonidae, ORDER: Salmoniformes, CLASS: Pisces.

WHITING *Merlangius merlangus*, a fish related to the cod found in the eastern North Atlantic but rare in the Mediterranean. The whiting is so commonly seen on fishmonger's slabs that a colour description would seem to be superfluous. When the author saw live whiting for the first time, however, he was momentarily perplexed by the yellow-brown fishes with golden mottlings on the belly and superb pink and purple reflections playing along the flanks. The dead whiting is a pale image of the live fish. As in the cod, there are three dorsal fins and two anal fins but there is no barbel under the chin. The lateral line series of scales are brown and curve downwards half way along the body. There is a black blotch at the bases of the pectoral fins. Whiting are slender fishes and smaller than the cod, growing to about 14 in (36 cm) and weighing about 3 lb (1·2 kg). The largest fish caught weighed 8 lb (3½ kg).

The whiting is found in the northeastern Atlantic but wanders a little farther south than the cod. It lives in large shoals that usually swim and feed near the bottom, especially over sand or mud. They are carnivores, feeding mainly on small fishes and crustaceans and will swim nearer the surface if tempted by shoals of fishes.

A female whiting lays about 200,000 eggs in spring, usually at depths of about 150 ft (50 m). During the spawning season the shoals stay together, but afterwards they break up and intensive feeding begins, usually in deeper waters. In early summer

Whiting with brittlestars on the rock in the background.

the shoals begin to reform over rich feeding grounds in moderately deep water of about 100 ft (30 m). They remain there during the summer but as winter approaches they move into shallower waters and can be readily caught on rod and line at dusk. Temperature and the availability of food seem to determine when the whiting move inshore. When spring comes they seek deeper water again. Prior to spawning they do not seem to feed so voraciously as they have during the winter. Small whiting can be a nuisance to anglers since they keep nibbling at the bait.

The closely related poutassou *Micromesistius poutassou* is a deeper-water species which occasionally comes inshore along British coasts.

In the United States, the name whiting is given to a species of hake (family Merluccidae). FAMILY: Gadidae, ORDER: Gadiformes, CLASS: Pisces.

WRASSES, a family of perch-like fishes related to the parrotfishes, typically having fairly elongated bodies with a long-based dome fin (the first part spinous) and a shorter anal fin. The lips are fleshy and in addition to strong teeth in the jaws there is a set of powerful molar teeth in the throat, the pharyngeal teeth, the lower set being fused into a triangular plate. In size, the wrasses range from small reef-fishes of 3 in (8 cm) to large species reaching 10 ft (3 m) in length.

Many of the Cleaner fishes, which remove parasites from larger fishes, are wrasses.

The tropical wrasses are usually more brightly coloured than those from temperate waters, but one of the prettiest is the Cuckoo wrasse *Labrus mixtus* of European coasts, a species which grows to about 12 in (30 cm) in length. Like many wrasses, the colours of the males differ from those of the females. The male has bright blue on the head and back, while the flanks, belly and dorsal and anal fins are yellow. There is also a blue longitudinal stripe running across the cheek and along the flank. In the females the colour is similar to that of the young, the general background being orange to red with three dark spots on the back. These fishes commonly occur in about 100 ft (30 m) of water but will often come inshore. In northern latitudes they tend to swim singly, but form shoals farther south.

The goldsinny *Ctenolabrus rupestris* is another European wrasse with golden brown or red colouring. The 'gold' in its common name clearly refers to its colour, but the derivation of 'sinny' is problematical. It has been suggested that 'sinny' is a corruption of 'finny' or fin, the 's' used in old books having been misread as an 'f'. This species, which inhabits rocky areas, is rare in the North Sea, but is common off the west coast of England. The Rock cock *Centrolabrus exoletus* is a small wrasse of northern Euro-

The Saddled rainbowfish, of Australia.

The male Cuckoo wrasse in its breeding colouration.

Small cleaner fishes at work picking parasites off the larger fish. The larger fishes present themselves voluntarily for this operation, even at times queueing up to do so.

pean waters distinguished by the broad crescentic mark on the tail. The Ballan wrasse *Labrus bergylta* is the most common of the British species. It is found mostly on rocky shores where it feeds on worms and other small creatures living amongst the weeds. The colour varies somewhat depending on the fish's habitat background, from brown or greenish brown to brick red with lighter spots on the head and on the scales and often dark bars on the body. The nest of the Ballan wrasse consists of thin pieces of seaweed pushed into crevices in rocks and cemented with a sticky secretion. The eggs are laid in early summer and they adhere to the nest. This species grows to 20 in (50 cm).

Although many wrasses feed on small marine animals (crustaceans, molluscs, etc), some have highly specialized feeding habits. The Hawaiian saddle wrasse, *Thalassoma duperryi*, for example, feeds on the eyes and fins of other fishes, including members of its own species. Its large and protruding front teeth are well adapted for obtaining its food.

Many wrasses, and especially those found in tropical seas, 'go to bed' at night. Normally, when fishes sleep—if indeed they do this in the sense in which we understand sleep—they rest on the bottom, but the tropical wrasses bury themselves in the sand for safety.

The larger wrasses are important as food fishes. The hogfish *Lachnolaimus maximus*, a species which grows to 2 ft (60 cm) in length, is important to the fisheries of the American Atlantic coast. FAMILY: Labridae, ORDER: Perciformes, CLASS: Pisces.

WRECKFISH or Stone basse *Polyprion americanus*, a marine perch-like fish that derives its common name from its habit of frequenting wrecks and pieces of floating debris. It lives in the open waters of the

tropical Atlantic and Mediterranean. The wreckfish has a deep and compressed body with a long dorsal fin, the soft-rayed parts of the dorsal and anal fins being prolonged into lobes. Reported to attain 6 ft (1·8 m) in length and to weigh up to 100 lb (45 kg), it is occasionally caught in British waters but is generally found in the warmer parts of the Atlantic. FAMILY: Serranidae, ORDER: Perciformes, CLASS: Pisces.

ZAMBEZI SHARK *Carcharinus leucas*, a species probably worldwide in tropical and subtropical waters but remarkable for entering estuaries and rivers and even living permanently in freshwater. This species has many different common names: in Australia it is known as the Whaler shark, in Central America the Lake Nicaragua shark and in the United States the Bull, Cub or Ground shark. It has a broad head with short rounded snout and small ears. The body is heavy, up to 10 ft (3 m) long and weighing over 400 lb (200 kg), with a prominent triangular first dorsal fin and a small second one set well back towards the tail. The teeth are triangular with saw edges. The back and flanks are light to dark

Corkwing, small European wrasse often found inshore.

grey, the underside white. Wherever it occurs the Zambezi shark has a reputation for being aggressive. It attacks large fish including other sharks and will attack human bathers and even boats. There seems to be a connection between the shark's attacks and the presence of freshwater, there being a greater incidence of attack on bathers in the freshwater Lake Nicaragua than in coastal waters. FAMILY: Carcharinidae, ORDER: Pleurotremata, CLASS: Chondrichthyes.

The wreckfish *Polyprion americanum*, a grouper.